Macroeconomic Theory

Macroeconomic Theory

A Short Course

Thomas R. Michl

M.E. Sharpe
Armonk, New York
London, England

Library of Congress Cataloging-in-Publication Data

Michl, Thomas R.
    Macroeconomic theory : a short course / Thomas R. Michl.
      p. cm.
    Includes bibliographical references and index.
    ISBN 0-7656-1141-4 (alk. paper) — ISBN 0-7656-1142-2 (pbk. : alk. paper)
    1. Macroeconomics—Mathematical models. I. Title.

HB172.5 .M42 2003
339′.01—dc21   2002026842

Contents

0.1 Preface

Experience has convinced me that there is a place for a truly concise treatment of the basic theory used by macroeconomic policymakers. This book is based on intermediate lectures in macroeconomics that have evolved over many years teaching the subject at Colgate University. Most textbooks today are so weighed down with material that students can hardly be blamed for not reading them. This one gets to the point.

This book boils macroeconomic theory down to the simplest mathematical models possible, using relatively easy algebra (and some light calculus in the footnotes and appendices). Formal mathematical presentation makes the subject easier, in my opinion, because it highlights the causal linkages of economic theory. I considered titling the book *Macroeconomics Made Easy* after the classic mathematics text by Sylvanus P. Thompson, *Calculus Made Easy* (revised by Martin Gardner, New York: St. Martin's Press, 1998), because I agree with Thompson's pedagogical philosophy so well summed-up by the aphorism that appears in his frontispiece: "What one fool can do, another can."

After reading this text, a student should be able to conduct a thought experiment in her imagination that traces out the effects that a monetary policy, fiscal policy, or other major shock would have over time on the major macroeconomic variables such as interest rates, inflation, or unemployment. This kind of ability is indispensable for understanding how monetary authorities operate, or understanding the debates about fiscal policy. And it's not that hard to achieve such mastery.

Graduate students in economics are another possible audience for this book, strangely. High-level macroeconomics as it is practiced in academia considers the basic macroeconomic theory presented here to be too low-brow to bother with, and it rarely shows up in the curriculum. But if you want to teach macroeconomics, or if you want to be able to function effectively in policy-making discussions, the basic models developed here are indispensable.

Chapter 1

Macroeconomic Accounting

Macroeconomic theory focuses on the determinants of the level of economic activity. National income accounting concerns the measurement of economic activity. Modern national income accounting is a complex and sophisticated branch of macroeconomics, but we need only develop the basic concepts we will need to understand macroeconomic theory[1].

For simplicity, let us begin with a *closed economy* that does no exporting and lending to, or importing and borrowing from, the rest of the world. Then we can progress to an *open economy* to include such transactions with the rest of the world.

1.1   Output and income

The *gross domestic product*, the most useful general measure of economic activity, is defined as the value of the final goods and services produced in an economy in one time period, which we can take to be one year. The value of goods and services is measured by their prices. Final goods and services are those that are either consumed by households (consumption goods) or carried over into future periods to be used productively (investment goods) later on. Goods and services that are used up in the production of other goods, such as the coal, iron ore, and scrap metal used to make steel or the services an accounting firm sells to a steel company, are called intermediate goods and

---

[1]Good discussions of the details of national income accounting can be found in the *Survey of Current Business*, and an excellent source of general macroeconomic data is the statistical appendix to the *Economic Report of the President*.

they are not directly counted as part of the GDP. Thus, if you were to add up all the output produced in a country in a given year, you would overstate its GDP because you would be double counting the intermediate goods.

This definition of output, based on the value of final goods and services, offers an advantage over other possible definitions because it links up the amount of output with the amount of income it generates in the form of the wages and salaries of workers and the profits of company owners[2]. An alternative way to measure GDP is to sum up the income (wages and profits) generated by all the firms in the economy. Since the income generated in a firm is just the difference between the firm's sales and its expenditures on raw materials and intermediate goods, it is called the firm's *value added*. Value-added accounting defines GDP so that income and output are identical, and we will in fact use these terms interchangeably throughout this book. This correspondence clarifies the relationship between production, income and spending in a macroeconomic theory.

Because the GDP is measured by summing the values of all the final goods and services produced in a given year, it can change either because prices change or because the volume of production changes. The number of jobs and the standard of living in a country depend on the volume of production, so economists distinguish between the real GDP (which measures the volume of production) and the nominal GDP (which measures the value of output at current prices). To translate our measure of nominal GDP into real terms, we need to deflate it by a suitable price index. This procedure measures the volume of production in some particular year's prices (called the *base year*). In this book, we will simplify reality considerably by assuming somewhat heroically that there is only one kind of good produced, and that it is an all-purpose good that can be used for consumption or investment purposes. Let us refer to the price index for the all-purpose good as P, setting $P = 1$ in the base year. For the volume of production of the all-purpose good we will use the symbol Y. The real GDP, Y, is calculated by dividing the nominal GDP, PY, by the price index, P.

Nominal variables are measured in \$; for example, the nominal GDP is measured in \$ trillions per year. Real variables are measured in base year prices, or constant \$. For example, the real GDP is measured in trillions of constant \$ per year.

---

[2]The GDP includes (is gross of) depreciation of the capital stock. Thus, the relevant definition of profit is gross profit or cash flow, which includes depreciation.

In real economies with literally millions of different final goods and services, the construction of accurate price indices is a major challenge. One simple kind of price index, called a *Paasche* index, illustrates the basic procedure. Let p_{it} and q_{it} represent the price and quantity of the i-th final good in period t, labelling the goods from 1 to n. Then the Paasche index for any year (identified by a subscript t) is just the nominal GDP in that year divided by the GDP in base year prices, or, taking $t = 0$ to be the base year:

$$P_t = \frac{\sum_{i=1}^{n} p_{it}q_{it}}{\sum_{i=1}^{n} p_{i0}q_{it}}$$

Notice that in the base year ($t = 0$), this index will be equal to 1.

The Paasche index computes the overall price level by weighting each price by the current year quantity of that good. An alternative index, the *Laspeyres* index, weights each price by the base year quantity of that good. To compute the real GDP more accurately and consistently, the U.S. Commerce Department now uses a *chain-type* price index that averages these two types of index each year (utilizing a geometric mean).

We can represent the output-income relationship by means of an accounting identity (an equation that is true by definition). Output consists of labor income (wages and salaries) plus profits. If we use W to represent the nominal wage per worker, N to represent the number of workers, and Π to represent profits in real terms, we then have the *output-income identity*:

$$PY = WN + P\Pi \tag{1.1}$$

Equation (1.1) can be used to calculate the GDP, and in fact is one method used by the Bureau of Economic Analysis of the U.S. Department of Commerce.

We can also divide through by P to express the output-income identity in real terms. The wage divided by the price level (W/P) is called the *real product wage* (or the real wage or the product wage) because it shows how much product a worker can buy with her wage. The nominal wage, W, is also called the *money wage* to distinguish it from the real wage. Using the symbol w to represent the real wage, we have

$$Y = wN + \Pi$$

We focus on the determinants of real GDP because the level of production plays such a key role in regulating the economic health of a country and therefore is the target of economic policies. Macroeconomic theory owes its existence to the need for policymakers in modern economies to have a workable model of the economy that helps them understand the effects of their policies. We will focus on the determinants of the price level in connection with inflation, the persistent increase in the price level that so concerns policymakers, particularly central bankers.

In this book, we will often need to identify the time period relevant to a particular variable. Time is assumed to come in discrete intervals of some appropriate length, such as one year. All the decisions in the economy are assumed to be made at the beginning of the period, and they can only be changed at the beginning of the next period. This treatment of time is admittedly crude, but more sophisticated treatments can quickly lead to difficulties.

We will identify the time period for a variable by a subscript, so that Y_0 represents GDP in period 0, Y_t represents GDP in the t−th period, and so on. (There are a few exceptions when subscripts do not refer to time.) When we need to identify the lagged value of a variable, such as its value in period $t - 1$, we will abbreviate the notation by writing Y_{-1}. Similarly, when the time subscript is obvious from context or irrelevant, we will simply leave it implicit to eliminate clutter.

1.2   Income and expenditure

Firms produce output because they hope to sell it, so we need to measure the total spending on final goods and services. Value-added accounting suggests that it would be useful to measure spending in such a way that it too is equivalent to output and income. Spending on final goods and services, as we have seen, is made up of either consumption spending, C, or investment spending, I, both of which are measured in real terms (the corresponding nominal values are PC and PI). Consumption spending is just the amount of real spending on consumer goods. We will assume that households are able to consume fully all the consumption goods they have purchased within the relevant time period, so that actual consumption equals planned consumption. In practice, the consumption in official national income accounts includes spending on durable goods that last longer than one year. Technically, these goods have some of the attributes of investment goods.

In macroeconomic theory, investment refers to spending on newly produced goods that add to the productive capacity of the economy[3]. This sense of the term differs from the everyday sense of investment. A household can add to its private wealth through the purchase of a real or financial asset, including a share of stock representing a title to existing capital. In the everyday sense, any of these purchases might be called an investment but from a macroeconomic perspective the transfer of title to existing productive capacity doesn't create any new social wealth and is therefore not considered investment spending.

Private investment spending consists concretely of three different kinds of expenditure: purchases of plant and equipment by firms, purchases of new residential housing by households, and finally, any change in the inventories of firms, which is called *inventory investment*. The first two categories are self-explanatory, but inventory investment requires some elaboration. If a firm is unable to sell all its annual output, then some goods will be placed in inventory and kept in a warehouse. This positive change in inventories is treated as an act of investment spending because these goods are available for future use, which satisfies the technical definition of investment. We call this investment spending even though no money has changed hands; it is as if the firm has bought these goods from itself. In the opposite case, when a firm has underproduced and satisfies demand by dipping into its inventories, the negative change in inventories is treated as an act of disinvestment or negative investment spending.

Using this definition of investment spending creates a potential confusion because a firm may wind up doing more or less investment spending than it desired if its inventories unexpectedly grow or shrink. The level of actual (sometimes called *ex post* or "after the fact") investment can exceed or fall short of the level of planned (sometimes called *ex ante* or "before the fact") investment. Unplanned changes in inventories make up the difference between the two. The distinction between actual and planned investment is clearly of great importance. Theories of investment spending concentrate on how firms plan their level of investment spending. The level of actual investment spending cannot be determined by the individual firms because it depends on how much they are able to sell at the end of the day, which is in fact the central question in macroeconomic theory.

---

[3]To be more precise, investment is measured gross of spending to replace depreciated capital. Deducting replacement investment would give us net investment, which truly increases the capital stock.

There is a simple fact, however, that makes this distinction less confusing than it seems. When firms are running their inventories up or down, it means they have incorrectly predicted the level of sales. They are not in any kind of equilibrium because they will respond to their error by adjusting production levels appropriately. If they have produced too much, for example, they will have to warehouse some output. This sends a signal to the firm's managers to cut back on production so as not to make the same mistake twice. Only when the economy achieves an equilibrium level of output will the managers have no incentive to change the level of production. But then there will be no unplanned changes in inventories, and actual investment will exactly correspond to planned investment.

Using the symbol I to represent actual investment spending, it is clearly true as a matter of accounting definition that the output of final goods and services equals expenditures, or

$$Y = C + I \tag{1.2}$$

We call this the *income-expenditure identity.*

Most textbooks on macroeconomics and official government national income and product accounts distinguish a third type of expenditure, government spending on goods and services. Technically, government spending is not a unique kind of spending because it can either be classified as consumption (as when the government provides firefighting services) or investment (as when the government builds a new school). However, because the level of government spending has been such a valuable instrument of fiscal policy, along with changes in taxes, it is convenient to separate this kind of spending by concentrating on government consumption, represented by G, and including public investment in I. There is no harm in doing this as long as we remember that not all government spending as it is officially reported represents consumption. With this convention, the income-expenditure identity becomes

$$Y = C + I + G \tag{1.3}$$

It is important to realize that government spending on goods and services does not include payments for programs like unemployment insurance or social security, which are called *transfer payments* because they merely transfer funds from taxpayers to recipients. Transfer payments are important in practice, and play a major role in real fiscal policies, but we gain much simplicity at little cost if we ignore them in constructing a basic theory of macroeconomics.

1.3   Saving and investment

Saving is defined passively as income not spent. This contrasts with the active nature of investment spending, and a big question in macroeconomic theory is how saving and investment are related to one another.

The government's income consists of its tax collections. We assume for simplicity that the government levies a lump-sum tax on all the households, represented by T. The government's saving is just $T - G$. This is also called *public saving*. In many discussions, public saving is called the government budget surplus or the fiscal surplus. A budget deficit represents negative public saving.

Note that the practice of treating all government spending as consumption understates the true extent of public saving by ignoring government investment. Some specialists have recommended that the government adopt a *capital budget* that distinguishes investment from consumption, as do corporations and other business enterprises.

The households earn income from wages, salaries, and property income like profits or interest, but they can only spend their after-tax or *disposable* income, $Y - T$. Their saving is therefore equal to $Y - T - C$ and this is called *private saving*. If you substitute the definitions of public and private saving into the income-expenditure identity given by Equation (1.3), you arrive at another great macroeconomic accounting relationship, the *investment-saving identity*:

$$I = S + (T - G) \tag{1.4}$$

The right-hand side of this identity, called *national saving*, is the sum of private and public saving. It represents the total saving generated internally by country. Investment cannot exceed this amount unless the economy is open, in which case the country could borrowing from the rest of the world to finance some of its investment, as we see below.

1.4   Accounting in an open economy

The same basic accounting definitions carry over easily to an open economy that trades with the rest of the world. The income-expenditure identity needs to recognize that other countries buy some of the goods and services produced in a given year, in the form of exports, X. Moreover, some consumption and investment spending is directed toward imports, represented by the symbol Q since other obvious choices will be used for other things. For now, let us assume that an imported good can be purchased by swapping one domestically produced good, so that Q and X are both measurable in the same units, which is to say constant dollars of domestically produced final goods and services. The excess of exports over imports, $X - Q$, is called *net exports*[4] and represented by NX. Net exports measure a country's balance of trade, called a trade surplus or deficit when net exports are positive or negative. With these definitions, the income-expenditure identity becomes

$$Y = C + I + G + (X - Q) = C + I + G + NX \qquad (1.5)$$

When we substitute the definitions of public and private saving into Equation (1.5), we arrive at the open-economy version of the investment-saving identity, or

$$I = S + (T - G) + (Q - X) = S + (T - G) - NX \qquad (1.6)$$

Like its closed-economy counterpart, Equation (1.6) shows that a country's investment spending must be equal to the sum of the saving available. An open economy can borrow from the rest of the world in addition to relying on national saving (which you may recall equals public plus private saving). The last term in Equation (1.6), or $(Q - X)$, represents *net capital flows*. We might more accurately say net capital *in*flows. Thus, this equation tells us that a country's investment is financed through its private saving plus public saving plus net capital flows from the rest of the world, i.e., through national saving plus net capital flows. A country that lends to the rest of the world does so because it has more national saving than is required by its own investment level.

Notice that Equation (1.6) implies that a country running a trade deficit (i.e., having negative net exports) must be experiencing an inflow of capital

---

[4]This definition implicitly assumes that the real exchange rate equals one. We will relax that assumption (and define the real exchange rate) later in the book.

funds, in effect borrowing from the rest of the world. Vice versa, a trade surplus implies lending to the rest of the world. We can visualize why this is true by imagining that money is the only financial asset. A country that runs a trade deficit is paying for its excess imports with its own currency, which other countries accept as payment. This means the other countries are building up claims on the country's future output, as if they had lent funds. Of course, real economies relying on foreign capital issue financial liabilities like stocks and bonds, or sell titles to real property.

It is also useful to consider the outflow of capital, which is directed toward purchasing foreign assets. Net exports must be equal to the net purchase of foreign assets, or *net foreign investment*, NFI. Using the equality $NFI = NX$, we can re-write the investment-saving identity to show that a country's national saving is absorbed by domestic investment and net foreign investment:

$$S + (T - G) = I + NFI$$

At the level of the entire globe, of course, all the trade deficits and surpluses cancel out. The entire globe is a closed system (as long as we have not yet opened up trade with the Moon!).

In practice, national income accounting can get very complex. Fortunately, the output-income, income-expenditure, and investment-saving identities are sufficient for the purpose of understanding basic macroeconomic theory.

1.5   Stocks and flows

National income, consumption, investment, saving, and the like are examples of *flows*: variables that are measured in \$ per year or constant \$ per year (or other time unit). In accounting terms, flows are recorded in the profit and loss statement of a business enterprise.

Macroeconomic theory also deals with *stocks*: variables that are measured in \$ or constant \$ at some point in time, without any time unit. Examples include money, the capital stock, bonds, and bank reserves. In accounting terms, stocks are recorded on the balance sheet of a business enterprise or household. (The term is also used in the U.S. in an unrelated sense to refer to the shares issued by companies that are traded on the stock exchange, and, in the U.K., to refer to inventories.)

The balance sheet reports the complete list of an accounting unit's assets and liabilities. Assets are things the unit owns; liabilities are things the unit owes. The left-hand side of a balance sheet lists assets while the right-hand side reports liabilities. A balance sheet is an accounting device that uses double-entry bookkeeping; assets must equal liabilities by definition. For example, consider the account for a typical household that maintains a balance in its checking account (called a demand deposit), currency, and bonds, and owes its creditors for loans (such as mortgage, car, or student loans):

Household

Assets	Liabilities
Demand Deposits	Loans
Currency	
Bonds	
	Net Worth = A – L

The difference between assets and liabilities is called net worth, and it is treated as a self-liability (something you owe yourself).

1.6   The money supply

1.6.1   Interlocking balance sheets

In a closed economy, the balance sheets of all the accounting units must be consistent with one another, forming a network of interlocking balance sheets, because one unit's liability is another unit's asset. Table 1.1 shows the accounts for the major sectors of the economy that are relevant to the operation of the banking system and the conduct of monetary policy. The U.S. Federal Reserve Board compiles statistics on the balance sheets of major sectors of the economy and reports them in the *Flow of Funds Accounts of the United States*.

The government sector collects taxes and pays for its expenditures on goods and services and for the interest on its outstanding debt, which takes the form of government bonds. The *primary fiscal surplus* is the difference between tax revenues and non-interest expenditures. The present discounted value of all future primary surpluses constitutes the main asset of the government[5].

---

[5]Discounting translates a stream of future values into its equivalent value as a current

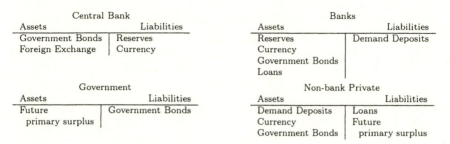

Central Bank	
Assets	Liabilities
Government Bonds	Reserves
Foreign Exchange	Currency

Banks	
Assets	Liabilities
Reserves	Demand Deposits
Currency	
Government Bonds	
Loans	

Government	
Assets	Liabilities
Future	Government Bonds
primary surplus	

Non-bank Private	
Assets	Liabilities
Demand Deposits	Loans
Currency	Future
Government Bonds	primary surplus

Table 1.1: The balance sheets for all the accounting units in a closed system interlock because one agent's asset is another agent's liability.

The non-bank private sector consists of households and businesses. They own money, in the form of currency and deposits in banks, and owe the banks for loans extended in the past. They also own government bonds, which are loans to the government. Since the private sector ultimately pays the taxes that service this debt, the present discounted value of the future primary surpluses of the government represents a liability to the private sector.

Private banks own deposits held at the central bank, called *bank reserves*. These special accounts are used to back up the liabilities of the private banks, which are the deposits of the non-bank sector. In a *fractional reserve* banking system, banks hold reserve funds equal to only a fraction of their deposit liabilities. The central bank sets a minimum legal reserve requirement. In practice, U.S. banks often operate with a margin of safety, and when they fall short of reserve funds, they borrow from banks with a surplus of reserves in the *federal funds* market. The rate of interest on these overnight loans is called the *federal funds rate*. Banks can also borrow from the central bank, paying a rate of interest called the *discount rate* in the U.S. For simplicity, we will assume that banks operate with a fixed desired reserve requirement.

Banks are in the business of extending loans to businesses and households, from which they earn profits. These loans are the performing assets of the banking system, along with holdings of government bonds. Any funds that are not required for reserve purposes, called *excess reserves*, will be loaned out. Banks also hold currency in the form of vault cash.

---

asset earning a rate of return called the discount rate. For example, $100 paid out next year is worth (has a present value of) $90.91 today if the discount rate is 10% per year, since $90.91 invested at 10% becomes $100 in one year. A stream of $100 payments over two years would be worth $173.55 today with the same discount rate, or $100/.1 + $100/(1.1)^2$.

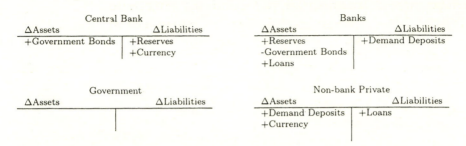

Table 1.2: An open market purchase increases the supply of high-powered money and the money supply proper. The T-accounts represent *changes* in assets or liabilities. Balance sheet items that do not change are not shown.

The central bank's liabilities are the currency of the nation (for which the central bank assumes responsibility) and bank reserves (the central bank is the bankers' bank). The central bank's most important asset is its holdings of government debt. In an open economy, central banks also hold foreign exchange and foreign-denominated liquid assets, which are sometimes called *foreign reserves.*

Central banks such as the U.S. Federal Reserve Bank control the money supply through *open market operations*, meaning buying or selling government bonds. Central banks can only use open market operations in countries that enjoy a broad and deep market for government bonds. In principle, the monetary authority can change the reserve requirement or its discount rate, although these are not used as often as primary instruments of monetary policy. Balance sheets that represent changes in assets and liabilities (indicated by + and −) are called *T-accounts.* We can see how an open market purchase from a bank creates money by studying the T-accounts shown in Table 1.2. The central bank pays reserve funds to the private bank that sells the bond. Since the reserve funds are not required, the bank promptly lends them out. The loan in turn leads some household or company to make a deposit in another bank, to which the reserve funds will go. This second bank now experiences a simultaneous increase in deposits and reserves, but it only needs to keep a fraction of the new reserves so it lends its excess reserves out. Once again, the loan leads to a new deposit somewhere else, which creates excess reserves, and another loan. This is called the money multiplier process. Some funds leak out of the multiplier process when firms or households choose to keep currency rather than demand deposits.

1.6.2 The money multiplier

How large is the money multiplier? We can answer this with a brief model. Let the reserve ratio be represented by $\theta = R/D$, where R stands for bank reserves and D for demand deposits. Let the currency ratio chosen by the private sector be represented by $c = CU/D$, where CU stands for currency. Then we can write the amount of central bank liabilities as $H = CU + R = cD + \theta D = (c + \theta)D$, where H is often called *high powered money* or *base money*. The money supply itself is defined as currency plus demand deposits, or $M = CU + D$. Into this definition, substitute $D = H/(c+\theta)$ and $CU = cD$, and we have:

$$M = \left(\frac{1+c}{c+\theta}\right) H$$

The money multiplier follows by using the difference operator on this equation[6]:

$$\Delta M = \left(\frac{1+c}{c+\theta}\right) \Delta H$$

In the U.S., the currency ratio is around .5 and the reserve ratio is around .1, so the money multiplier, $(1 + c)/(c + \theta)$, is around 2.5. Each \$100 bond purchase by the Fed results in a \$250 increase in the money supply of the U.S. The arm of the Fed that decides on open market operations is the Federal Open Market Committee, while the trading desk of the New York Federal Reserve Bank actually implements the instructions of the FOMC through trades with a select group of large banks, called primary dealers, which are privileged to participate in this market. These activities are closely watched by financial markets because millions of dollars ride on every basis point (hundredth of a percentage point) in the short-term interest rate that open market operations influence.

In practice the definition of money is not self-evident, and central banks generally publish estimates of several different monetary aggregates. In the U.S., the narrowest definition of money, called M1, consists of currency plus checkable deposits, while broader definitions, called M2 and M3, also include various other financial instruments (such as saving accounts and money market deposit accounts) that are less liquid than cash but can still be turned into cash quickly and cheaply.

---

[6]Alternatively, differentiate to obtain $dM = (1 + c)/(c + \theta)dH$.

1.7   The equation of exchange

There is one important accounting identity, the *equation of exchange*, which links the stock of money with the flow of income. It is an identity by virtue of the definition of the *income velocity of money*:

$$V = \frac{PY}{M}$$

The best way to think about the velocity of money is in terms of units of measurement. Using dim x to indicate the dimension of the variable x, we can write[7]

$$\dim V = \frac{\dim(PY)}{\dim M} = \frac{\$/\text{year}}{\$} = \frac{[1]}{\text{year}}$$

The velocity of money is measured as a pure number per year because it represents the number of times the average dollar changes hands as the result of transactions involving the sale of final goods and services[8]. Take the reciprocal of the velocity of money, and you have $M/(PY)$, or the ratio of money balances to income. This is measured in years, which makes sense because it represents the length of time we could support our expenditures using our current money holdings. This can also be conceptualized as the amount of time the average dollar stays in someone's possession before it is spent. If people hold on to their money for a longer time, the average dollar will circulate more slowly and participate in fewer transactions.

The equation of exchange is most often written by rearranging the definition of velocity:

$$MV = PY \tag{1.7}$$

This equation is useful for understanding the monetarist theory of prices and inflation.

---

[7]Don't underestimate the value of analyzing the units of measurement of economic variables, even in the simplest cases. Michal Kalecki, the famous Polish economist, once complained that "macroeconomics is the art of confusing stocks and flows."

[8]This last qualification is necessary because there is also a transactions velocity of money that involves all transactions, not just those involving final goods and services.

1.8 The Marshallian short run

The macroeconomic theory in this book, except for the last two chapters, is used to inform policy makers about how fiscal and monetary policy affect the economy in the short run. It is designed to deal with stabilization issues, such as unemployment and inflation. The Marshallian short run (named after British economist Alfred Marshall) is a period defined by the assumption that the capital stock and other forms of wealth remain constant. The rationale for this assumption is that because wealth changes very slowly, it does little harm to assume it is constant when dealing with a short period of time. The benefit is that we can overlook the complications created by wealth accumulation.

This theoretical device creates some potential sources of confusion. For example, we will assume that households are actively saving (not consuming all their income), yet their wealth remains fixed. This is an economic impossibility, of course, but if their wealth is growing slowly, it is a reasonable approximation. The assumption that wealth is fixed is critical for understanding the households' decisions about how much money to carry on their balance sheets. If their total wealth is constant, they can only increase their cash balances by selling off some other asset (and vice versa).

Within our hypothetical Marshallian time period, we will need to distinguish between different degrees of adjustment to economic imbalances. We will say the model is in a long-run equilibrium when it is fully adjusted, and in a short-run equilibrium when it is only temporarily adjusted to economic imbalance.

Growth models study the accumulation of wealth over the true Marshallian long run, a period defined by the condition that the capital stock and other forms of wealth have fully adjusted to economic circumstances. Growth theory has become increasingly significant in policy discussions as the long-run implications of budget deficits, social security, and other policies have become more evident. We will complete this survey of macroeconomic theory with two chapters on the theory of growth that focus on the long-term effects of an increase in national saving.

1.9   Components of a macroeconomic model

Any model of an entire economy must at a minimum describe the major markets that make up the macroeconomy: the product (or goods and services) market, the asset markets, and the labor market. The economy is pictured as a large number of firms (business enterprises) that hire workers in the labor market and rent capital goods from households in order to produce goods and services that are sold back to workers and households in the product market. The firms choose a level of production, which determines how many workers are employed and how many are unemployed. The households and firms must decide how much of their incomes to spend on consumption and investment, and how much to save. They must also make portfolio decisions about how much of their wealth should be held in liquid, monetary form and how much should be held in interest-bearing form. These decisions determine the demand for financial assets, money and bonds, in their respective markets.

Because macroeconomic theory is a general equilibrium theory—everything depends on everything else—it makes good sense to start simply and build up an increasingly complex model in steps. This will be our strategy. As the model gets more complex, it is always possible to look back at each simpler model as a specialized form of the complex model, valid under certain assumptions. Pay careful attention to the assumptions that separate the different layers of complexity in this book.

Macroeconomic theory starts with a basic model of the product market, making implicit assumptions about the other markets that cut them out of the action. We then add first the asset markets and then the labor market to the basic model. The asset markets give us insights about how interest rates and monetary policy affect the product market. The labor market provides insight about how wages and prices are determined, which is important for understanding inflation and unemployment.

Modern macroeconomic theory has made great progress in understanding the decisions underlying these markets at the level of individual firms, households, workers, and central banks, which is often called the microeconomic foundations of macroeconomics. This area is a casualty of the approach of this text, which focuses on how the whole macroeconomic model works at the expense of detailed exposition of its microeconomic foundations. Another topic that has been lost to the cutting room floor is doctrinal controversy in macroeconomics—i.e., debate between competing schools of thought. The most important split is between the New Keynesian economists, who maintain that the major markets are imperfectly competitive, and the New Classical economists, who insist that these markets are perfectly competitive[9]. This text follows the New Keynesian economists because they seem to be more influential in terms of policy analysis and decision making outside of academia. The macroeconomic theory presented here should not be taken to be some kind of scientific truth, and students should maintain a healthy amount of skepticism about the theory explained here. Be aware that there are many heterodox economists, from post-Keynesians to neo-Marxists, who have articulated thoughtful critiques of the dominant orthodoxy, as well as positive models in their own traditions (see Baiman et al., 2000). But before you can intelligently criticize a macroeconomic theory, you need to understand it, so let's get started.

Problems for Chapter 1

1. Imagine a two-industry economy. Industry A employs 10 workers each paid $50 per year to produce an intermediate good worth $1100 per year and uses $100 of its own output as an input (think of seed corn). Industry B produces $4000 per year of a consumption good, using $1000 in materials purchased from Industry A and 20 workers, each paid $50 per year. Calculate the GDP by (i) measuring the value of final output (ii) measuring the total value-added.

2. Consider an economy with three final goods industries, A, B, and C. In years 1 and 2, the prices (p) in $ per unit and outputs (q) in units of type A, B, and C per year are:

---

[9]Excellent surveys of these competing schools of thought and their microeconomic foundations are given by Carlin and Soskice (1990) and Snowdon et al. (1994). The New Keynesians are sometimes called "saltwater" economists because their strongholds at Harvard, MIT, and Berkeley are close to the oceans, while the New Classicals are "freshwater" economists because they dominate Chicago, Minnesota, and Rochester. Who says economists lack personality?

	Year 1		Year 2	
Industry	p	q	p	q
A	2.00	100	2.50	120
B	3.00	50	3.25	60
C	1.00	25	2.00	25

Calculate the GDP in each of the two years in (i) current prices and (ii) year 1 prices (constant year 1 dollars). Calculate the Paasche price index for year 2, taking year 1 as the base year. By what percentage has the economy grown in real terms? By what percentage have prices increased?

3. The GDP is $10 trillion per year measured in current prices. Measured in the prices prevailing in year 2000, the GDP is 9 trillion constant dollars per year. Calculate the Paasche price index with base year 2000.

4. In a closed economy, consumption spending is $100 per year, government spending is $50 per year, and $250 worth of final goods and services were actually produced. Calculate the level of actual investment. If planned investment spending is $75 per year, calculate the unplanned change in inventories.

5. An open economy with GDP equal to $10 trillion per year has investment spending of $2 trillion per year, consumption spending of $6.5 trillion per year, and government spending of $1.8 trillion per year. Calculate the value of net foreign investment. Calculate the level of national saving.

6. The reserve ratio is .2, the currency-deposit ratio is .6, and there are $375 in currency and $125 in bank reserves. Calculate the money supply. If the central bank purchased a bond for $100, by how much would the money supply change?

7. Show the T-accounts of the central bank, the banking sector, and the nonbank private sector after an open market sale of a bond by the central bank.

8. Use the balance sheets of the commercial banks and the monetary authority in the *Flow of Funds Accounts of the United States* to calculate the size of the money multiplier.

9. Use the statistical appendix of the *Economic Report of the President* to find data on each term in the income-expenditure identity for a closed economy. Make a graph describing the percentage composition of real GDP in the U.S. over time. How has it changed from 1970 to the present?

Chapter 2

Prices and Output

In an economic boom, firms experience increased demand for their products. Do they respond by raising prices, by producing more, or by some combination of the two? In this chapter, we answer this question with a simple model of the firm. In this model, as long as wages remain constant the firm will respond by producing more output without changing its price. Understanding this response is crucial for the subsequent chapters, which develop complete macroeconomic models resting on this microeconomic foundation.

In a simple macroeconomic model, all the firms are assumed to be identical. In this case, we have only to consider one *representative firm* in order to understand the whole economy. The firm's managers have two fundamental decisions: how much output to produce and what price to charge for it. We know from microeconomic theory that these decisions can get quite complex, but for purposes of building a model of the whole economy we must forego subtlety. A good approximation to the price-setting behavior found in modern economies, at least in the short run, is given by the theory of imperfect competition[1].

2.1 Price setting

In order to remind ourselves that we are viewing matters from the standpoint of an individual firm, we will attach a subscript i to variables that represent

---

[1]The tradition of building a macroeconomic model on the assumption of imperfectly competitive product markets begins with Kalecki (1971). For a survey of theoretical and empirical work on price setting, consult Layard et al. (1991).

the i-th firm. (Note that this is a rare instance when the subscript does not represent time.) Since all the firms are the same, we have only to drop the i subscript in order to make a useful statement about the whole economy; this is sometimes called the symmetry property. Thus, once we determine the price, P_i, charged by the typical firm, we have also determined the price level, P, for the whole economy.

One form of imperfect competition that is particularly tractable is monopoly. We will assume that firms have some monopoly power, which means that they are *price setters*. Under perfect competition, firms are *price takers* because they are too small to control prices in the face of vigorous competition.

2.1.1 Costs of production

The typical firm produces final output using no intermediate goods; labor is the only variable input in production. The simplest short-run *production function* displays constant returns to labor, so that output is a constant multiple of labor input, $Y = yN$. The constant y measures the productivity of labor, or output per labor unit. We can save on symbols by choosing labor units so that this multiple is exactly one, in which case our typical firm's production function is simply

$$Y_i = N_i$$

where N_i refers to the number of units of labor, and a unit of labor is defined so that one unit of labor produces one unit of output[2]. For example, if the employed labor force is 100 workers and the output is 1,000 units per year, we take each actual worker to be equivalent to 10 units of labor. Then each unit of labor, so defined, produces exactly one unit of output per year. We will call the labor unit a "worker-year" or just a "worker," even though it may not be equal to one actual person.

The cost of labor is the wage, W, which we will take to be constant for the first six chapters of this book. Later, we drop this assumption in favor of a theory of wage-driven inflation that originates in the labor market. The point is to build up a macroeconomic model one step at a time, starting simply and progressively relaxing assumptions to achieve greater realism.

---

[2]We do need to remember the existence of the constant, y, because it translates dimensions so that both sides of the equation are measured in the same units.

We can summarize the assumptions about the firm's costs briefly. The marginal product of labor is constant, which means it is equal to the average product of labor, and both are made to equal one by the choice of labor units. To produce one more unit of output requires one more worker: the marginal cost is equal to the wage.

2.1.2 Demand for output of the firm

The typical firm faces a demand curve for its output, which we will represent as $Y_i^d = D(P_i, Y)$. The quantity demanded, Y_i^d, is a function of the price, P_i, and the aggregate income of the households, Y. Economic theory suggests that this will be an inverse function, or that the demand curve will slope downward, because when the price of one good is increased, consumers will seek out substitute goods, and they will also feel poorer in general and less able to afford goods of all types.

Note that the whole demand curve facing the firm shifts out when the economy expands (Y goes up), and shifts in when the economy contracts.

A convenient assumption is that the demand for the typical firm's output has a constant elasticity over all price ranges and for all income levels. With this assumption, it can be shown through a proof found in the Appendix (or in any intermediate-level microeconomics textbook) that the profit-maximizing price will be a *mark-up* over marginal costs. Since marginal cost equals the wage under our assumptions, we have

$$P_i = (1 + \mu)W$$

where μ represents the mark-up. The mark-up depends on the elasticity of demand for the product. For example, a lower elasticity of demand means consumers are less price-sensitive, and firms with monopoly power will be able to raise prices above marginal costs more aggressively before reaching the point where the loss of sales makes further increases unprofitable. That is why the mark-up will be larger the lower the elasticity of demand.

Since the firm receives a price of P_i and has unit costs of W, its profit per unit sold is just $P_i - W$. The mark-up maximizes the firm's total profit, or $(P_i - W)Y_i$. We can express total profit as a share of output by dividing it by the firm's revenues, P_iY_i. By substituting the pricing equation, we see that this *profit share* will be equal to $\mu/(1 + \mu)$. Thus, it is possible to estimate the mark-up using data for the profit share (or the wage share which is just one minus the profit share), or to estimate the profit share using data for the mark-up.

The mark-up pricing equation is not restricted to the special case of monopoly. Other forms of imperfect competition, such as oligopoly or monopolistic competition, give rise to similar pricing equations.

2.2   Endogenous and exogenous variables

A macroeconomic model is a mathematical formalization of a theory. The theory suggests that some variables influence or determine other variables, and the model specifies particular mathematical forms for these determinations. A model is a system of equations. The variables that are determined within the model are called *endogenous variables*. Some examples of endogenous variables encountered so far are the price level, the level of output, and the level of employment. The variables that are taken to be constant, and determined outside the model are called *exogenous variables* or *parameters*. The mark-up, μ, is an example of an exogenous parameter. A macroeconomic model lets us study the effects that changes in each parameter have on the endogenous variables in the model. For example, it is obvious that an increase in the mark-up results in an increase in the price. It is always easier to understand a macroeconomic model if you carefully distinguish between the endogenous variables and the exogenous parameters.

2.3   Production levels

With firms setting prices by adding on a mark-up to their marginal cost, and with constant marginal cost, the firms' managers have a straightforward task in determining the appropriate level of production. They have only to predict the quantity demanded at the price they have already established.

If the economy operated at one level of output all the time, the managers would only have to solve this problem once. But real economies are in a state of fluctuation, which is the chief object of analysis for macroeconomic theory. How do fluctuations in the overall level of activity affect the typical firm? Remember that the demand curve for the firm's output is a function of price and the level of income of the whole community, Y (note: no subscript). When households experience an increase in income during an expansion in

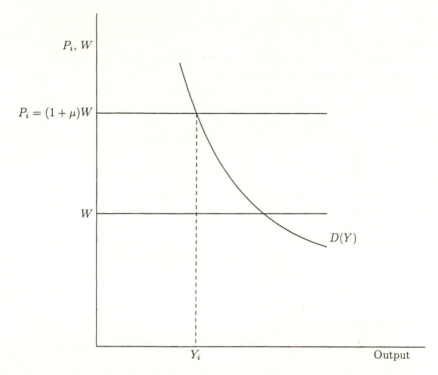

Figure 2.1: A monopolist facing a constant elasticity of product demand will set prices as a constant mark-up over marginal cost. Here the marginal cost is equal to the wage because labor is the only input and constant returns to labor prevail.

the economy, they will demand more of everything and the typical firm will see the demand curve it faces shift outward. To respond to this increase in demand, the firm does not have to change its price, since under the assumptions we have made it always charges the same mark-up over marginal cost. The firm's managers will have to find the new quantity demanded at that price, however. Managers need to predict the position of the demand curve for their product, and that is why businesses are willing to pay professional economists for their forecasts of GDP.

We can visualize the problem by referring to Figure (2.1). There we see that the typical firm sets the same price no matter how much or little demand there is for its output. In effect, there is a horizontal "pricing curve" for the firm's output[3]. For example, if there were an increase in the economy's income, Y, the demand curve for each firm's output would shift outward because its consumers could afford to buy more. Then more output would be produced and sold at the same price.

Since all the firms are identical, we can generalize this point to the aggregate level. For an economy that satisfies the assumptions we have made, particularly the assumption that the money wage is constant, the aggregate pricing curve is horizontal. This curve has come to be known as the *aggregate supply curve*, and even though this terminology is not very accurate, we will adopt it. The horizontal aggregate supply curve has an extremely important implication. Changes in the level of demand will be reflected entirely in changes in output, as managers try to match production to sales, and will not result in changes in prices.

Of course, this simplified picture depends on the special assumptions that we have made. But it turns out that empirical studies of pricing behavior support the position that our simplified picture is a good first approximation to reality.

2.4   Aggregate price, output, and employment

Most of the results we have established with respect to the individual firm carry over when we aggregate over all the firms because they are identical in every important respect. However, one concept that does not survive aggregation is that of the demand curve. The reason is simple: the microeconomic demand curve exists mainly because an increase in P_i, *holding all other prices constant,* stimulates consumers to seek substitutes for the typical good. When we aggregate over all the goods, we are considering a simultaneous increase in all the prices, so that all the relative prices remain constant. That is why an aggregate demand curve cannot be formed by simply adding up all the individual demand curves. We will see that nonetheless, macroeconomic theory does suggest reasons of a purely macroeconomic nature for the existence of an aggregate demand curve, but the aggregate demand curve can be vertical or even positively sloped, even when individual demand curves have

---

[3]There is no true supply curve under imperfect competition because the firm chooses the price depending on properties of the demand curve, rather than by responding to some given price. Here the price chosen is constant because we have assumed that the elasticity of product demand is constant.

their usual negatively sloped shape. This illustrates why macroeconomics is more than an extension of microeconomics: the whole is often different from the sum of its parts.

Aggregating the pricing equation over all the firms results in an aggregate pricing equation

$$P = (1 + \mu)W$$

which, once again, tells us that as long as the wage is fixed, firms will charge the same price no matter how much demand they experience for their products. Again, it is conventional to call the horizontal line at the price given by this equation the aggregate supply curve, although it would be more accurate to call it the aggregate price curve. When we drop the assumption that wages are constant in later chapters, we will find that the aggregate supply curve may slope upward.

Just as we can find the profit share at the firm level from the mark-up, so too can we find the aggregate profit share, Π/Y, which will be equal to $\mu/(1 + \mu)$.

Aggregating the production function over all the firms results in an aggregate production function[4].

$$Y = N$$

Obviously, if firms choose to expand output, they must hire more units of labor. In practice, this can be accomplished through longer hours per worker, or through hiring. We simplify by assuming that hours per worker are constant, so that changes in labor input are equivalent to changes in the number of employed workers.

Modern macroeconomic theory originated in the Great Depression of the 1930's, when unemployment levels in advanced countries reached levels of 25 per cent or more, and policy makers sought methods for creating jobs. The aggregate production function shows that the secret to increasing employment lies in increasing the level of production. The next chapter introduces the Keynesian model of output determination that emerged from the political and intellectual ferment of the Great Depression.

---

[4]The constant $y = 1$, which is left implicit, has the dimension constant dollars per worker per year to ensure that the production function is dimensionally consistent.

Problems for Chapter 2

1. If 200 million workers produce $10 trillion per year in output, in what units should labor be measured so that the production function is $Y = N$?

2. If the wage is $5 per worker, each worker produces one unit of output, and firms charge a 50% mark-up over marginal cost, what price will the firms charge?

3. The firm described in the previous question sells 100 units of its output. Calculate its total profits, profits as a share of output, and wages as a share of output.

4. The firm (firm i) described in question 2 thinks its demand curve has the form $Y_i^d = P_i^{-3}Y$, where Y represents aggregate income. It forecasts that the level of GDP will be $1000 per year. What price will it charge and how much should it produce, assuming its output is divisible so that fractions are permitted? How much more would it produce if it expected GDP to be $2000 per year?

5. The elasticity of product demand in the previous question has a value of 3. Verify that the mark-up is 50% (see appendix).

6. Use the statistical appendix of the *Economic Report of the President* to find data on prices and costs for nonfinancial corporate businesses in the U.S. Calculate the mark-up, the wage share of output, and the gross profit share of output in each year over the last two decades. How stable are the mark-up and profit share?

Chapter 3

Keynesian Theory

The central ideas of the Keynesian theory of macroeconomics are that the level of aggregate (or total) demand depends on the level of income, and that in equilibrium the level of income (aka output) adjusts so that it conforms to the level of demand[1].

3.1 Components of aggregate demand

We model these ideas by writing down equations that describe each of the components of aggregate demand, combining them, and solving for the level of GDP that equates aggregate demand and output. The consumption function and investment function play central roles.

3.1.1 Consumption

The consumption function describes how consumer spending by households responds to changes in their disposable income. It is written in general form as $C = C(Y, T)$, which says that consumption depends on income and taxes, the two variables that determine disposable income, $Y - T$. It makes sense to assume that consumption depends positively on income, Y, and negatively on taxes, T. Rather than work with a general form (which expresses qualitative information), we will work with a particular form of the consumption function (and other functions) in order to make our macroeconomic model as

---

[1]The theory originates with the seminal work of Keynes (1936), of course, but also with the independent discoveries of Kalecki (1971).

concrete as possible. Whenever possible, we use linear equations. The linear consumption function is written as follows,

$$C = c_0 + c_1(Y - T) \tag{3.1}$$

where c_0 and c_1 $(0 < c_1 < 1)$ are parameters referred to as *autonomous consumption* and the *marginal propensity to consume*[2]. Autonomous consumption does not require any disposable income, for example, because it is financed out of past accumulations of wealth. The marginal propensity to consume describes how much consumption spending increases in response to each \$1 increase in disposable income. Note that it is a fraction less than one.

It is also possible that consumer spending depends on the interest rate, the distribution of income, or wealth, as some theories of consumption predict, but we will stick to the simplest case, represented by Equation (3.1).

Because saving is defined as disposable income that is not consumed, the consumption function implicitly defines a companion saving function, $S(Y, T)$. The companion to Equation (3.1) is the saving function

$$S = -c_0 + (1 - c_1)(Y - T) \tag{3.2}$$

The marginal propensity to save is $1 - c_1$.

3.1.2   Investment

Investment spending takes three main forms in practice: spending by businesses on new plant and equipment (business fixed investment), spending by households on new residential housing (residential fixed investment), and changes in inventories (inventory investment). It seems reasonable to believe that investment spending ought to respond to changes in the interest rate. The most obvious example is residential investment; households are reluctant to build new houses (or add to existing housing) when mortgage interest rates are high. Business fixed investment, too, is predicted to respond to interest rates by some theories of investment because it represents the cost of funding for major projects. Even if businesses do not have to borrow to finance an expansion, they will still regard the interest rate as an opportunity cost of the funds used for that purpose since they could have lent them out at that rate.

---

[2]Notice that we use subscripts on parameters for identifying purposes, not to represent a time period as we will do with variables.

It also seems reasonable to suppose that investment responds to changes in income. Households whose incomes have increased are better able to afford new houses. Businesses that enjoy higher profits have more funds available to finance new projects.

We can summarize these ideas through an investment function of the general form $I^p = I(Y, i)$, where i represents the interest rate. The superscript p is a reminder that the investment function describes planned investment. A linear investment function is written

$$I^p = b_0 + b_1 Y - b_2 i \tag{3.3}$$

where b_0, b_1 ($0 < b_1 < 1$), and b_2 are parameters, called *autonomous investment*, the *marginal propensity to invest*, and the *interest sensitivity of investment*. We might interpret autonomous investment as at least in part a reflection of government investment spending, which does not depend closely on income or credit conditions.

In order to reduce the Keynesian theory to its most fundamental terms, we will impose two restrictive assumptions in this chapter. First, we assume a constant interest rate, eliminating one possible source of variation in investment. (This might be rationalized by the underlying assumption that the central bank maintains a constant interest rate.) Second, we will assume initially that the parameter b_1 is zero, eliminating the second possible source of variation in investment. In other words, we assume that investment spending itself is constant, and we represent a constant by using the bar ($^-$) notation:

$$I^p = b_0 - b_2 \bar{i} = \bar{I}$$

Later in this chapter, we will consider what effect the marginal propensity to invest has in the Keynesian model.

3.1.3 Government

The final category of spending is government expenditure. It is determined by the political authorities, e.g., Congress and the president of the United States. Government spending and taxation are the tools of fiscal policy. We will assume that both are determined exogenously. In practice, both government spending and taxation do respond to changes in the level of economic activity, but we will be ignoring these details. One of the key

questions we will want to answer is how fiscal policies affect the level of GDP
and other endogenous variables.

3.2   Theories of consumption and investment

The most influential explanations of consumption are the *life-cycle theory*
and the *bequest theory*.   The life-cycle theory (Modigliani and Brumberg,
1954) predicts that people save during their working lives to finance retirement. In this case, the private marginal propensity to consume depends on
how many years you plan on working relative to how many years you plan
on living in retirement. The fewer the working years, the greater the need to
save for retirement, and the lower the propensity to consume. The aggregate
marginal propensity to consume depends on the distribution of households in
different stages of their life-cycles. The more young households, the lower the
aggregate propensity to consume. There will be no aggregate saving unless
the population is growing, which ensures there are more young households
(savers) than old ones (dissavers).

The bequest theory assumes that people are altruistic toward their children, and save in order to leave them an inheritance. The bequest motive
underpins the theory of Ricardian equivalence (Barro, 1974), which predicts
that consumers who receive a tax cut will actually save all their tax rebate
in anticipation of the future tax increase (even when this mostly affects their
heirs) made necessary by the tax cut. Since consumers do not respond to the
government's choice to borrow rather than tax, debt and taxes have equivalent effects. Under some conditions, this conflicts with the Keynesian theory
that fiscal deficits stimulate demand.

A third theory of consumption is the Classical theory that saving propensities differ by social class (see Kalecki, 1971). In a Classical model, workers
own no wealth, live off their wages, and consume most or all of their income,
while capitalists own wealth, live off profit-type income, and have a smaller
propensity to consume than workers. Since capitalists save more, a redistribution of income toward profits reduces the aggregate propensity to consume.
In this book, we will generally assume that the real wage and distribution of
income are constant, which suppresses these effects.

The most influential theory of investment is the *neoclassical theory*. It
is based on the hypothesis that capital can be substituted for labor subject
to continuously diminishing returns. As the cost of capital (i.e., the interest

rate) declines, it makes a larger capital stock economical to firms and they respond by increasing their investment, which is in fact the change in their capital stock. Another theory states that firms plan their investment needs based on the expected level of sales. This *accelerator theory* predicts that investment is a function of the expected change in GDP. The neoclassical theory and the accelerator theory can be combined, or the accelerator theory can stand by itself for economists who think capital and labor are complements rather than substitutes. The third theory of investment emphasizes the role that cash flow (profits plus depreciation) plays in financing investment expenditures. This theory is based on the hypothesis that profit overcomes a *credit constraint* on investment, so that the more profit businesses earn, the more investment spending they are able to finance. We acknowledge this theory by making investment depend on GDP, a large fraction of which is profit.

Investment projects represent a sort of bet on the future, and this presents a real theoretical problem. The decision to build a new factory or develop a new product is often made under conditions of great uncertainty about the future. Will the demand materialize when the factory is completed or the new product launched? Keynes (1936) suggested that it is futile to treat this decision with the same theoretical tools used to describe a consumer choosing between competing goods whose characteristics are known with certainty. He proposed that investment depends at least partly upon the mood of business managers and entrepreneurs, which he called their *animal spirits*. To a large extent, this perspective resists the kind of formal, mathematical modelling that we rely upon in this book. The best way to bring this perspective back into these models is to recognize that the investment function may be subject to considerable instability due to changes in the animal spirits of investors.

3.3 Aggregate demand

Aggregate demand is the sum of consumption, investment, and government spending. In general, the aggregate demand function is written $Z = Z(Y) = C(Y) + I(Y, i) + G$, where Z represents aggregate demand. Since both consumption and investment are direct functions of the level of income, we expect aggregate demand to be directly related to income. As a first approximation, we are assuming that investment is constant. The linear form of the aggregate demand equation is derived by substituting the linear consumption equation and the constant level of investment into this equation. It is written,

$$Z = [c_0 - c_1 T + \bar{I} + G] + c_1 Y \tag{3.4}$$

Notice that the aggregate demand function is presented above in intercept-slope form. The slope of the aggregate demand function is the marginal propensity to consume. This makes good sense, because consumption spending is the only kind of spending that responds to changes in the level of income under the assumption that the marginal propensity to invest is zero.

3.4   Equilibrium in the product market

The aggregate demand function expresses total planned spending as a function of the level of income or output (recall that they are equivalent). The economy will be in equilibrium when the firms have collectively chosen to produce the level of output that exactly corresponds to the level of demand. Mathematically, we write the condition for equilibrium in the product market, where final goods and services are bought and sold, as

$$Z = Y \tag{3.5}$$

By substituting Equation (3.4) into this equilibrium condition, we can solve for the equilibrium level of output since we are left with one equation and one unknown. The solution is

$$Y^* = (\frac{1}{1 - c_1})[c_0 - c_1 T + \bar{I} + G] \tag{3.6}$$

The first part of the right hand side, enclosed by parentheses, is called the *multiplier*. Let us represent the multiplier using the symbol γ, where

$$\gamma = \frac{1}{1 - c_1}$$

The second part, enclosed in brackets, represents all the spending that is independent of the level of GDP, called *autonomous spending*. In the Keynesian theory the economy achieves an equilibrium level of GDP equal to autonomous spending blown up or magnified by the multiplier.

3.5 The multiplier

Any change in autonomous spending will result in a change in equilibrium GDP. For example, suppose government spending increased by ΔG, where the Δ notation indicates a change in G. From Equation (3.6), it is clear that[3]

$$\Delta Y = \gamma \Delta G$$

If the marginal propensity to consume is .75, the multiplier is 4 and a $1 increase in government spending results in a $4 increase in equilibrium GDP. Government spending has a multiplier effect on GDP, as does a decrease in taxes (although the multiplier effect of a tax cut will be smaller in magnitude). The multiplier is the basic analytical tool for understanding how fiscal policy works in the short run. An increase in autonomous consumption spending or an increase in investment spending also has a multiplier effect on GDP. This is also the basic analytical tool for understanding economic fluctuations. Changes in consumption spending and especially changes in investment spending lead to corresponding changes in GDP, but of larger magnitude. Investment spending is more important in practice in this regard because it is the most volatile element of spending in modern economies. In a sense, with its multiplier effects, investment spending is like the tail that wags the dog.

3.6 The Keynesian cross

We can visualize the basic Keynesian model of aggregate demand by means of a diagram. Figure (3.1) shows the level of output (aka income) on the horizontal axis and the level of aggregate demand on the vertical axis. The 45-degree ray through the origin graphs the equilibrium condition, Equation (3.5). The equilibrium level of GDP must lie along this ray.

To pin down where along the ray the equilibrium GDP lies, we graph the aggregate demand function, Equation (3.4). Notice that the vertical intercept for this function is autonomous spending, $[c_0 - c_1 T + \bar{I} + G]$, while the slope of the function is the marginal propensity to consume. That reflects the fact that consumption is the only kind of spending that responds to changes in income under the assumptions we maintain.

---

[3]You can reach the same conclusion by differentiating Equation (3.6) to find $dY/dG = \gamma$ or $dY = \gamma dG$. The multiplier was introduced by Kahn (1931).

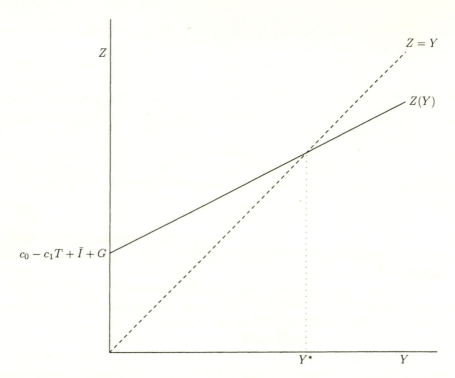

Figure 3.1: The Keynesian cross diagram shows the equilibrium level of output where aggregate demand just equals output. At levels above the equilibrium, output exceeds demand so inventories will accumulate. At levels below the equilibrium, demand exceeds output so inventories will be drawn down. These changes in inventories provide signals to managers to adjust the level of output.

The equilibrium level of GDP, Y^*, occurs where the aggregate demand curve intersects the 45-degree ray. For obvious reasons, this diagram has come to be called the *Keynesian cross*.

3.7   Investment-saving equilibrium

The investment-saving identity provides an alternative way to think about equilibrium GDP. Recall that this condition says that actual investment must equal national saving, or $I = S + (T - G)$. This identity is true by virtue of the fact that actual investment has been defined to include any change in inventories. In our model, planned investment is represented by $\bar{I}$. The difference between planned and actual investment is unplanned changes in inventories. In equilibrium, when production levels have been chosen correctly, there will be no unplanned changes in inventories. That is why equality between planned investment and national saving is an alternative way to express the equilibrium condition, Equation (3.5), and we can write the alternative equilibrium condition

$$\bar{I} = S + (T - G) \tag{3.7}$$

All the terms in this equation are exogenous, except for private saving, S. Substituting the saving function, Equation (3.2), gives us:

$$\bar{I} = S + (T - G) = -c_0 + c_1 T - G + (1 - c_1)Y \tag{3.8}$$

If we solve this equation, we obtain the expression for equilibrium GDP we found earlier, Equation (3.6). Equilibrium occurs at the level of GDP that brings about an equality between the (pre-determined) amount of planned investment spending, $\bar{I}$, on the left-hand side of Equation (3.8) and national saving as specified on the right-hand side of Equation (3.8).

We can visualize this in Figure (3.2), which displays an alternative way of representing the equilibrium level of GDP. The upward sloping function shows that national saving increases with the level of national income because private saving is a function of disposable income. The horizontal function shows that planned investment is constant (by assumption). Equilibrium GDP occurs where these functions intersect, and planned investment equals national saving. That is why we can either define equilibrium in terms of the product market or in terms of the investment-saving (IS) relationship. We will use the symbol IS as a synonym for product market equilibrium.

3.8 Dynamics

Before we can conduct an analysis of the effects of changes in parameters on the level of GDP, we need to establish that this model will return to its equilibrium GDP following some disturbance. First, let us review what we know about inventory changes, which provide signals to managers to raise or lower production levels. The difference between output and sales (i.e., demand) is inventory change, or, expressed mathematically,

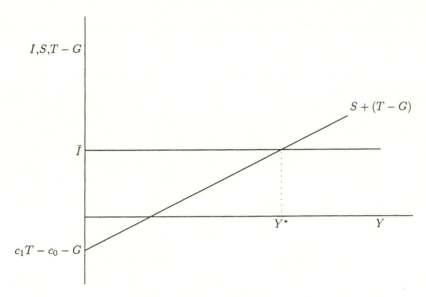

Figure 3.2: The equilibrium level of output in the Keynesian model can also be found by equating planned investment with national saving. That is why an equilibrium in the product market is called *IS* equilibrium.

$$\Delta\text{inventories} = Y - Z = C + I + G - (C + \bar{I} + G)$$

Simplifying the right-hand expression shows that the difference between actual investment and planned investment also describes inventory change:

$$\Delta\text{inventories} = Y - Z = I - \bar{I}$$

Consider a level of GDP that lies below the equilibrium level, for example. In this case, it is clear from Figure (3.1) that the level of aggregate demand, Z, will exceed the level of output, Y, since the aggregate demand function lies above the 45-degree line (demand and output are equal on the 45-degree line). In this case, because the firms have under-produced in relation to the demand for their products, they will have to satisfy their customers by drawing down their inventories, selling goods from the warehouse rather than freshly produced goods. A natural assumption is that this inventory reduction will signal the firms' managers to boost the level of production in the next period. So, as long as output lies below the equilibrium level, managers will be increasing output over time and this will move the economy toward its equilibrium level.

On the other hand, if the level of output exceeds the equilibrium level, the same line of reasoning should convince you that firms will experience a unwanted accumulation of inventories of unsold goods. This signals the managers to cut back on production in the next period. This reasoning demonstrates that the equilibrium level of GDP is indeed a point of attraction, so that the model will in fact gravitate toward its equilibrium after a disturbance.

A formal analysis of the dynamics of the Keynesian cross model appears in the Appendix.

3.9 Comparative equilibrium analysis

3.9.1 Fiscal policy

The purpose of the Keynesian model is to help us understand the effects of fiscal policy on the level of activity. The best way to understand the effects of fiscal policy, or any other change in a parameter, is to conduct a comparative equilibrium analysis in which we change just one parameter, such as government spending or taxes in the case of fiscal policy, and study the effect this has on the endogenous variables of the model, in particular the level of equilibrium GDP. It is important to change just one parameter so we can isolate the effects it has on the endogenous variables.

Multiplier for government spending

An increase in government spending will clearly increase the intercept in Equation (3.4) without affecting the slope term. This fiscal policy shifts the aggregate demand function, $Z(Y)$, upward. Clearly, the equilibrium level of GDP increases, as we see graphically in Figure (3.3). We have already calculated the magnitude of the change. Each \$1 increase in government spending increases GDP by \$$\gamma$, where γ is the multiplier.

Another way to understand the multiplier is through the dynamic process of adjustment itself. Suppose the increase in government spending is \$1 (one constant dollar). The first year, firms will experience an increase in demand equal to \$1, which will reduce their inventories. In response, in the

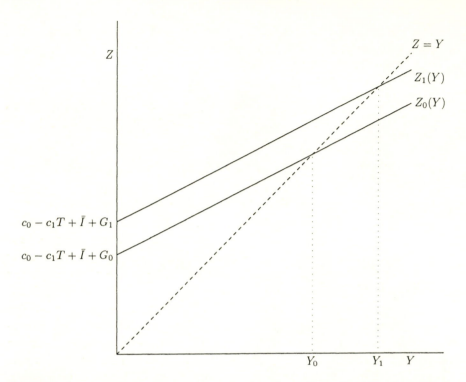

Figure 3.3: An increase in government spending from G_0 to G_1 shifts the aggregate demand function upward and creates a multiplier effect. The change in output, $Y_1 - Y_0$, is equal to the multiplier times the change in government spending, or $\gamma(G_1 - G_0)$.

second year they increase output by \$1. This results in additional income, of which \$$c_1$ are spent. But this results in yet another increase in demand and reduction in inventories. When firms respond to that by another increase in output, equal to \$$c_1$, they raise incomes again by this amount. Thus another increase in demand emerges, this time equal to \$$c_1^2$. The economy experiences successive rounds of a multiplier process. To calculate the total increase in output at its end, we have only to add up an infinite geometric series[4]:

---

[4]To sum this series, write out a finite series $V_n = 1 + c_1 + c_1^2 + \cdots + c_1^n$. Now multiply both sides by c_1 and subtract the result from the original. This gives $V_n - c_1 V_n = 1 - c_1^{n+1}$ or $V_n = (1 - c_1^{n+1})/(1 - c_1)$. Then take the limit (and remember that $c_1 < 1$): $\lim_{n \to \infty} V_n = 1/(1 - c_1)$.

$$\Delta Y = 1 + c_1 + c_1^2 + \cdots = \frac{1}{1 - c_1} = \gamma$$

Reassuringly, this is the same expression for the multiplier we got using other methods. This dynamic process is surely too mechanical to be realistic, but it should help fix the idea of the multiplier.

Funding the government

An important question is where the government gets the funding for an increase in spending. If it starts with a balanced budget, $G = T$, then an increase in government spending requires that the government borrow to fund the increase. Implicit in the Keynesian model is a financial system standing in the background, with a market for government debt where this borrowing could be arranged. But that raises yet another question. Where do the funds that the government borrows come from? The answer may surprise you. The economy responds to the fiscal stimulus by generating new saving in the private sector, which provides the funds for the government to borrow. We can see how this works by referring to Equation (3.7), which shows the alternative method of determining equilibrium using the investment-saving identity. As long as the level of investment remains constant, the level of national saving must also stay constant. So a reduction in government saving, $(T - G)$, means the system responds by increasing private saving, S, correspondingly. Private saving depends on the level of GDP, so the multiplier process that increases GDP can be conceived as a process of increasing private saving by exactly the amount that public saving has been reduced.

This way of thinking about saving was a major innovation of the Keynesian revolution. Previous to Keynes, many economists subscribed to a belief in *Say's Law*, named after French economist Jean-Baptiste Say. Say's Law asserts that there cannot be a general overproduction of goods; supply always creates enough aggregate demand to take whatever has been produced off the market ("Supply creates its own demand"). In other words, if people choose to save more, they will demand less for consumption purposes but that means they will have to buy more investment goods, either directly or indirectly, and in this way, saving determines investment. Keynes objects that people could save by acquiring more financial assets like money, which need not lead to more investment purchases at all. His basic insight is that

the level of output adjusts so that saving matches the pre-determined amount
of investment spending. This is called *the principle of effective demand*. It
suggests that investment determines saving.

Tax multiplier

A decrease in taxes, T, will also have a multiplier effect. A tax cut of $-\Delta T$
will increase consumer spending by $c_1\Delta T$. The *tax multiplier* can be derived
from Equation (3.6). It will be: $\Delta Y/\Delta T = -c_1/(1 - c_1) = -c_1\gamma$.

3.9.2   The paradox of thrift

Another interesting question is how an increase in private saving would affect
the level of GDP. Before the Keynesian revolution, economists generally associated an increase in saving with economic growth. The implicit assumption
behind this thinking was that saving would automatically generate investment according to Say's Law. But the principle of effective demand suggests
a much different relationship.

In the Keynesian model an increase in planned saving on the part of
households will actually reduce the level of GDP. We can see this by inspecting Equation (3.6). Increased saving can be effected by either a decrease in
c_0 or in c_1, and either of these changes will clearly reduce equilibrium GDP.
The reason is that increased saving implies reduced consumer demand, which
causes firms to cut back on production.

Another way of seeing how this works is to visualize the investment-saving
relationship, as in Figure (3.4), which shows how a decrease in autonomous
consumption (which is the same as an increase in autonomous saving) would
affect equilibrium by shifting the national saving function upward. The critical point is that the amount of saving is strictly limited by the amount of
planned investment, represented by the horizontal line at the level $\bar{I}$. When
households, consulting their own individual tastes, attempt to increase their
saving, the result is that they are prevented from doing so by the drop in
income that ensues. This result is called the *paradox of thrift*. In the Keynesian model, because it is investment that determines saving through the
principle of effective demand, an attempted increase in saving is doomed to
fail. In direct contradiction to the pre-Keynesian conventional wisdom, which
was based on the theory that saving determines investment, an increase in
saving actually causes a lower level of economic activity in the Keynesian

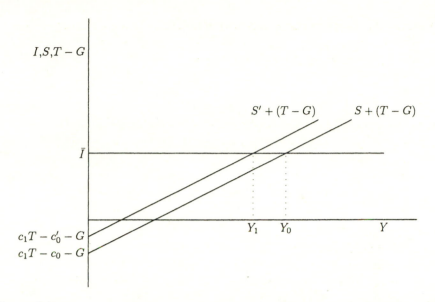

Figure 3.4: An increase in saving, represented by an upward shift in the saving function, has no effect on national saving in the Keynesian model. This is called the paradox of thrift. In the Keynesian model, the level of investment determines the level of saving, rather than the other way around. As long as the level of investment remains constant, households or the government cannot change the level of national saving.

model. This pessimism about the ability of financial markets to translate additional saving into additional investment spending pervades Keynesian economic theory[5].

An increase in public saving, in the form of a fiscal surplus, can also be interpreted as a form of the paradox of thrift. For example, a decrease in government spending will contribute to a fiscal surplus and it will reduce the level of output, through the multiplier process discussed above.

---

[5]A variant of the paradox of thrift occurs with a redistribution of income toward profit. Under the Classical consumption function, this will lower the aggregate propensity to consume and result in a lower level of output. Put another way, lowering the real wage will actually destroy jobs through its effects on aggregate demand. See Foley and Michl (1999) for more details.

3.9.3   Balanced budget multiplier

We have seen that the government spending multiplier is γ, which is also the multiplier for any other type of autonomous spending. An increase in government spending is self-financing in the sense that it causes an increase in private saving, which can be lent out to the government. Obviously, government borrowing faces some limitations, so the question arises, can fiscal policy be effective once these limitations on government borrowing are recognized? It is a remarkable fact that in the Keynesian model, a fiscal policy that leaves the government budget unchanged by increasing tax revenues one-for-one with the increased spending will have a multiplier effect. (This is sometimes called "pay as you go" financing, and abbreviated as PAYGO.) In other words, fiscal policy can stimulate without deficit spending.

This fact was discovered by the early pioneers of Keynesian theory (Baumol and Preston, 1955). Previous economists had been unaware of it because they reasoned erroneously that an increase in government spending would increase aggregate demand but that an equal increase in taxes would decrease aggregate demand, and the two effects would cancel each other out. We can now see that this is not true because only a fraction—the marginal propensity to consume—of the increase in taxes goes toward reducing consumption spending. The rest goes toward reducing saving.

Mathematically, we can determine the multiplier effect of a tax-financed fiscal policy by applying the difference operator, Δ, to Equation (3.6), giving us

$$\Delta Y = (\frac{1}{1 - c_1})[-c_1 \Delta T + \Delta G]$$

By substituting the tax-finance condition $\Delta T = \Delta G$, we obtain

$$\Delta Y = \Delta T = \Delta G$$

This remarkable result is called the *balanced budget multiplier theorem*. This terminology is somewhat misleading, since there is no requirement that the budget be balanced, only that any change in spending is financed one-for-one by a change in taxes. It might better be called the PAYGO multiplier. The balanced budget multiplier turns out to be equal to unity (one) no matter what the marginal propensity to consume, a strikingly elegant result.

3.10 Marginal propensity to invest

Including the marginal propensity to invest in the investment function changes slightly the equations that describe product market equilibrium. First, let us continue to assume that the interest rate is constant. Investment spending is now

$$I^P = b_0 + b_1 Y - b_2 \bar{i} \qquad (3.9)$$

When we follow the procedure for deriving the equilibrium solution by substituting the investment equation and consumption equation into the equilibrium condition, we arrive at an extended version of the equation for equilibrium GDP, which is

$$Y = (\frac{1}{1 - c_1 - b_1})[c_0 - c_1 T + b_0 - b_2 \bar{i} + G] \qquad (3.10)$$

As before, the first term on the right hand side is the multiplier, now written:

$$\gamma = \frac{1}{1 - c_1 - b_1}$$

Note that the presence of the marginal propensity to invest makes the multiplier larger, which makes good sense from an economic standpoint.

To avoid an ill-conditioned model with a negative or infinite multiplier, we must impose the parameter restriction that the marginal propensity to invest is less than the marginal propensity to save, or

$$b_1 < 1 - c_1$$

With this restriction in place, the main results of the Keynesian cross model go through without difficulty and with minor changes. The main difference is that now investment is variable, and its level depends on the equilibrium level of GDP. A fiscal expansion will increase investment by increasing the overall level of GDP. The paradox of thrift becomes more paradoxical because an increase in *ex ante* private saving will actually cause the overall level of investment (and therefore national saving) to fall.

3.11   Limitations of the Keynesian model

Many economists regard the Keynesian cross model of aggregate demand as a good first approximation to the short-run behavior of modern market economies. But it is important to keep in mind the restrictions that we have imposed through special assumptions.

First, we have assumed that wages and prices are constant, and do not change even though employment and output are changing. We will continue to maintain this assumption for several more chapters.

Second, we have assumed that if investment spending is sensitive to the interest rate, the interest rate remains constant even when the level of income changes. We will relax this assumption in the next chapter and see that our results must be modified to take into account the role of the interest rate. In fact, we will see throughout this book that relaxing special assumptions transforms the macroeconomic theory we are building into one that is less and less "Keynesian" and more and more "pre-Keynesian." We will see this by checking the status of the government spending multiplier and the paradox of thrift as we progress to more complex models.

Problems for Chapter 3

These problems make use of the following data for a hypothetical economy:

$$C = 140 + .6(Y - T)$$

$$\bar{I} = 200$$

$$G = 150$$

$$T = 150$$

All variables are in units of constant dollars per year, which we will represent by the $ symbol. Unless the problem states otherwise, always go back to these original data.

1. Calculate the equilibrium level of output.

2. Derive the equation for aggregate demand. Calculate the level of demand and unplanned inventory change when output is $500 per year, and describe the supply response. Repeat when output is $1200 per year.

3. Draw the Keynesian cross diagram and identify the positions described in the previous two problems.

4. The government wants to increase GDP by \$250. Calculate the level of government spending required.

5. Use the investment-saving identity to explain where the government will get the funding for its fiscal policy in the previous question. What has the fiscal deficit done to national saving?

6. Go back to the original data, but replace the investment equation above with $I^p = 100 + .1Y$ and calculate the level of national saving. Now suppose households attempt to save more of their income, so that the consumption function shifts to $C = 100 + .6(Y - T)$. Calculate the new level of national saving and explain what has happened.

7. Set up a spreadsheet that lets you change the parameters of the Keynesian model experimentally. Make two copies of the model in your spreadsheet, one to use as a control (with the original parameter values), and the other to test changes in a single parameter. Graph the aggregate demand equations from the control and test models along with the equilibrium condition $Z = Y$ to visualize the Keynesian cross. Use the spreadsheet to verify your answers to the previous problems, and to conduct comparative equilibrium experiments of your own design.

Chapter 4

The IS Curve

In the last chapter we developed a simple Keynesian model of the equilibrium level of GDP under the assumption that the interest rate is constant. In this chapter we will relax that assumption and examine the effects of changes in the interest rate (for example, caused by monetary policy) on the equilibrium level of GDP. The IS curve represents the relationship between interest rates and the equilibrium level of GDP. By bringing together the IS curve with the LM curve to be developed in the next chapter (which represents a theory of interest rate determination), we will construct the IS-LM system that forms the core of macroeconomic theory.

4.1   Interest rate effects on aggregate demand

We are now ready to examine how the interest rate affects the level of GDP. Let us suppose that the central bank controls the interest rate. How would a rate reduction affect GDP? First, we work out the effects graphically, and then mathematically. (Obviously, we could just as easily ask how a rate increase works, and this makes a good exercise for the reader.)

4.1.1   Visualizing the IS Curve

An interest rate reduction increases investment spending. There is little controversy that one of the main components of investment spending, residential fixed investment, does respond to lower interest rates. When households see mortgage rates fall, they are more inclined to start planning a new house

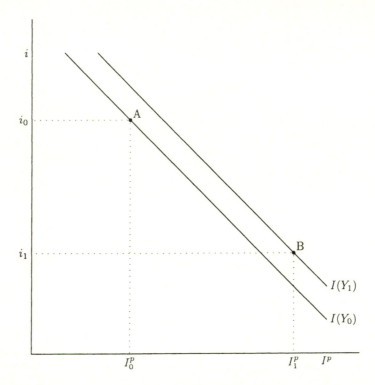

Figure 4.1: The investment function shows that planned investment increases when the interest rate is reduced. This gives the central bank the ability to influence investment demand. Here a rate reduction has caused an expansion of GDP, which has shifted the investment schedule to the right since $I = I(Y, i)$, augmenting the effect on spending.

or addition. There is controversy about whether business fixed investment responds much or at all to interest rates.

Consider a rate reduction from i_0 to i_1. Figure 4.1 shows the investment function, Equation (3.9), with the interest rate on the vertical axis and investment on the horizontal axis. The position of the investment function depends on the level of income. With a lower interest rate and no change in GDP, investment would increase along the curve labeled $I(Y_0)$. But, as we will see, this increase in investment generates a multiplier effect that raises the level of income and shifts the investment function out to the position labeled $I(Y_1)$.

To visualize how a lower interest rate generates a multiplier effect, Fig-

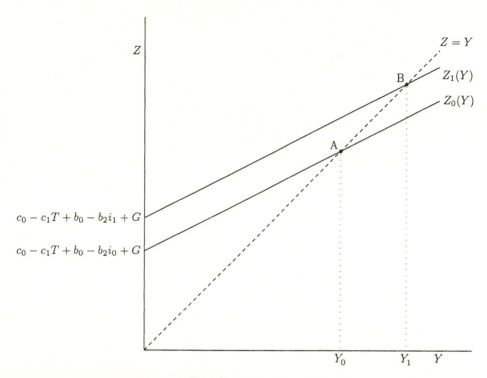

Figure 4.2: Lower interest rates cause an upward shift in the aggregate demand function, through their effect on investment spending. The increase in investment spending has a multiplier effect on the economy.

ure 4.2 shows how the increase in investment induced by lower interest rates affects the Keynesian cross diagram. By increasing the part of investment spending not related to income, $b_0 - b_2i$, the rate reduction shifts the aggregate demand function upward and stimulates an expansion of GDP. Because investment also depends upon the level of GDP, through the marginal propensity to invest, the level of investment will increase further during the multiplier process as a result of the feedback from income to investment. Now we can see why the investment function represented in Figure 4.1 shifts out.

Figure 4.3 brings all this information together and represents the original and new equilibrium in (Y, i) space. We can see that lower interest rates are associated with higher levels of equilibrium GDP in the product market.

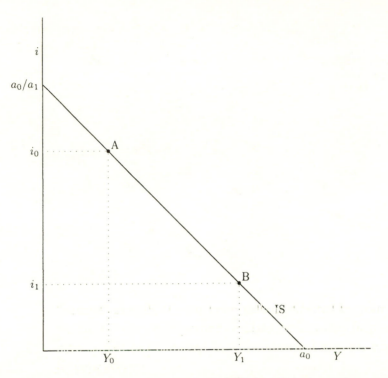

Figure 4.3: The IS curve shows all the levels of GDP for which the product market is in equilibrium. The IS curve slopes down because a lower interest rate is associated with more investment spending, more aggregate demand, and therefore more output. Points A and B in Figures 4.1 – 4.3 correspond to one another. Study these three figures carefully.

Because equilibrium in the product market requires that planned investment equal national saving, the set of points satisfying product market equilibrium is called the *IS curve*.

4.1.2   Deriving the IS curve

As we have seen, the consumption function and the investment function are written:

$$C = c_0 + c_1(Y - T)$$

$$I = b_0 + b_1Y - b_2i$$

In these equations, we call terms like c_1 or b_2 the *structural parameters*.

Substitute these equations into $Z = C + I + G$ and use the equilibrium condition $Z = Y$ to derive the IS curve:

$$Y = \frac{1}{1 - c_1 - b_1}(c_0 - c_1 T + b_0 + G) - \frac{b_2}{1 - c_1 - b_1}i$$

It helps to eliminate notational clutter by defining some handy *consolidating parameters*[1]:

$$a_0 = \frac{1}{1 - c_1 - b_1}(c_0 - c_1 T + b_0 + G) = \gamma(c_0 - c_1 T + b_0 + G)$$

$$a_1 = \frac{b_2}{1 - c_1 - b_1} = \gamma b_2$$

The IS curve can now be written concisely, to emphasize its simple linear structure:

$$Y = a_0 - a_1 i \tag{4.1}$$

Written out in this form, the IS curve remains true to its causal structure, which is based on the theory that changes in interest rates cause changes in investment spending that in turn cause changes in aggregate demand and output. Be sure you understand this causal structure because it explains why the IS curve generally slopes downward[2].

Since we will be graphing the IS curve with i on the vertical axis, it also will be useful to rearrange it with i as dependent variable,

$$i = \frac{c_0 - c_1 T + b_0 + G}{b_2} - \frac{1 - c_1 - b_1}{b_2}Y \tag{4.2}$$

This version of the IS curve is appropriate for gaining familiarity with the properties of the IS curve. Note that in Figure 4.3 the vertical intercept of the IS curve is a_0/a_1, using the consolidating parameters, while the horizontal intercept is a_0.

---

[1]We will form consolidating parameters throughout this book. If you ever need to look up their definitions, you can find them in the index.

[2]It is technically possible for the IS curve to slope upward, but we assume that the parameters lie in a range prohibiting this. The IS curve slopes up if the marginal propensity to invest exceeds the marginal propensity to save.

4.2   Properties of the IS curve

It is important to become familiar with the effects of changes in the structural parameters on the slope and intercept of the IS curve. We will do this by looking back at Equation (4.2) to see how changes in the structural parameters affect the slope and/or intercept of the IS curve.

4.2.1   Fiscal policy

Increases in government spending and reductions in taxes both shift the vertical and horizontal intercepts of the IS curve outward without changing the curve's slope. In other words, fiscal policy generates a parallel shift in the IS curve. Any comparative equilibrium analysis of fiscal policy using the IS curve will start by shifting the curve out (for a fiscal expansion) or in (for a contraction).

We illustrate such an analysis on the assumption that the interest rate is constant Figure 4.4. An increase in government spending shifts the IS curve to the right. The equilibrium level of GDP increases from Y_0 to Y_1. We can be specific about just how much GDP has increased. Since the interest rate is constant, there will be no interest rate-induced changes in investment. Thus we can analyze this case using the Keynesian cross model developed in the previous chapter. The increase in GDP will just be the multiplier[3] effect of an increase in government spending, or $\Delta Y = Y_1 - Y_0 = \gamma \Delta G$. This fact will be valuable when we study the IS-LM model in subsequent chapters.

4.2.2   The slope of the IS curve

To get a deeper understanding of the economic meaning of changes in the slope of the IS curve, it helps to consider the basic causal structure of the IS curve, which is represented by using arrows to indicate causation:

$$\Delta i \Rightarrow \Delta I \Rightarrow \Delta Z \Rightarrow \Delta Y$$

For example, an interest rate reduction leads to an increase in investment, whose magnitude depends on the interest sensitivity of investment, b_2. The

---

[3]Do not forget that the multiplier depends on the marginal propensities to consume and to invest in the full version of the Keynesian cross model.

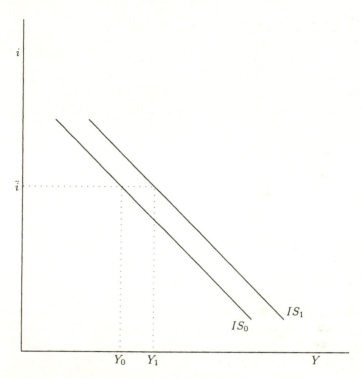

Figure 4.4: An increase in government spending shifts the IS curve to the right. For the given interest rate shown here, the shift is exactly equal to the multiplier effect of the increase in spending, or $Y_1 - Y_0 = \gamma\Delta G$.

increase in investment then leads to an upward shift in the aggregate demand curve, which has a multiplier effect on equilibrium GDP whose magnitude depends on the multiplier. Thus, a given rate reduction causes a larger ultimate increase in GDP the larger the interest sensitivity of investment, and/or the larger the multiplier. Invoking the definition of the slope of a straight line, a larger increase in GDP for a given rate reduction implies a shallower slope ($\Delta i/\Delta Y$) for the IS curve.

The propensity to consume or invest

Increasing either the marginal propensity to consume or to invest will increase the multiplier, which reduces the slope of the IS curve. This makes good sense. Compare two economies with the same interest sensitivity to

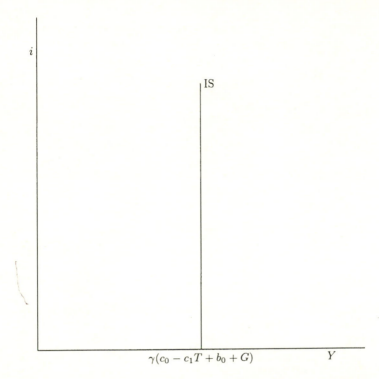

Figure 4.5: When investment is completely insensitive to the interest rate, the IS curve becomes vertical.

investment. The same rate reduction increases investment spending by the same amount in each one, raising the aggregate demand function by the same amount. But in the economy with the larger propensity to consume (or invest), there will be a more vigorous multiplier process because the initial stimulus will induce more consumption (or investment) spending. That economy will expand by more, and its IS curve has a shallower slope.

Interest sensitivity of investment

Changes in the interest sensitivity of investment similarly affect the slope of the IS curve. Consider two economies having the same multiplier. A given interest rate reduction will cause a larger initial increase in investment spending and an upward shift in the aggregate demand function in the economy having a larger interest sensitivity of investment. That economy will therefore experience a larger expansion in equilibrium output, which expresses itself in a shallower slope in the IS curve.

There is one special case, illustrated by Figure 4.5, that is particularly important. When investment spending is completely insensitive to interest rates, $b_2 = 0$, the IS curve becomes vertical. This is best seen by setting $b_2 = 0$ in Equation (4.1), which reduces it to

$$Y = a_0 = \gamma(c_0 - c_1 T + b_0 + G)$$

In this case, interest rates have no way to affect aggregate demand because there is no category of spending that is interest-sensitive. Some economists think this is true of real economies. If that is right, it makes the simple Keynesian-cross model a particularly good approximation of reality. But there is good reason to think that some spending, particularly residential investment (housing), is interest-sensitive.

The IS model offers a theory of how interest rates affect aggregate demand, but not a theory of how interest rates are themselves determined. For that we turn to the market for financial assets like money and bonds.

Problems for Chapter 4

1. The investment equation takes the form $I^p = 50 + .2Y - 2000i$. Calculate planned investment spending when $i = .05$ per year (5% per year) and $Y = \$1000$ per year. Repeat for $i = .05$ per year and $Y = \$700$ per year. Repeat for $i = .08$ per year and Y = \$700 per year.

2. The consumption function is C = 120 + .6(Y - T), T = \$200 per year, G = \$250 per year, and the investment equation is given in the previous problem. Derive the IS curve.

3. Use the IS curve from the previous problem to decide whether firms have produced too much or too little output to achieve equilibrium in the product market if the interest rate is .08 per year and the level of output is \$1000 per year. Describe the changes in inventories they experience, and their supply response.

4. Government spending increases to \$300 per year. How will this affect the IS curve in problem 2? Calculate the change in Y when $i = .05$ per year.

5. Graph the investment equation in problem 1. Determine which of the positions on the investment equation in problem 1 are on the IS curve in problem 2. Refer to Figure 4.1.

6. List the parameter changes that make the IS curve steeper, and explain the economic rationale.

Chapter 5

The LM Curve

Up to this point in this book, we have concerned ourselves with *flows* of income and spending. Flows are measured in units like \$/year. The interest rate is determined in the market for financial assets, which are *stocks* measured in timeless units like \$. For example, the value of the real estate I own at the end of this year is a stock. We will simplify reality considerably by considering an economy in which only two assets are available, money and bonds.

5.1 Money and bonds

We first describe money and bonds, and then explain the portfolio choice that households make in allocating their wealth between money and bonds.

5.1.1 Money

Money is a financial asset whose distinguishing features are liquidity and zero interest. Liquidity refers to the widespread acceptance of money as means of payment in settling transactions of all types. Money offers its owners the advantage of liquidity at the cost of interest foregone, since the same wealth could be held in the form of a bond, earning interest. The interest rate thus represents the opportunity cost of holding money. In real economies, there are many financial assets that do earn some interest but which are also highly liquid, such as cash management accounts, but there is always an interest penalty for greater liquidity. In our model, money takes the form of currency.

5.1.2 Bonds

Bonds are financial instruments that originate when a company or the government borrows from the private sector. The company or the government agrees to pay the owner of the bond a fixed amount of money each year (called the coupon) to cover interest on the loan plus a single repayment of the principal when the bond matures. In real economies, the spectrum of financial assets is enormous, ranging from stocks that give ownership rights in corporations to bonds of varying maturity and riskiness. These assets offer a broad spectrum of returns or yields. As the maturity of bonds of similar quality increases, the yield tends to increase as well. This pattern, called the *yield curve*, is closely watched on financial markets because it is thought to depend upon expectations of future interest rates. We simplify substantially by collapsing the highly charged world of finance into one all-purpose asset, called a bond for convenience, with one rate of return, the interest rate. Abstracting from the yield curve keeps the model manageable, at the cost of some realism.

In our model, bonds are illiquid because in order to settle a transaction, agents must first sell their bonds for money in the market for bonds. The market for bonds should not be confused with the market for new loans, or newly issued bonds. The market for bonds is a second-hand market, where bonds that have not yet reached maturity are bought and sold. The owner of a bond may not be the person who purchased it when it was issued by a company or government borrowing money. The interest rate is determined in the market for bonds.

To see how this works, consider a bond with a one-year maturity. The owner of the bond receives a fixed coupon after one year, which represents the interest payment, plus the initial repayment of principal. Thus, a bond in year t will be worth a known amount after one year, or $P_{t+1}^B = \bar{P}$. The nominal rate of interest is defined as the yield on the funds advanced to purchase the bond at its current price, P_t^B, or

$$i = \frac{\bar{P} - P_t^B}{P_t^B}$$

Rearrange this equation and the relationship between the price of the bond and the interest rate comes sharply into focus:

$$P_t^B = \frac{\bar{P}}{1 + i}$$

From these equations it should be clear that the price of bonds and the interest rate are inversely related[1]. A lower bond price means that the total return from buying the bond, $\bar{P} - P_t^B$, is greater, and thus the interest rate, which is this return expressed as a proportion of the bond price, must by definition be greater as well. Financial reports in the press routinely slip back and forth between bond prices (e.g., "bond prices fell yesterday") and interest rates (e.g., "yields rose yesterday"), since these are two equivalent ways of describing the same financial event. This inverse relationship between bond prices and interest rates generalizes to all maturities and risk classes.

We exploit this basic financial fact to help visualize how the markets for money and bonds interact. If, for example, people try to liquidate (sell) their bonds, the sudden increase in supply will depress bond prices and raise interest rates.

5.1.3 Portfolio choice

In real economies, the idea of portfolio choice has become so familiar as to be the subject of television commercials for financial products. A good example of portfolio choice faces college professors who choose how to allocate their retirement funds in TIAA-CREF between various kinds of financial instruments. In our simplified economic world, financial wealth consists of money and bonds. Our model is a short-run model, which strictly speaking means that the period of time we are studying is short enough that we can safely take the amount of wealth to be constant. The typical (or representative) household chooses to allocate its wealth between money and bonds. It is important to see that the representative household's total amount of wealth never changes, but its composition is subject to change. An individual household can choose to reallocate its portfolio, shifting from bonds into money for example. (This is what happens when people liquidate their bonds.)

However, the quantity of money and the quantity of bonds are fixed at the aggregate level. The quantity of money is determined by the central bank. The quantity of bonds represents the bonds inherited from the past. Thus, one agent can sell her bonds only if another agent is willing to make room for them in his portfolio. But we are assuming that all the agents are identical, ruling out this asymmetry. If one agent is behaving rationally, and

---

[1]Financial analysts would say that the current price of the bond is the present discounted value of its price at maturity.

selling bonds, all the others will want to do the same. How do we resolve
this dilemma?

The answer is that the total supply of money and bonds, $M + B$, must
be equal to the total demand for money and bonds, $M^d + B^d$, since people
who are trying to sell bonds (to stick with this example) are trying to obtain money. The demands for money and bonds show the desired portfolio
allocation. Thus, we can write

$$M + B = M^d + B^d$$

and then rearrange this identity to obtain

$$(M^d - M) + (B^d - B) = 0$$

This expression states that the excess demand for money plus the excess
demand for bonds must add up to zero. When people are trying to shift their
wealth from bonds to money, they desire more money in their portfolios and
have an excess demand for money. If there is an excess demand for money,
there must be an equal and opposite excess demand (i.e., an excess supply)
for bonds. Similarly, an excess supply of money implies an excess demand
for bonds.

When the excess demand for money goes to zero, people have achieved
their desired allocation of wealth, and the excess demand for bonds will also
be zero. Another way of putting this is to say that when the market for
money clears (i.e., quantity demanded equals supply), the market for bonds
will also clear. This is an example (albeit trivial) of *Walras's Law*, which
states that in a closed demand system of n markets, when $n - 1$ markets
clear, the n-th market will also be in equilibrium (here $n = 2$). Walras's Law
lets us analyze the asset markets without paying any attention at all to one
of the two assets. It is conventional to choose to focus on the market for
money, and to leave the events in the bond market implicit.

For example, suppose we find that there is an excess demand for money.
We can see that this implies an excess supply of bonds. People are all trying
to liquidate their bonds. This will put downward pressure on the price of
bonds, and upward pressure on the interest rate since it always moves in the
direction opposite to the price of bonds. Changes in the interest rate are a
potential source of equilibration.

5.2 The demand for money

In everyday language, we use the word money loosely. In macroeconomic theory, money has a precise meaning. It is the quantity of the most liquid financial asset, which is a stock measured in $ at a particular date (e.g., this year). It should never be confused with income, which is a flow measured as $/year. Even though in everyday language we often say that Bill Gates makes a lot of money, we really should say that he receives a large income. We might also say that Bill Gates has a lot of money to convey the fact that he is wealthy. Much of his income comes in the form of interest and dividends on his substantial wealth consisting of money, stocks, bonds and other assets.

The representative household faces a straightforward asset-allocation problem. Given that the household's wealth is fixed, any decision to increase the amount of money in its portfolio must imply a decision to reduce (liquidate) bonds. The existing theories of the demand for money all conclude that the portfolio decision depends on two variables, income and the interest rate.

Income affects our demand for money because we need money to support our expenditures, which is called the *transactions motive*. This part of the demand for money is called the transactions demand for money. If our income goes up, we will spend more on consumer goods and therefore we will need to have liquidity available in the form of cash or a checking account balance.

The interest rate affects our demand for money because any wealth held in money form cannot earn interest. The interest rate is the opportunity cost or penalty for holding wealth in liquid form. Because the interest rate is the cost of liquidity, we will desire less money and more bonds in our optimal portfolio as the interest rate increases. This is the *asset motive*, or *speculative motive* for holding money, and this part of the demand for money is called the speculative demand. (We will explain why the peculiar term speculative is used later.)

In general, the demand for money is written as a function $M^d = PL(Y, i)$, where PY represents nominal income. The symbol L derives from the fact that this function describes the demand for liquidity, and this approach to asset markets is called the theory of liquidity preference. The simplest linear form of the demand for money is

$$M^d = P(d_1 Y - d_2 i)$$

The price level appears outside the parenthesis in conformity with economic theory. If prices double (say), the demand for money should also double. The parameters d_1 and d_2 will be called the *income sensitivity* and the *interest sensitivity* of the demand for money. According to economic theory, their values depend on the underlying preferences of the households and on institutional details of business organizations and the financial system.

The demand for money in real terms is also called the demand for *real balances*. By simply rearranging terms in the linear demand for money, it is written

$$\frac{M^d}{P} = d_1 Y - d_2 i \qquad (5.1)$$

It turns out to be much easier to work with the demand for and supply of real balances.

When economic agents choose a demand for money, they also choose the velocity of money. For example, under Equation (5.1), the velocity of money would be defined by $V = PY/M = Y/(d_1 Y - d_2 i)$. In general, the velocity of money is a function of real income and interest rates, or $V = V(Y, i)$. This fact helps us understand the quantity theory of money in later chapters.

There are (at least) two influential kinds of theory of the demand for money, distinguished by the motive for holding money that they emphasize. The *inventory-theoretic* approach (Baumol, 1952; Tobin, 1956) emphasizes the transactions motive for holding money. The basic idea of this theory is that we balance out the costs of holding money, measured by foregone interest, and the benefits that arise because storing wealth in non-monetary (interest-bearing) form imposes transactions costs. If the interest rate goes up, that makes it worthwhile to put more wealth in interest-bearing form even though it imposes higher transactions costs, such as more frequent trips to our savings bank or financial manager. The *portfolio* theory of the demand for money (Tobin, 1958) focuses on the speculative or asset motive for holding money. Money can be thought of as a store of wealth with very low risk but a zero return. A risk-averse investor will want to put some of her wealth in such a safe asset in order to diversify, or balance out the more risky assets in her portfolio. Both these theories predict that the demand for real balances is directly related to income and inversely related to the interest rate.

5.3 The supply of money

The supply of money, M, refers to the quantity of liquid assets held by the private sector. We will assume that the central bank controls the supply of money. Changes in the money supply are thus the chief instrument of monetary policy.

In practice, the central bank in the U.S. and other rich countries manipulates the money supply through open market operations—buying and selling government bonds. When the central bank buys bonds, it pays the sellers (usually large money-center banks) by issuing new liabilities. The money supply (cash and demand deposits) is a liability of the central bank. An open market purchase therefore increases the money supply by swapping bonds for money in the private sector's portfolio. An open market sale reduces the money supply by swapping money for bonds in the private sector's portfolio. In effect, the central bank has the power to "print" money with a few computer keystrokes.

In the theoretical model we are constructing, however, banks play no role[2]. The money supply consists entirely of currency. An open market purchase is effected by the central bank issuing new currency and increasing the supply of money on a one-for-one basis, while an open market sale reduces the money supply. In this way, the central bank can regulate the supply of money in nominal terms, M.

The supply of real balances, M/P, however has two sources of variation. First, monetary policy can alter the nominal money supply, M, through open market operations. Second, changes in the price level, P, have effects on the purchasing power of an existing quantity of money. A general price increase reduces the purchasing power of the money supply, resulting in a decline in the real money supply. Conversely, a decline in prices increases the real money supply. These sources of variation become important when we relax the assumption that prices are constant.

We will consider two kinds of monetary policy. When the central bank sets the supply of money, it adopts an essentially passive monetary policy

---

[2]Many economists find a macroeconomic theory that ignores the role of banks to be too simplistic. One alternative approach, developed by Hyman Minsky (1982), stresses the interactions between uncertainty, investment, and credit in generating macroeconomic instability. Minsky (1975) outlines the differences between his theory and the IS-LM model, as well as providing a superb explanation of subtleties of Keynes's macroeconomic theory not well captured by the IS-LM model.

that lets the economy adjust to a given money supply. This will be the main assumption we use in deriving and using the LM curve. When we study inflation, we will modify this assumption so that the central bank sets a constant growth rate of the money supply. In either case, the central bank targets the money supply. While there have been brief episodes when central banks have claimed to target the money supply, this assumption is not very realistic. Its main virtue is that it isolates the effects of monetary policy on the economy.

When the central bank changes the supply of money in response to economic conditions, particularly unemployment and inflation, it adopts an active monetary policy. Econometricians (economists specializing in statistical analysis) who study the behavior of the U.S. central bank describe it by the *Fed reaction function*. Many modern central banks have adopted some sort of target inflation rate. When the inflation rate exceeds the target rate, they increase interest rates by reducing the money supply in order to slow the economy. Inflation targeting and other reaction functions are more realistic than monetary targeting. We will extend the model to them only when we have achieved a good understanding of inflation.

5.4   Asset market equilibrium

Through Walras's Law, we can understand the asset markets by studying the market for money while leaving the bond market in the background. Figure 5.1 shows the demand for real balances as a downward sloping function of the interest rate. A decrease in the interest rate reduces the cost of liquidity, and stimulates movement along the demand curve for money as people seek to liquidate their bonds. Figure 5.1 shows the real money supply as a vertical line because the nominal money supply has been chosen exogenously by the monetary authority and the price level is constant[3].

Note that the position of the demand curve depends on the level of income, Y, and the demand curve shown is only valid for one particular level of GDP. Obviously, for this particular level of GDP there is one interest rate that clears the money market, equating the demand for money with the sup-

---

[3]In a model with an explicit banking sector, the money supply may be positively related to the interest rate, because higher interest rates make it attractive for banks to lend out any reserves not legally required, which increases the money multiplier. For a given supply of high-powered money, the money supply expands as the interest rate increases.

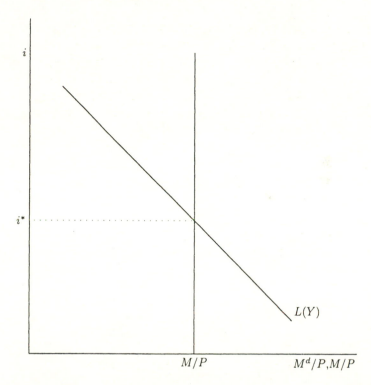

Figure 5.1: The interest rate clears the market for money for a given money supply and a given level of income. At higher interest rates, there will be an excess supply of money, as people want to move more wealth into bonds. This drives up the bond prices and drives down interest rates. At lower rates, people want to move wealth into money, driving down bond prices and driving interest rates upward.

ply of money. This equilibrium interest rate clears both assets markets, the money market and the bond market.

What happens if the interest rate falls short of its equilibrium level? From Figure 5.1 it is clear that a low interest rate creates an excess demand for money. (The demand for money, given by the demand curve, lies to the right of the money supply.) This means that there must be an excess supply of bonds. People are trying to liquidate their bonds in order to build up their real balances at such low interest rates. As they sell bonds, the price of bonds must fall and the interest rate must rise. But this is exactly the change required to get rid of the excess demand for money. Eventually, the interest rate will rise to its equilibrium level. Similar reasoning should convince you

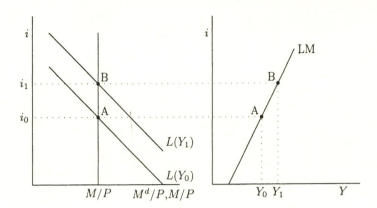

Figure 5.2: The LM curve consists of all the interest rates that clear the money market for each possible level of income. As income increases, people want to hold more money in their portfolios for transactions purposes. Since there is a fixed supply of money, the interest rate rises as a result.

that the interest rate will fall when it starts out above the equilibrium level. Even though the interest rate is technically determined in the bond market by the price of bonds, we can focus our attention on the market for money by virtue of Walras's Law.

The process of adjustment described in the previous paragraph takes place rapidly in real economies. Financial markets move information at electronic speeds. It is reasonable to believe that the time it takes to achieve equilibrium in the asset markets is small in relation to the time it takes to achieve equilibrium in the product markets (which involves changing the level of production in response to inventory signals). We will assume that for all practical purposes the economy achieves asset market equilibrium instantaneously.

5.5   Income variations and the interest rate

The asset market equilibrium represented in Figure 5.1 is valid for the particular level of GDP assumed there. There will generally be a unique equilibrium interest rate for each possible level of GDP. Let us first develop this point graphically before we derive the relevant equations. Consider the way an increase in income affects the asset markets, ignoring for the time being why the level of income has increased.

5.5.1   Visualizing the LM curve

Figure 5.2 shows what happens to the equilibrium interest rate when the level of GDP increases from Y_0 to Y_1. The increased income shifts the demand curve for money outward. There is a larger transactions demand for money. The supply of money remains constant by assumption. With more demand and a fixed supply, it makes sense that the equilibrium interest rate (which is the cost of liquidity) should rise.

When income first increases, the outward shift in the demand curve for money creates an excess demand for money. We have already seen that an excess demand for money implies an excess supply of bonds, which leads to falling bond prices and rising interest rates. The equilibrating process is no mystery. An increase in income will cause the interest rate to rise until it achieves a new equilibrium.

We have identified the points in (Y, i) space where the asset markets are clearing in the right panel of Figure 5.2. Since each level of GDP is associated with its own unique equilibrium interest rate, there will be a locus of such points, which is called the *LM curve* because it involves equality between the demand for liquidity (L) and the supply of money (M).

5.5.2   Deriving the LM curve

To derive the LM curve algebraically, we need only recognize that by definition, it represents positions where the asset markets clear. By virtue of Walras' Law, we know that when the money market clears, or $M^d/P = M/P$, the bond market will be in supply-demand equilibrium as well. Substituting Equation (5.1) into this equilibrium condition gives us the equation for the LM curve

$$i = (\frac{-M}{d_2})\frac{1}{P} + (\frac{d_1}{d_2})Y$$

Again, define consolidating parameters

$$a_2 = \frac{1}{d_2} \qquad a_3 = \frac{d_1}{d_2}$$

so we can write the LM curve concisely to emphasize its linear form:

$$i = -a_2(M/P) + a_3Y \tag{5.2}$$

This form remains true to the theory behind the LM curve, which states that increases (or decreases) in income cause increases (or decreases) in the demand for money, in turn causing interest rates to rise. Note that the LM curve has been written in intercept-slope form, which will ease the understanding of its properties.

The reason for leaving the variables M and P out of the consolidating parameter scheme will become evident when we study aggregate demand as a function of the price level.

5.6   Properties of the LM curve

5.6.1   Monetary policy

We derived the LM curve under the supposition that the real money supply, M/P, was constant because the monetary authority had determined the money supply and because prices are constant by assumption. An increase in the money supply shifts the vertical supply of money to the right. Each level of GDP will be associated with a lower equilibrium interest rate than before the money supply increased. An expansionary monetary policy shifts the LM curve to the right.

Mathematically, an increase in the money supply reduces the vertical intercept of the LM curve in Equation (5.2). Increasing the money supply shifts the LM curve to the right, while decreasing the money supply shifts the LM curve to the left. With our linear model, these shifts are parallel shifts that do not alter the slope of the LM curve.

Decreasing the price level, P, has exactly the same effect as an increase in the nominal money supply, M. In both cases, the real money supply increases, shifting the LM curve to the right. Obviously, reducing the price level shifts the LM curve to the left. We will take advantage of this remarkable isomorphism between monetary policy and price changes extensively in later chapters.

5.6.2   The slope of the LM curve

The slope of the LM curve depends on the income and interest sensitivities of money demand. The causal structure of the theory behind the LM curve can be well represented using arrows:

$$\Delta Y \to \Delta L \to \Delta i$$

An expansion in the economy causes an increase in the demand for money. The size of this effect depends on how sensitive money demand is to income. The increase in money demand results in a rise in interest rates. Because the supply of money is fixed, interest rates must rise by just enough to convince people that despite their higher transactions demand for money, they really don't want to change the composition of their portfolios after all. How much interest rates rise depends on the interest sensitivity of money demand.

Thus, a given increase in income will result in a larger increase in interest rates the greater the income sensitivity of money demand and the lower the interest sensitivity of money demand. The slope of the LM curve is directly related to the income sensitivity of money demand and inversely related to the interest sensitivity of money demand.

5.6.3 The interest sensitivity of money demand

The most important question related to the LM curve concerns the interest sensitivity of money demand. There are two special cases that have theoretical, and perhaps practical, significance.

First, when the demand for money is completely insensitive to interest rates, the LM curve will be vertical. You can see this by substituting $d_2 = 0$ into Equation (5.2), which reduces to

$$Y = (1/d_1)\frac{M}{P}$$

In this case, illustrated in Figure 5.3, there is only one level of GDP that brings about equality between the demand for money and the supply of money, at any level of the interest rate. The position of the vertical money demand curve is determined by the level of GDP, and it will only meet the vertical supply curve at a unique level of GDP.

Second, when the demand for money is infinitely elastic with respect to the interest rate, the LM curve will be horizontal[4], as illustrated in Figure

---

[4]The LM curve can also become horizontal if the supply of money is infinitely elastic with respect to interest rates, making the supply curve for money horizontal. This is one theory of *endogenous money*, which denies that the central bank actually controls the money supply. Endogenous money arises from the operation of a credit system capable of financial innovation.

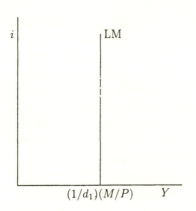

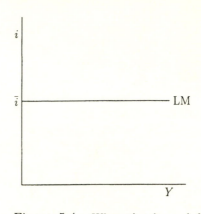

Figure 5.3: When the demand for money is completely insensitive to interest rates, the LM curve becomes vertical. Equilibrium in the money market can only be achieved at one unique level of GDP.

Figure 5.4: When the demand for money approaches infinite sensitivity to interest rates, the LM curve becomes horizontal. Changes in the money supply do not affect the position of the LM curve in this case. Keynes called this case the liquidity trap.

5.4. An infinite elasticity occurs when the parameter d_2 approaches ∞, and the money demand curve becomes horizontal, in the form

$$i = \bar{i}$$

where $\bar{i}$ is the level of the demand curve. With an infinite elasticity, households are willing to hold onto any amount of money at that interest rate, and therefore would like to get rid of all their bonds. In this case, the asset markets never clear because the supply of bonds exceeds the demand for bonds at every price and interest rate.

Keynes called this state of affairs a *liquidity trap*. His explanation was that when the interest rate reaches some very low level, as it does in deep recessions or depressions, households become convinced that the interest rate will eventually return to normal levels. In this case, they will become preoccupied with interest rate risk—the possibility that they will experience a capital loss when the price of the bonds they own collapses and interest rates rise. Keynes argued that under normal circumstances, opinions would be divided about the future path of bond prices, but in a liquidity trap, the financial markets become unanimous in speculating that bond prices are going to rise. (This is why the asset motive for holding money is also called the speculative motive.) When the central bank tries to lower interest rates in order to stimulate the economy, it finds that the open market purchases that usually push up bond prices and lower rates have no effect because people are willing to swap bonds for money at the existing bond price and interest rate. Portfolios become traps for any money the central bank prints, rendering monetary policy impotent as a way to reduce interest rates.

While it was once thought to be a theoretical curiosity, many observers have argued that in the 1990's the Japanese economy fell into a liquidity trap.

5.7 Whose perspective?

The LM curve shows how the interest rate is determined by the available supply of money and the level of income. In a sense, it represents the way the world looks to the central banks that control the money supply. Central banks know that if they increase the money supply, that will lower interest rates, while if they decrease the money supply, that will raise rates. They control the position of the LM curve, and can use it to manage the economy. In most of this book we will adopt this perspective on the world by asking how the economy responds to any given money supply. In more technical terms, we assume that the central bank targets the money supply. But from the Olympian perspective of an economist, the central bank's behavior can be modelled just like any other agent's. Central banks respond to changes in unemployment, inflation, and other variables by actively changing the money supply. In Chapter 11 we will ultimately find that this alternative perspective leads to a powerful model of how the economy works when the central bank uses the interest rate as a policy instrument in response to variations in the unemployment and inflation rates.

Problems for Chapter 5

1. The demand for money is $M^d = P(2Y - 8000\ i)$. Find the demand for real balances when $i = .05$ per year and Y = $1000 per year. Repeat when $i = .08$ per year and Y = $1000 per year. Repeat when $i = .08$ and Y = $1120 per year.

2. The supply of money is $1600 and the price level is 1. Use the demand

for money from the previous problem to derive the LM curve.

3. Use the LM curve from the previous two problems to decide whether agents experience an excess supply or excess demand with respect to their money holdings when the interest rate is .08 per year and the level of income is $1000 per year. Describe their response in the bond market, and the effect this will have on the price of bonds and the interest rate.

4. The central bank sells $500 in bonds in an open market operation. There are no banks, so the money supply consists only of currency. Using the LM curve from problem 2, calculate the shift in the LM curve, and carefully state its direction.

5. List all the parameter changes that might make the LM curve steeper, and explain the economic rationale.

Chapter 6

The IS-LM Model

The IS curve describes positions in which the product market is in equilibrium. On the IS curve, at each interest rate the level of production matches the level of aggregate demand, and the planned level of investment corresponds to the level of national saving. But the IS curve does not explain how the interest rate is determined, or say anything about asset markets. The LM curve describes positions in which the asset markets (money and bond markets) clear. On the LM curve, each level of output begets a unique equilibrium interest rate that makes the available money supply welcome in the portfolios of households. But the LM curve does not explain how the level of GDP is determined, or say anything about the product market. The IS-LM system puts the two subsystems together in order to describe a nearly general equilibrium in which the product, money and bond markets clear simultaneously (only the labor market is left out). This allows economists to make precise statements about how monetary policy, fiscal policy, and various shocks that change the underlying parameters of the model affect the equilibrium values of key endogenous variables. In the basic IS-LM model, fiscal policy operates through the IS curve and monetary policy operates through the LM curve. The IS-LM system is an elaboration of the Keynesian model first introduced by Hicks (1937).

6.1 The IS-LM equations

From the previous two chapters, we learned that the IS-LM system could be written as a pair of linear equations. Using the consolidating parameters introduced earlier to reduce clutter, these are:

$$Y = a_0 - a_1 i$$
$$i = -a_2(M/P) + a_3 Y$$

These equations are called the *structural equations* of the IS-LM model. Notice that the structural equations show the dependent variables, Y and i, as functions of each other. They have to be solved simultaneously to find the equilibrium solution, which can either be done using substitution or by using Cramer's Rule as shown in the Appendix. The solution takes the form of the *reduced form equations*:

$$Y^* = \frac{a_0}{1 + a_1 a_3} + \frac{a_1 a_2}{1 + a_1 a_3}(M/P) \qquad (6.1)$$

$$i^* = \frac{a_0 a_3}{1 + a_1 a_3} - \frac{a_2}{1 + a_1 a_3}(M/P) \qquad (6.2)$$

The reduced form equations show the endogenous variables as functions of exogenous variables and parameters. The asterisk ($*$) denotes the equilibrium value of a variable. Notice that using consolidating parameters gets rid of a lot of clutter, but we do lose an immediate sense of how the underlying parameters affect these solutions. It is a good exercise to work out the effect of changes in key exogenous variables on the consolidating parameters and on the reduced form equations.

We can visualize IS-LM equilibrium in Figure 6.1 as the intersection between the IS and LM curves.

6.2 Dynamics in the IS-LM model

Before we can perform a comparative equilibrium analysis, we need to be assured that the IS-LM equilibrium is stable. If the system begins at some arbitrary level of GDP, will it gravitate toward the equilibrium level of GDP and interest rate? Recall that points on the IS curve represent product market equilibria while points on the LM curve represent asset market equilibria. At some arbitrary level of GDP, such as Y_0 in Figure 6.2, will the system be on the IS curve, the LM curve, or neither?

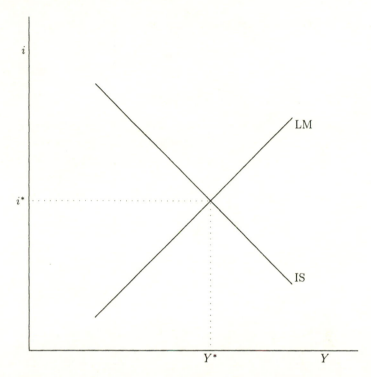

Figure 6.1: The IS curve represents positions in which the product market clears. The LM curve represents positions in which the asset markets clear. The intersection of IS and LM represents a general equilibrium, in which product, money, and bond markets simultaneously clear.

We argued in the previous chapter that the speed of adjustment in the financial markets is quick enough to be considered instantaneous. After all, if there were an excess demand for money, people would contact their financial representatives, perhaps through the Internet, and issue orders to sell bonds, which could be executed without delay. By contrast, if the product markets are out of equilibrium, there will be a time lag between when the extent of the imbalance is recognized by managers and when they are able to make adjustments in the level of production by hiring or laying off workers. That is why it is reasonable to assume that the economy will always be on the LM curve, as shown in Figure 6.2. The interest rate i_0 clears the asset markets when GDP is Y_0. At this interest rate, the economy is producing too little to achieve IS equilibrium. In the product market, firms perceive an

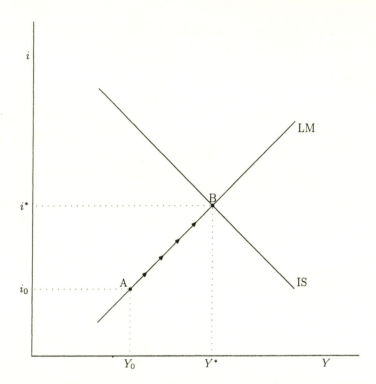

Figure 6.2: It is reasonable to believe that the asset markets clear more quickly than the product market. If we assume that the asset markets clear instantaneously, the economy will always be on its LM curve. Here, the initial level of GDP is low. The resulting low interest rate is stimulating investment spending and causing an expansion; the economy lies below the IS curve, so there is an excess demand for goods. Over time, the economy moves along the LM curve following the arrows until it reaches the general equilibrium.

excess demand that is signaled by unexpected accumulations of inventory. Alternatively, we could say that the level of planned investment exceeds the level of national saving, so there is an excess demand for investment. The managers of firms respond to the signals from inventory changes by increasing production to meet the unsatisfied demand. As the economy expands in this way, the level of output and income increase over time. Models that describe the movements of an economy over time are called *dynamic (or dynamical) models*. Our dynamic model will remain purely informal since we have no pressing need to formalize it mathematically.

As the economy expands over time, the increases in income feed back to the asset markets and cause increases in the demand for money, shifting the demand curve outward. These shocks are processed quickly by the financial markets, which manage to stay in equilibrium continuously. Thus the trajectory of the economy (its path over time) lies along the LM curve, with interest rates rising as the economy expands. This trajectory will bring the economy to its equilibrium position, (Y^*, i^*). The interest rate will rise until there is no longer any excess demand in the product market, and hence no motivation for managers to change the level of output.

If we repeated this thought experiment starting from an arbitrary level of GDP above the equilibrium level, we would find that the trajectory takes the economy down the LM curve. Thus, the equilibrium is stable[1]. We can safely undertake a comparative equilibrium analysis, which is the main application of the IS-LM model.

6.3 Fiscal policy

In a comparative equilibrium exercise, we change one parameter and compare the new equilibrium to the old equilibrium before the change. This purely static analysis does not predict the exact path that takes the system from the old to the new equilibrium.

A fiscal stimulus, in the form of an increase in government spending, shifts the IS curve outward. As we can see in Figure 6.3, the economy enjoys a higher level of income in the new equilibrium at (Y_1, i_1), but it also experiences a higher interest rate. The purpose of a fiscal stimulus is to increase the level of output and employment, typically when the economy has fallen into a stubborn recession that policy makers want to escape. Will this plan work?

It is clear from Figure 6.3 that as long as the LM curve is not too steep, a fiscal stimulus will succeed in generating an expansion of GDP. The increased interest rate could discourage investment spending. However, investment spending also depends on the level of income, through the marginal propensity to invest, and the expansion of GDP will encourage investment. Which of these counteracting influences will predominate depends on the magnitude

---

[1]This analysis would be more involved if the IS curve were to slope upward, which we have simply assumed away. In this case, it can be shown that the model will only be stable if the IS curve cuts the LM curve from above, i.e., if the IS curve is less steep than the LM curve.

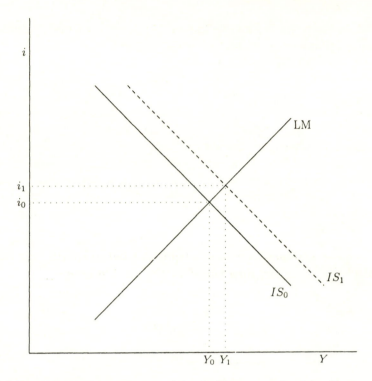

Figure 6.3: A stimulative fiscal policy shifts the IS curve to the right. Because interest rates rise, the change in GDP will be less than the full multiplier effect of the increase in government spending. The fiscal policy shown is a bond-financed budget deficit.

of the relevant parameters and cannot be determined a priori.

When an increase in government spending causes investment spending to fall, this is called *crowding out*. When an increase in government spending causes investment spending to rise, it is called *crowding in*. The IS-LM model cannot decide on the basis of principle the question of whether crowding out or crowding in is more likely. The direction of crowding depends on the slopes of the LM and IS curves.

How does the government finance its increase in spending, assuming it starts out with a balanced budget? The government can finance a fiscal deficit by borrowing, either issuing bonds that are sold directly to the public, or selling bonds to the central bank. If the bonds are sold to the central bank, as we learned in Chapter 1, the supply of high-powered money will increase, and that will ultimately increase the supply of money itself. Therefore, the government's *finance constraint* is

$$G - T = \Delta B + \Delta M$$

where the Δ identifies a change in the variable[2]. This constraint shows that the government can finance a deficit by *bond financing* or by *money financing*. With a bond-financed deficit, $\Delta M = 0$, while with a money-financed deficit, $\Delta B = 0$. A bond-financed deficit is a pure fiscal policy, shifting only the IS curve as in Figure 6.3. In this section, we stick to a bond-financed deficit for this reason. We will return to the question of a money-financed deficit when we discuss the mix of fiscal and monetary policy.

6.3.1 Fiscal policy effectiveness and the LM curve

Policy makers have a vested interest in determining how effective fiscal policy will be in affecting the level of output, employment and other macroeconomic variables. The answer depends on the underlying parameters of the LM and IS curves.

In the extreme case of a vertical LM curve, created by an underlying lack of sensitivity of money demand to interest rates, crowding out will occur and it will be complete. With complete crowding out, investment spending declines one-for-one with government spending, or $\Delta I = -\Delta G$. Figure 6.4 shows the IS-LM diagram with complete crowding out. In this case, because there is no increase in GDP, the only factor affecting investment is the rise in interest rates. You can deduce that the crowding out is complete by using the income-expenditure identity, $Y = C + I + G$. Since income has not changed, consumption (which is a function of disposable income) remains constant. With C and Y constant, it follows that the increase in G has led to a corresponding decline in I.

In the 1930s, economists advised that government programs to create jobs through fiscal policy were unlikely to succeed in combating unemployment because the jobs gained through the government spending would be cancelled out by jobs lost in the investment goods industries through crowding out.

---

[2]Careful readers will notice that the left-hand side does not take account of interest on the government's outstanding debt. A more rigorous analysis would do so, but it would bring up dynamic issues that are best left for more advanced treatments. The implications of bond-financing versus money-financing are explored by Blinder and Solow (1973).

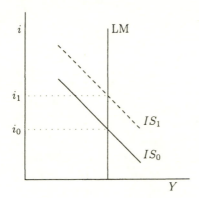

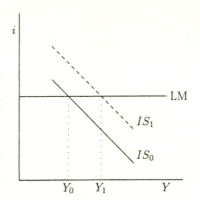

Figure 6.4:   When the LM curve
is vertical, fiscal policy does not affect GDP. The interest rate rises just
enough to crowd out investment by the
full amount of the fiscal stimulus.

Figure 6.5:   When the LM curve is
horizontal, fiscal policy has powerful effects on GDP. Since the interest rate
does not rise, there will no crowding out
of investment.

In the UK, this pessimistic assessment was called the *Treasury view*.   In
the IS-LM model, the Treasury view requires a vertical LM curve. In this
case, an increase in government spending triggers a corresponding fall in
investment spending, but not because the economy has any shortage of real
resources. In fact, we are implicitly assuming a recessed economy in need of
fiscal stimulus. The economy is constrained by a shortage of money. If the
monetary authority were to increase the money supply at the same time that
the fiscal authority increases government spending, crowding out would no
longer threaten to be a problem.

At the other extreme, crowding out cannot occur in an economy suffering
a liquidity trap, as in Figure 6.5. In this case, the demand for money is
infinitely elastic and both the demand curve for money and the LM curve
are horizontal. A fiscal stimulus has no effect on interest rates. That is why a
fiscal stimulus results in the full multiplier effect of an increase in government
spending, or $\Delta Y = \gamma \Delta G$, when the economy is in a liquidity trap. In this
case, fiscal policy is clearly effective without any added help from monetary
policy.

Real economies probably lie somewhere between these extremes.   But
policymakers need to be aware of the fact that a low interest sensitivity of
money demand can reduce the effectiveness of a fiscal expansion by increasing
the likelihood that it will be dissipated in crowding out.

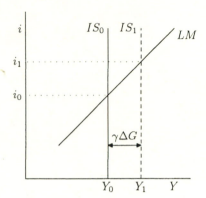

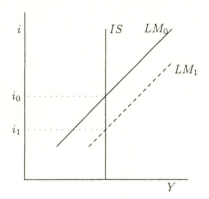

Figure 6.6: When the IS curve is vertical, a fiscal stimulus from increased government spending does not cause crowding out. Unencumbered by crowding out, demand grows by the full multiplier effect of the fiscal policy.

Figure 6.7: When the IS curve is vertical, monetary policy cannot change the level of aggregate demand. Monetary policy depends on the existence of some interest-sensitive spending for its success.

6.3.2 Fiscal policy effectiveness and the IS curve

The other factor that conditions crowding out is the slope of the IS curve as determined by the interest sensitivity of investment spending. The extreme case is a vertical IS curve, reflecting an investment function that is completely insensitive to interest rates. This case is illustrated in Figure 6.6. As long as the LM curve is not horizontal, the IS curve shifts outward and causes an interest rate rise. But in this case, the interest rate rise is harmless because investment spending does not react to it. Crowding-in will prevail. Again, the full multiplier effect of the increased government spending results, or $\Delta Y = \gamma \Delta G$, since we know that this is the distance the IS curve has shifted to the right. In sum, if the IS curve is steep owing to low interest sensitivity of investment, fiscal policy will be an effective tool for stimulating demand without causing much crowding out.

The Appendix presents a formal (mathematical) derivation of all the results relating to the effectiveness of fiscal policy for readers who seek a deeper understanding of them.

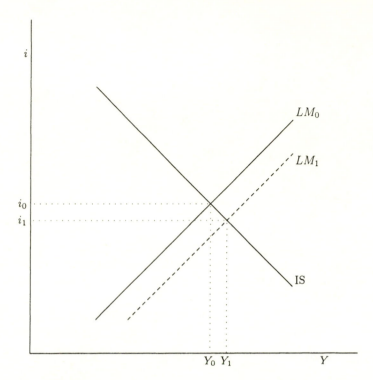

Figure 6.8: An expansionary monetary policy shifts the LM curve to the right, and stimulates aggregate demand by lowering interest rates and encouraging investment.

6.4   Monetary policy

Monetary policy shifts the LM curve. An expansionary monetary policy shifts the LM curve to the right. It is clear in Figure 6.8 that an increase in the money supply reduces the equilibrium interest rate and increases the level of GDP.

In the IS-LM model, the *transmission mechanism* for monetary policy works through the effect of the money supply on the interest rate. This mechanism is sometimes called the *monetary channel*[3]. We can visualize the

[3]Some theories of the financial system suggest the existence of a *credit* or *bank lending channel*, which works through the availability of credit rather than the interest rate. These theories assume that firms are constrained from borrowing as much as they want by the amount of equity they can put up for collateral. A monetary expansion can increase the firms' profits, giving them more equity for collateral. In this theory, both the LM curve

monetary channel using causal arrows:

$$\Delta M \to \Delta i \to \Delta I \to \Delta Y$$

The effectiveness of monetary policy as a tool for stimulating the economy depends on the strength of each of the causal relationships.

6.4.1 Monetary policy effectiveness and the IS curve

Because monetary policy operates through interest rates, it obviously requires that some category of spending, normally taken to be investment, is sensitive to interest rates. This is the second linkage in the monetary channel.

In the extreme case in which investment spending is insensitive to interest rates, the IS curve is vertical. In this case, illustrated in Figure 6.7, even though monetary authorities succeed in reducing rates, it does no good in terms of stimulating investment spending or aggregate demand.

Some economists believe that investment spending is not very responsive to lower interest rates during sharp recessions, but that higher interest rates do have a dampening effect on business activity even in prosperous times. This view has been captured by the aphorism "Monetary policy is like pushing on a string." You can pull an economy into a recession through a monetary contraction, but recovery requires a judicious mix of fiscal and monetary stimulus.

6.4.2 Monetary policy effectiveness and the LM curve

The effect of monetary policy on interest rates—the first linkage in the monetary channel—depends on the parameters of the demand for money, in particular its interest sensitivity. In the most extreme case, the demand for money is infinitely elastic, the LM curve is horizontal, and the economy is in a liquidity trap. In a liquidity trap, as we have already seen, trying to reduce interest rates by increasing the money supply is an exercise in futility. The LM curve remains in its current position when the money supply is increased. Thus, in a liquidity trap, monetary policy can have no effects on the level of GDP, even if investment spending is responsive to interest rates.

---

and the IS curve will shift outward after an increase in the money supply.

As the demand for money becomes less elastic or less sensitive to interest rates, monetary policy will become a more effective instrument for stimulating aggregate demand.

The Appendix presents a formal treatment of these conclusions about the effectiveness of monetary policy.

6.4.3   Monetary policy and the yield curve

An important practical constraint on monetary policy is that open market operations affect only short-term interest rates (such as the federal funds rate) directly. Rates on longer maturity financial instruments are affected indirectly, through changes in expectations about future short-term interest rates. But investment spending is far more sensitive to these long-term rates than it is to short-term rates, since investment projects usually take many years to complete. Thus, the central bank has the least amount of control over the rates that matter the most. Monetary policy usually changes the short end of the yield curve by more than it changes the long end. This is one reason why monetary policy operates with a lag.

6.4.4   Monetary policy targets

There are two quite distinct ways in which monetary policy can be conducted. Under *monetary targeting*, the central bank focuses on the supply of money. This means that in each period, the central bank attempts to fix the position of the LM curve, and allows the position of the IS curve to determine the equilibrium position of the economy. Under *interest rate targeting*, the central bank focuses on the interest rate. This means that in each period, the central bank adjusts the money supply in order to achieve its interest rate objective, allowing the position of the LM curve to change accordingly.

While few if any central banks pursue monetary targeting, this policy makes it particularly easy to learn how to use the IS-LM model as an analytical framework. For this pedagogical reason, we assume that the central bank does pursue monetary targeting in this and subsequent chapters. Only when we have built up a good understanding of the macroeconomic theory of inflation, will we be able to appreciate the alternative strategy of interest rate targeting.

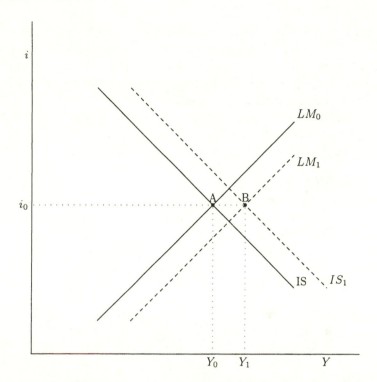

Figure 6.9: With the right policy mix, a stimulative fiscal policy will generate the full multiplier effect without any drag from crowding out.

6.5 Policy mix

At one time, economists debated the relative merits of fiscal versus monetary policy as tools of economic stabilization, but there is no need to view them as competitors. Fiscal and monetary policies can work together to achieve desired effects by the choice of the appropriate policy mix.

For example, as illustrated in Figure 6.9, a fiscal expansion ("loose fiscal policy") can raise the level of GDP without unwanted crowding out if it is combined with an accommodating ("loose") monetary policy. If policy makers know the size of the parameters of the IS-LM model, they can design such a policy mix.

The need for a policy mix arises because of *Tinbergen's Rule*, which states that the number of policy instruments must be as great as the number of policy goals or targets[4]. Tinbergen's Rule stems from the mathematical fact that the IS-LM model is a system of simultaneous equations. If policy makers want to achieve a desired level of GDP as well as a desired level of investment (e.g., a level at least as great as the current level), they must generally pursue a policy mix combining fiscal and monetary policy.

A loose-fiscal, loose-monetary policy mix arises automatically when a fiscal deficit is money-financed. Recall that any purchase of an asset (in this case a government bond) by the central bank results in an increase in the money supply. When deficits are financed by borrowing from the central bank, they are said to be *monetized*. In the U.S., the central bank is legally prohibited from lending money directly to the government, but it can still monetize a deficit by purchasing bonds from the public more or less immediately after they are issued.

6.6   The paradox of thrift

As a final comparative equilibrium exercise, consider the effect of an increase in private saving modeled by a decline in autonomous consumption (i.e., an increase in autonomous saving). In the simple Keynesian model, such an increase in private saving ultimately has no affect on national saving, which is limited by the amount of planned investment. One of the defining features of the simple Keynesian model is that planned investment is constant. Elaborating the Keynesian model by recognizing the existence of a marginal propensity to invest out of income only deepens the paradox of thrift. In this case, an increase in autonomous saving actually reduces the overall level of investment and saving.

In the IS-LM model, the dependence of investment on the interest rate creates the possibility of overcoming the paradox of thrift, under some conditions. An increase in autonomous saving shifts the IS curve to the left. Unless the LM curve is horizontal, this will reduce interest rates, which encourages investment. But because GDP declines, which discourages investment, the net effect on investment spending is indeterminate, just as it was in the case of fiscal policy.

In the special case of a vertical LM curve, only the interest rate effects on investment operate and an increase in autonomous saving will result, dollar

---

[4]The Dutch economist Jan Tinbergen (1952) was a pioneer in the study of achieving optimal policy objectives using the reduced form of the IS-LM model.

for dollar, in an increase in investment spending. Thus, the composition of GDP shifts away from consumption and toward investment; there is no paradox of thrift here. The same underlying conditions that favor crowding out from fiscal policy also work toward the neutralization of the paradox of thrift.

6.7 Policy objectives

Our analysis shows how fiscal and monetary policy work, but it does not tell us how these policies are conducted in practice. In particular, we have said nothing about the policy objectives that decision-makers pursue. Our analysis shows that both policies can be used to manipulate the level of demand, depending on the relevant parameter values, and that a mix of monetary and fiscal policy works well. The IS-LM model was designed to guide policy makers toward full employment or high employment, which is achieved at a high level of GDP. The implicit assumption in our discussion is that the economy is operating below this desired level of GDP, and it needs a boost.

The IS-LM model invites us to interpret the business cycle of booms and slumps in terms of erratic shifts in aggregate demand. Demand shocks can either arise because of changes in investment or consumption spending, in which case they affect the IS curve, or because of changes in the character-istics of money demand or supply, in which case they affect the LM curve.

There are basically two underlying visions of the business cycle. The orig-inal Keynesian view is that modern economies are subjected to asymmetric or one-sided shocks that regularly reduce output below its full capacity value. In particular, Keynes was quite pessimistic about the likelihood that invest-ment spending would maintain sufficient vigor (recall that he spoke of the animal spirits of entrepreneurs) to generate full employment continuously. This vision builds a case for a policy directed at filling the gap between actual output and capacity. Such gap-filling policies are an example of *dis-cretionary policies*, where decision-makers react to every situation without following some pre-set formula.

A more modern (though not necessarily correct) view is that the shocks are symmetric, sometimes causing slumps and sometimes causing expansions, and that there are powerful self-equilibrating forces (the subject of future chapters) arising in the supply side of the economy. This vision has led to the idea that discretionary policies might make things worse, especially considering the long and variable lags associated with both fiscal policy (where the political process can be very slow) and monetary policy (where responses to interest rates often take from six months to two years to materialize). The modern view recommends that policy makers adopt *policy rules* that stabilize the economy over time.

An early monetary policy rule was suggested by Milton Friedman (1956), who advocates a strict money supply target that increases by around 2 per cent a year to allow for economic growth. A good example of a fiscal policy rule is given by the fiscal surplus under an income tax[5]. When the economy booms, tax collections rise and the fiscal budget moves toward surplus. When demand slumps, tax collections fall off and the fiscal deficit widens. This kind of fiscal policy smooths out the swings in the level of GDP without requiring any discretionary judgments by policymakers. Such a policy is called an *automatic stabilizer*[6]. Other programs that function as automatic stabilizers include unemployment insurance and welfare.

Problems for Chapter 6

These problems make use of the following data for a hypothetical economy:

$$C = 120 + .6(Y - T)$$

$$I = 50 + .2Y - 2000i$$

$$G = 250$$

$$T = 200$$

$$M^d = P(2Y - 8000i)$$

$$M = 1600$$

$$P = 1$$

---

[5]We could formalize an income tax in our model by letting $T = \tau Y$, where $0 < \tau < 1$ represents the tax rate.

[6]If the U.S. passes a recently proposed constitutional amendment requiring a balanced budget, that would constitute a fiscal policy rule, but it would not be stabilizing. Many economists have criticized such an amendment on the grounds that it would in fact be destabilizing.

All variables (except P) are in units of constant dollars (per year for flows), which we will represent by the $ symbol. Unless the problem states otherwise, always go back to these original data.

1. Derive the IS and LM curves for this economy.

2. Calculate the equilibrium level of GDP and the interest rate.

3. The government increases spending by $200. Calculate the new level of GDP and the new interest rate.

4. The central bank increases the money supply by $280. Calculate the new level of GDP and the new interest rate.

5. Determine if crowding out or crowding in occurred in problem 3.

6. If the investment equation in this economy were $I = 50 + .2Y$, would monetary or fiscal policy be more effective as a stabilization tool?

7. If the demand for money in this economy were $M^d = P(2Y)$, would monetary or fiscal policy be more effective as a stabilization tool?

8. Design a policy plan to increase national saving without changing the level of GDP, using any combination of fiscal and monetary policy.

9. Set up a spreadsheet that lets you change the parameters of the IS-LM model experimentally. Make two copies of the model in your spreadsheet, one to use as a control (with the original parameter values), and the other to test changes in a single parameter. Graph the IS and LM equations from the control and test models. Use the spreadsheet to verify your answers to the previous problems and to conduct comparative equilibrium experiments of your own design.

10. Draw the IS-LM diagram that describes a tax cut. Label carefully, and explain the effects of the tax cut on each of the variables in the income-expenditure and investment-saving identities.

11. Draw the IS-LM diagram that describes a monetary contraction. Label carefully, and explain the effects of the contraction on each of the variables in the income-expenditure and investment-saving identities.

12. Use the statistical appendix of the *Economic Report of the President* to evaluate the effects of fiscal policy on the level of investment in the U.S. during the 1980s. Make a graph showing the percentage of real GDP comprising consumption, investment, and government purchases in each year from 1970 to 1990, and a separate graph showing the government's fiscal surplus and private investment. Did crowding out or crowding in occur?

Chapter 7

The Aggregate Demand Curve

In this book, macroeconomic theory from the Keynesian cross to the IS-LM model is predicated on the constancy of wages and prices. To be more specific, we have assumed that wages are constant, and have maintained that prices are set by imperfectly competitive firms that mark-up their labor costs, so that price constancy results from wage constancy. We have ignored the labor market, where wages are determined, in order to get a good understanding of the product, money and asset markets. Now we are ready to include the labor market in our macroeconomic theory as well, and when we do we will have to confront the following question: how do changes in prices affect the level of aggregate demand? In this chapter, we will not try to explain the price level. Rather, we examine how changes in the price level affect aggregate demand.

7.1   Visualizing the AD curve

As we have already observed, price changes have exactly the same effect on the IS-LM model as monetary policies; both change the real money supply and shift the LM curve. This insight leads to an inverse relationship between the level of aggregate demand and the price level that is called the aggregate demand (AD) curve. In general, the AD curve has the form $Y = Y(P)$, although we will always graph the AD curve with real income on the horizontal axis and the price level on the vertical axis.

We can visualize the AD curve by identifying two points on it that are defined by two arbitrary price levels, such as P_0 and P_1 in Figure 7.1. An increase in prices shifts the LM curve to the left as shown in the top panel

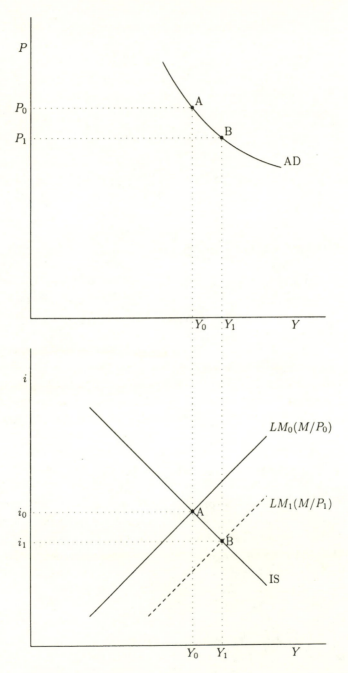

Figure 7.1: The AD curve shows that lower price levels are associated with higher real money supplies, and thus higher levels of aggregate demand. There is no analytical difference between a lower price level and an expansionary monetary policy.

because it reduces the real money supply for every given nominal quantity of money. This equivalence between price changes and monetary policy was discovered by Keynes, and is known as the *Keynes effect*. The reduction in the real money supply causes interest rates to rise, just as would a contractionary monetary policy, and that discourages investment. The new IS-LM equilibrium associated with the higher price level occurs at a lower level of GDP, Y_1. Thus, an increase in prices will generally reduce the level of aggregate demand as it is determined by the IS-LM equilibrium. We have shown the AD curve as a non-linear function to remain true to its mathematical form, but this non-linearity has no deep economic significance and we will hereafter draw a linear AD curve.

7.2 Deriving the AD curve

Deriving the AD curve based on the linear model involves nothing more than re-interpreting the reduced form of the IS-LM model, Equation (6.1) as an aggregate demand curve. The relevant reduced-form equation,

$$Y = \frac{a_0}{1 + a_1 a_3} + \frac{a_1 a_2}{1 + a_1 a_3}(M/P),$$

can now be interpreted as an AD curve. The AD curve shows precisely what happens to equilibrium income when the price level changes. Notice that all the terms on the RHS except P are parameters; now you should see why we left P out of the consolidating parameters. This equation shows that the equilibrium level of aggregate demand is an inverse function of the price level.

The structure of this equation can be brought into sharper relief by consolidating parameters to write the AD curve

$$Y = a_4 + a_5 M(1/P) \tag{7.1}$$

where the consolidating parameters are

$$a_4 = \frac{a_0}{1 + a_1 a_3} = \frac{\gamma(c_0 - c_1 T + b_0 + G)}{1 + \gamma b_2(d_1/d_2)}$$

$$a_5 = \frac{a_1 a_2}{1 + a_1 a_3} = \frac{\gamma(b_1/d_2)}{1 + \gamma b_2(d_1/d_2)}$$

For a given, constant money supply, this function takes the form of a rectangular hyperbola, even though the underlying IS-LM equations are linear. Be sure you know how to interpret the effects of changes in the structural parameters on the slope of the aggregate demand function, and how changes in the policy instruments G, T, and M affect the aggregate demand function.

7.3   Properties of the AD curve

Since the AD curve mirrors events in the IS-LM model, it will not be hard to master its properties. We will consider shifts in the AD curve and changes in the slope of the AD curve.

7.3.1   Policy changes and AD

Stimulative fiscal or monetary policies both shift the AD curve out, while contractionary policies shift the AD curve in. This can be seen either by working through the graphic visualization or by inspecting the AD equation. The non-linearity of the AD curve has no real economic significance, so for convenience we will draw a linear AD curve in subsequent chapters.

In general, any parameter change that would be stimulative in the IS-LM model results in an outward shift in the AD curve, and vice versa.

7.3.2   Slope of the AD curve

While the AD curve is not linear, we can still speak somewhat loosely of the slope of the AD curve, and exploit the isomorphism between price variation and monetary policy. Any parameter configuration that makes monetary policy more effective will make the AD flatter (putting P on the vertical axis). These include a larger interest sensitivity of investment spending, a larger multiplier, and a smaller interest sensitivity of money demand. Any parameter configuration that makes monetary policy less effective will make the AD curve steeper. In the extreme case, investment spending that is completely insensitive to interest rates or an infinitely elastic demand for money will both make the AD curve vertical. In the former case, this is because the IS curve is vertical, rendering any changes in interest rates irrelevant. In the latter case, it is because the LM curve is horizontal, and increases in the real money supply are absorbed by the liquidity trap.

7.4   Other factors influencing AD

In our textbook IS-LM model, the Keynes effect is the only factor that links the price level to the level of demand. But in more sophisticated models, other effects can also arise. The most famous such effect is the *Pigou effect* (Pigou, 1943) that refers to the relationship between wealth and consumption demand. When the Pigou effect is active, a lower price level increases the real value of the wealth owned by households, such as their monetary holdings, M. We know from the underlying theories of consumption demand that an increase in wealth can be expected to cause an increase in consumption. Thus, at lower price levels, households feel richer because their real balances (M/P) increase in worth, and they consume more. The Pigou effect shifts the IS curve to the right as prices decline. This works in the same direction as the Keynes effect and contributes to the existence of an aggregate demand curve. The Pigou effect is also known as the *real balance effect.*

There does seem to be evidence that increases in household wealth stimulate consumer spending, but the effects are modest. An increase of $1 in wealth generates a rise of around $.05 in consumption, according to most studies. This wealth effect finds some practical application in explaining the effects of stock market fluctuations on the real economy.

The Pigou effect played an important role in the history of economic doctrine. A great debate erupted in the 1940s over whether falling prices during a depression would eventually bring about recovery to full employment, or in other words, whether the market economy is self-regulating. Keynes believed that the Keynes effect would be incapable of returning a depressed economy to full employment when the IS curve is vertical by virtue of interest-insensitive investment. (Recall that the AD curve is vertical when the IS curve is vertical.) He envisioned a state of permanent depression, unless an activist government was prepared to launch a fiscal rescue. The Pigou effect was thought by many economists (Patinkin, 1948) to show, at least in principle, that if prices were to fall in a depression, that would eventually cause movement along the AD curve back to full employment.

The problem with this argument is that there are other plausible effects that work against the Pigou and Keynes effects. When prices fall, that makes it harder for debtors to pay off their debts, which have increased in real value[1]. If they go bankrupt, they bring down their creditors in a kind of chain-reaction. The resulting decline in spending caused by such a debt-deflation is called the *Fisher effect*. The Fisher effect works directly against the Pigou and Keynes effects. If this effect is strong enough, it can make the aggregate demand curve positively sloped. The relative importance of these three effects remains an unresolved issue in macroeconomics (see Tobin, 1980). The Japanese economy in the 1990s experienced high unemployment and falling prices, yet it did not recover, suggesting the presence of a vertical or even positively sloped aggregate demand curve arising from strong debt-deflation forces.

7.5   A preliminary AS-AD model

When wages are constant and firms set prices by applying a constant mark-up to their labor costs, they will be willing to satisfy any level of demand at the existing price level. In this case, the aggregate supply curve is horizontal, as shown earlier in Figure 2.1. The AD curve merely mirrors the underlying IS-LM model. We can think of the AS-AD equilibrium as a mapping of the IS-LM equilibrium we are already familiar with. All the comparative equilibrium exercises up to this point in this book can be represented in an AS-AD diagram as shifts in the AD curve along a stationary, horizontal AS curve. This should serve to warn students about the importance of getting behind the AS-AD model. In particular, avoid the temptation to regard these curves as aggregated versions of microeconomic supply and demand curves. We will want to generalize this model to accommodate the idea that wages (and thus prices) respond to the level of output, production, and employment.

---

[1]The Pigou effect does not relate to wealth that is based on lending and borrowing because falling prices generate winners among the lenders and losers among borrowers. The money supply relevant to the Pigou effect is thus the supply of high-powered money, which does not rest on credit. Economists call this "outside money" to distinguish it from the "inside money" that rests on credit. As we have observed, the IS-LM economy is a pure currency system, in which the money supply and high-powered money are identical. This also explains why the Keynes effect involves money but not bonds.

Problems for Chapter 7

Problems 1 and 2 make use of the following data for a hypothetical economy:

$$C = 120 + .6(Y - T)$$

$$I = 50 + .2Y - 2000i$$

$$G = 250$$

$$T = 200$$

$$M^d = P(2Y - 8000i)$$

$$M = 1600$$

All variables (except P) are in units of constant dollars (per year for flows), which we will represent by the $ symbol.

1. Find the IS-LM equilibrium in this economy when the price level P = 1. Repeat when P = 2 and when P = .75. Graph these three points, with P on the vertical and Y on the horizontal axis.

2. Derive the AD curve for this economy.

3. In general (i.e., without reference to the hypothetical data above), under what two conditions will the AD curve be vertical? One condition relates to the IS curve and the other condition relates to the LM curve.

Chapter 8

The Aggregate Supply Curve

Modern macroeconomic theorists have come around to a belief that labor markets, like the product markets, are best represented by the assumption of imperfect competition[1].

8.1 Wage setting models

There are two kinds of imperfectly competitive models of the labor market. One model, based on the dynamics of wage setting under trade unions, emphasizes collective bargaining power. Another model, based on efficiency wage models of the firm, emphasizes that individual workers have bargaining power. Both kinds of model lead to the same substantive conclusion: the bargained wage will tend to be higher at higher levels of output (lower unemployment rates).

These models create several potential sources of confusion. First, workers can bargain only over their *money wage*, W, measured in $ per labor unit, but if they are fully rational, they should be focused on their *real wage*, W/P, measured in real output per labor unit. Workers who are rational do not suffer from *money illusion*, or confusion between the real wage and the money wage[2]. The real wage represents the purchasing power of the money

---

[1]Kalecki (1971) was an early advocate of this position. For a thorough survey of theoretical and empirical work on wages and prices, see Layard et al. (1991).

[2]There is actually some good evidence that firms are reluctant to reduce money wages because of the effect on employee morale, so that a form of money illusion prevails. See Bewley (1999) for details.

wage. Workers act on their perception of the real wage, based on the price level they expect to prevail in the period when they receive the money wage. A macroeconomic theory of wage setting must come to grips with the issue of price expectations.

Second, workers (or their union leaders) bargain at the microeconomic level, and operate independently of each other. Each worker or union takes the wages of the rest of the labor force to be a given. But when all the workers or unions act similarly, the wages they took as given (and prices which those wages influence) may turn out differently than they expected. So the problem of price expectations is bound up with the *fallacy of composition* that what is true for the individual is not always true for the whole.

8.1.1   Wage setting under trade unions

There are many models of wage setting under trade unions, and while they do not always agree, they generally predict that the ability of an individual union to raise wages will be conditioned by the overall unemployment rate. The rationale is straightforward. In a bargaining situation, the employers can threaten to hold out in the event of a long strike. Workers can hold out only if they can get temporary jobs, which is more likely when the unemployment rate is low. Employers may even threaten (in the U.S., where this is legal) to replace strikers with non-union workers, but they are less likely to be able to find workers desperate enough to cross a picket line when the unemployment rate is low.

8.1.2   Efficiency wage models

Efficiency wage models regard the wage as an argument in the firm's production function, rather than as simply the price of labor input. There are several versions. One good example is the shirking model (Bowles, 1985). In the shirking model, employers have imperfect information about worker effort. Monitoring and surveillance are costly. Workers, on the other hand, are perfectly aware of when they are putting out full effort on the job. Consequently there is a structure of asymmetric information that creates interesting economic effects. How are employers to extract a profit-maximizing level of effort from their workers? In the shirking models, they use the wage as an incentive device. By paying workers slightly more than their reservation wage (the wage that lures them into the job), they can make job loss costly. A worker who shirks risks detection and firing. If she is fired, she will only be able to find a new job after a spell of unemployment and job search. Thus, the cost of job loss depends on the wage and the unemployment rate. A higher unemployment rate increases the cost of job loss and permits employers to elicit worker effort with a smaller wage.

8.2 The bargained real wage curve

In either case, the wage bargain depends on the unemployment rate. Whether they bargain collectively or individually, workers are in a better position to demand higher wages when the unemployment rate is low. The money wage settlement is conditioned on the price level that workers expect to prevail, P^e, and we will refer to the function that relates the wage settlement to the unemployment rate as the *bargained real wage curve*, or following Blanchflower and Oswald (1994), as the *wage curve* for short. The general form of the wage curve is $W/P^e = F(u)$, where $\partial F/\partial u < 0$. We will work with a linear version of the wage curve:

$$\frac{W}{P^e} = n_0 - n_1 u \tag{8.1}$$

The parameters n_0 and n_1 are based on the nature of the wage-setting institutions, and n_1 reflects the sensitivity of wage-setting to labor market forces.

One disadvantage of this form of the wage curve is that it relates wages to the unemployment rate rather than to GDP, but this is easily remedied. Recall that we are assuming a production function $Y = N$, where N refers to labor units or workers. The labor force, L, is assumed to be constant and the supply curve for labor is inelastic (vertical). The number of unemployed workers is just $L - N$, and the unemployment rate is defined by

$$u = \frac{L - N}{L}$$

Thus, using $Y = N$, we can write the wage curve

$$\frac{W}{P^e} = (n_0 - n_1) + \frac{n_1}{L}N = m_0 + m_1 Y \tag{8.2}$$

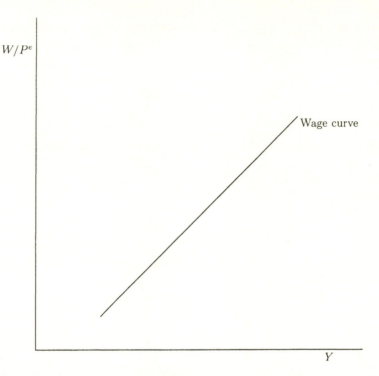

Figure 8.1: The wage curve slopes upward because at lower unemployment rates (higher levels of output), workers are in a stronger bargaining position and can extract wage concessions from employers.

where m_0 and m_1 are consolidating parameters. The wage curve is illustrated in Figure 8.1. It slopes upward because an increase in output requires an increase in employment, which lowers the unemployment rate, putting workers in a stronger bargaining position that allows them to win higher wage settlements.

8.3   The price-determined real wage

As we have already seen in Chapter 2, firms set prices by marking-up their labor costs. To be more precise, with the production function $Y = N$, the marginal product of labor is unity, and the marginal cost of production is equal to the money wage, W, since labor is the only variable cost. The firms are monopolies that face a demand curve with a constant elasticity of demand. The profit maximizing price will be

$$P = (1 + \mu)W$$

where μ is the mark-up, a function of the elasticity of demand. Note that the price here is the actual price. The fact that firms set prices after they observe their costs of production (i.e., the wages they pay) places them in a privileged position with respect to the real wage that workers receive.

The price-setting equation can be solved to yield the real wage that will prevail, called the *price-determined real wage* or PRW:

$$\frac{W}{P} = \frac{1}{1 + \mu} \tag{8.3}$$

The price-determined real wage does not depend on the level of employment or output. It depends only on the mark-up, which reflects the parameters of the representative product's demand curve and is therefore constant.

We are making an assumption about the timing of wage and price setting with an important implication. Prices are set immediately after wages have been negotiated. Consequently, workers will always receive the price-determined real wage, no matter what real wage they think they have bargained for. We are implicitly assuming that firms have better information than workers: firms know what their costs of production are, but workers do not know the price level that will prevail.

To see how this works, imagine that workers bargain for a higher wage. Firms will experience increases in their costs, and will raise prices by the same proportion that wages have risen. At the end of the day, the real wage will not have changed. What is going on here is that workers bargain independently of each other. Each worker (or union) acts as if the other workers' wages and therefore all other prices are constant. From this perspective, an increase in money wages will raise real wages. But when all the workers act this way, they will succeed only in raising the overall price level, without receiving any gain in purchasing power. The workers fall victim to the fallacy of composition just like fans at a sporting event who each stand up thinking it will give them a better view.

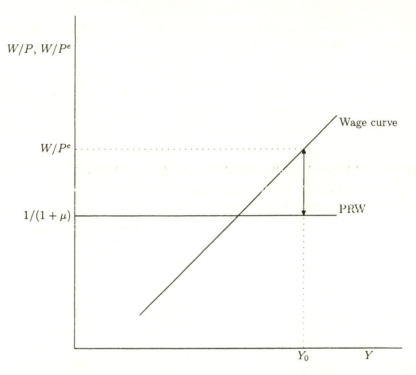

Figure 8.2: When the level of output is high, workers bargain for a real wage that exceeds the wage they will ultimately receive. Because firms set prices, the actual wage will always be the Price-determined Real Wage, or PRW. The double arrows show the size of the inflationary gap between workers' expectations and reality.

8.4   Wage and price setting dynamics

We can put these ideas together to give us a complete picture of how wage-setting in the labor market and price-setting in the product market interact dynamically. Figure 8.2 shows both the wage curve and the price-determined real wage. We need to interpret events at a level of GDP like Y_0, where the wage curve and price-determined real wage fail to intersect. At this level of GDP, the bargained real wage, W/P^e, is more than the the actual real wage, which is the price-determined real wage, W/P. This shows that workers have miscalculated since $P^e < P$. Workers are actually receiving a lower real wage than befits their strong bargaining position. Their bargaining position is strong because the unemployment rate is low when GDP is high. In the next round of wage negotiations, workers or unions, bargaining individually, will insist on increases in their wages in order to close the gap between the bargained and actual real wage, and they will prevail because of their favorable bargaining position. But when all the workers succeed in raising their pay, firms just pass these cost increases through to prices, and we are once again back where we started. A level of output like Y_0 gives rise to an *inflationary gap* between the bargained real wage and the price-determined real wage, which leads to rising wages and prices.

For example, suppose the price-determined real wage is .5 units of output per worker, but that at Y_0 the bargained real wage is .55 units. Workers will demand a 10 per cent increase (i.e., $[.55 - .5]/.5$) in their money wage to close the gap between the real wage they got last year (which by assumption will always be the price-determined real wage) and the real wage they are bargaining for this year. This wage increase will immediately be passed through into prices[3]. As long as output stays at Y_0, this cycle of wage and price increases will repeat itself.

For low levels of GDP, the tables are turned, and workers will receive a real wage that exceeds the bargained real wage. In this case, employers will press for money wage reductions and a downward spiral of wages and prices will ensue. A low level of output gives rise to a *deflationary gap* that leads to falling wages and prices.

Inflation comes about in this model when there is a gap between the aspirations of workers, measured by the bargained real wage, and the wage that is feasible given the market power of monopolistic firms. This is a *conflict theory of inflation*, as Rowthorn (1977) emphasizes.

There is one level of GDP that is consistent with stable wages and prices, and it occurs at the point in Figure 8.3 where the bargained real wage curve and the price-determined real wage intersect at the output level Y_n, which we call the *natural level of output*[4]. In this case, workers have not miscalculated, since $P^e = P$, and they receive precisely the real wage that befits their bargaining position.

Economists first conceived of this position in terms of the unemployment rate associated with it, u_n, which has been called the *natural rate of unemployment*. The natural rate of unemployment brings the aspirations of

---

[3]As we will see in Chapter 10, if the workers anticipate inflation, they will demand a 10 per cent increase on top of the expected inflation rate.

[4]The term "natural" was first used to describe an equilibrium value by Adam Smith, who distinguished between natural prices and market prices. It has no further connotation.

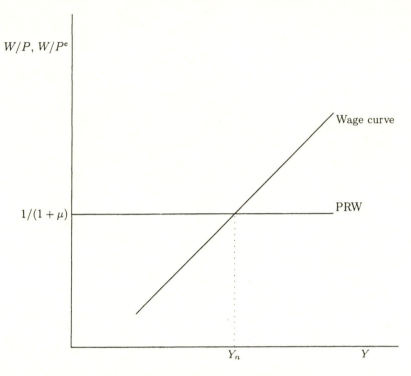

Figure 8.3: Workers' bargained real wage and the price-determined real wage are exactly consistent with one another when output is at its natural level and unemployment reaches the natural rate of unemployment.

workers into line with the feasible real wage. Other synonyms for the natural rate of unemployment include the NAIRU (an acronym for non-accelerating inflation rate of unemployment), the structural rate of unemployment, and the sustainable rate of unemployment (coined by the Council of Economic Advisors in the U.S., but unfortunately not used extensively). None of these names is particularly accurate. For example, there is nothing natural about the natural rate of unemployment since it depends on political and social institutions that could be and have been changed. Indeed, a spirited public debate rages about such changes affecting the natural rate.

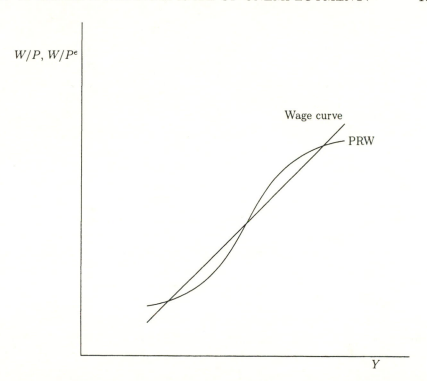

Figure 8.4: If the mark-up depends functionally on the level of demand, the PRW curve can intersect the wage curve at several points. Each of these intersections represents a potential natural rate of unemployment. The theoretical possibility of multiple equilibria suggests some skepticism about the existence of a unique natural rate of unemployment.

8.5 Is there a natural rate of unemployment?

Almost all public discussions of inflation and unemployment are premised on the existence of a well-defined natural rate of unemployment. It is important to be aware that the existence of the natural rate is predicted by the simplest macroeconomic models, such as the one offered here, but it is not necessarily predicted by more sophisticated models.

For example, we can illustrate the possibility of *multiple equilibria* within the framework of our simple model. Suppose that rather than remaining constant, the mark-up changes depending on the level of demand in the economy. If the mark-up is a function of demand, the price-determined real wage will similarly depend on the level of GDP. Figure 8.4 shows that in this case it is possible for the PRW curve to intersect the wage curve at several points. Each of these points represents a different natural rate of unemployment. Unless we can somehow rule out this kind of behavior on the part of the mark-up on theoretical grounds, we should not discount the possibility that there may actually be many unemployment rates at which inflation stabilizes.

To give another example of multiple equilibria, in one kind of economic model the wage curve shifts during a period of prolonged unemployment. If mass unemployment discourages workers and if idleness causes a decline in workers' skills and ambition, it can have the effect of weakening the threat that unemployed workers pose as replacements for those employed. This will shift the wage curve to the left, bringing about a reduction in the natural level of output and an increase in the natural rate of unemployment. In this model, mass unemployment becomes self-perpetuating, a phenomenon known as *hysteresis*. Rather than always returning to the same natural rate of unemployment, the economy will gravitate toward some rate that depends on its own past history, a phenomenon known as *path dependency*. Many economists believe that hysteresis helps explain the persistence of high unemployment in Europe during the 1980s and 1990s, often called *Eurosclerosis*. We will not pursue these more sophisticated models further[5], but the reader is advised to remain skeptical about any claims that there exists one unique and well-defined natural rate of unemployment. At best, this is a first approximation or a broad framework for conducting policy analysis.

There are two competing interpretations of the natural rate of unemployment. The first associates it with full employment, or the absence of involuntary unemployment. This interpretation is accepted by many New Classical and monetarist economists, but it is inconsistent with the model of the labor and product markets presented here. The second interpretation, which is associated with New Keynesian theory, accepts the existence of involuntary unemployment at the natural rate of unemployment. In our model, the labor supply is inelastic, so $L - Y_n$ workers are involuntarily unemployed in equilibrium. Much modern macroeconomic theory predicts that full employment is virtually impossible in a free market economy. For example, under the efficiency wage model, full employment implies that the cost of job loss is zero; workers would shirk universally, which rules out any full

---

[5]For a good theoretical and empirical treatment of hysteresis, consult Layard et al. (1991).

employment equilibrium. Some unemployment is necessary in these models to serve as a worker discipline device. This idea has roots in the Marxian theory of the reserve army of labor and was re-introduced to macroeconomics by Kalecki (1943).

8.6 Price expectations

It is clear that the dynamics described here involve an interaction between the expected price level and the actual price level. Workers are unable to foresee exactly where the wage and price dynamics are going, and they persistently over- or underpredict the price level. (An alternative interpretation, discussed below, is that there are significant time lags that prevent workers from acting quickly as new information comes in.) When workers use past information, mainly the past behavior of prices, to forecast future prices, this is called *adaptive expectations*. We will use the simplest form of adaptive expectations, which states that workers expect the price level to remain constant over time, or

$$P_t^e = P_{t-1} \tag{8.4}$$

where the subscript refers to the time period. (To save on notation, we will leave the t subscript implicit from now on, writing this equation $P^e = P_{-1}$.) This form of expectations implies that the expected rate of inflation is always zero, a limitation that we will overcome in Chapter 10.

There is something unsatisfying about adaptive expectations. Workers wind up making the same mistakes over and over again. One alternative is to assume that workers use other information besides past prices, such as their understanding of macroeconomic theory, to predict the future price level. When the mathematical expectation of the workers' price forecast is equal to the actual future price level, *rational expectations* prevail. Rational expectations does not imply clairvoyance; it asserts only that workers are accurate in some statistical sense, on average, without systematic errors. This approach is premised on the idea that much of the variation in prices in real economies is pure noise, so that workers face a signal extraction problem (separating real information from background noise). Only in the extreme case of *perfect foresight* are workers assumed to know the future price. But rational expectations, too, fails to provide an intellectually satisfying theory of perceptions. For example, rational expectations requires that workers know the underlying structure of the economy, and that they know that all the other workers have the same knowledge and act rationally upon it. The rational expectations hypothesis turns out to be just as arbitrary and unrealistic as adaptive expectations. From a plausibility perspective, in the one case workers have too little knowledge, but in the other case they have too much knowledge.

As in most macroeconomic theory that is used by policymakers, we will assume that adaptive expectations is closer to the truth than rational expectations. One good justification is that even if workers correctly perceive what is happening to prices, institutional obstacles prevent them from acting on their perceptions without delay. For example, unions typically sign multi-year contracts, so that any unforeseen price changes during the life of a contract must await its expiration before they affect wage settlements. Even in the absence of unions, business organizations often set wages and prices in annual cycles, which creates the same kind of lag effect. Wages and prices are thus said to be sticky. We could interpret the adaptive expectations equation as a reflection of the inertia built into wage-setting institutions and the stickiness of wages as much as a statement about how workers forecast the future.

8.7   The AS curve

Since changes in wages are immediately passed through to prices, and since wages depend on the level of output, it should be clear that prices also depend on the level of output. To formalize this idea, first substitute Equation (8.4) into the wage curve, Equation (8.2), and rearrange to give

$$W = P^e[m_0 + m_1 Y] = P_{-1}[m_0 + m_1 Y]$$

In each period, the past price level has obviously been determined. Variables that are inherited from history are called *predetermined variables*. The lagged price level, P_{-1}, is such a predetermined variable.

Next substitute this equation into the price setting equation to derive the relationship between the price level and the level of output:

$$P = P^e(1 + \mu)[m_0 + m_1 Y] = P_{-1}(1 + \mu)[m_0 + m_1 Y] \qquad (8.5)$$

This equation is called the *aggregate supply curve* or AS for short. It describes the relationship between output and prices at the macroeconomic or

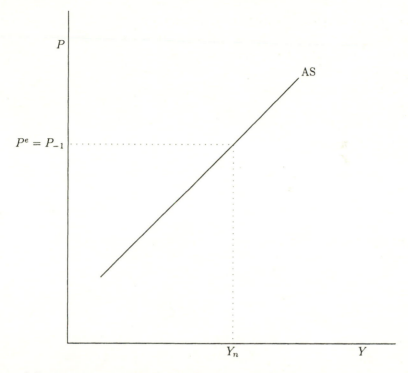

Figure 8.5: When the level of output reaches the natural level, the price that prevails will by definition be the price that workers expect.

aggregate level, given the expected price level. Each individual firm continues to operate with a horizontal pricing curve as in Chapter 2 because if it alone were to increase its output, this would not affect wages. But collectively firms generate an upward-sloping AS curve through the wage-setting behavior in the labor market.

8.8 Dynamic properties of the AS curve

We can see from Figure 8.5, which shows the aggregate supply curve in one particular year, that at the natural level of GDP and the natural rate of unemployment, workers have accurately predicted the actual price level. Because workers receive the real wage that they have bargained for, there is no incentive for wages to change, and prices will remain stable over time.

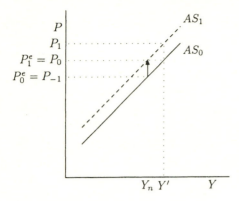

Figure 8.6: At high levels of GDP, $Y > Y_n$, the price level always exceeds the expected price level. The AS curve shifts upward in each period as price expectations change. The arrow shows how the change of price expectations repositions the AS curve.

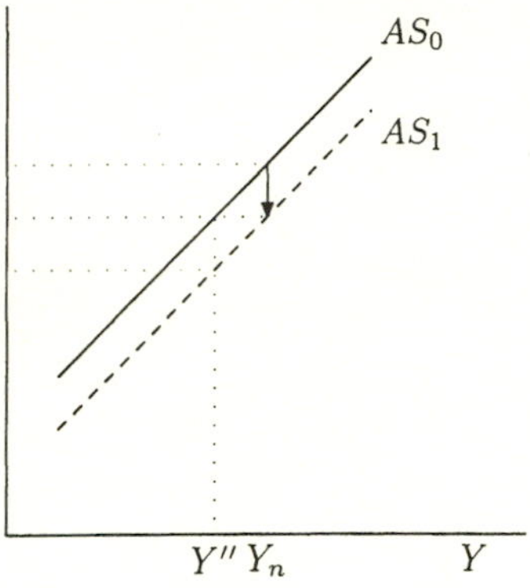

Figure 8.7: At low levels of GDP, $Y < Y_n$, the expected price always exceeds the actual price level. The AS curve shifts down in each period as price expectations change. Under adaptive expectations, the expected price chases after the actual price.

At levels of GDP above the natural level, the actual price level exceeds the expected price level, and an inflationary gap prevails. Workers will revise their forecast of the price level upward when this happens. Figure 8.6 shows how the economy evolves over time when GDP is above its natural level (so unemployment is below the natural rate). In period 0, the expected price level, P_0^e, is lower than the actual price level, P_0. This miscalculation on the part of workers means that they are receiving lower real wages than befits their strong bargaining position, and they will press for a higher wage in the next period, which is period 1. They base their expectations in period 1 on the price level in period 0, through Equation (8.4), and this conditions the wage that they will demand in period 1. These dynamics are represented by the shift in the AS curve shown in Figure 8.6. The new aggregate supply curve, AS_1, is positioned so that $P_1^e = P_0$. If the level of output remains constant, the new price level will be P_1. But at this point, the inflationary gap persists, so this cycle of wage setting, price setting and changing price expectations will continue to drive the price level up over time.

At levels of GDP below the natural level, the expected price level exceeds the actual price level, and a deflationary gap prevails. Workers will revise their forecast of the price level downward when this happens. Figure 8.7

shows this situation. As long as the deflationary gap persists, the AS curve and price level will drift down over time. (Careful readers will notice that technically speaking, changes in the expected price level alter the slope of the AS curve. The actual movements in the AS curve are not parallel shifts, a fine point we have ignored.)

When the level of GDP lies away from the natural level, that will initiate a cycle of wage setting, price setting, and changing price expectations. A high level of GDP leads to an upward spiral of wages and prices. A low level of GDP leads to a downward spiral of wages and prices.

These thought experiments are designed for gaining familiarity with the dynamic properties of the AS curve. But they are incomplete because they take the level of output to be constant and independent of the price level. We will get a better understanding of how price determination and output determination are mutually related by combining the AS curve with the AD curve to produce a complete model of the labor, product, money and asset markets.

Problems for Chapter 8

These problems make use of the following data for a hypothetical economy. The mark-up is .25, the wage curve is $W/P^e = 1 - 2.5u$, and the labor force is 100 workers. Recall that the production function is $Y = N$ and $P^e = P_{-1}$.

1. Calculate the price that firms will set when the wage is $5 per worker. Calculate the real wage the workers receive. Calculate the price-determined real wage.

2. Determine the natural rate of unemployment and the natural level of GDP for this economy.

3. If the level of GDP is $95 per year, what will the unemployment rate be? What real wage will workers expect to receive? If the money wage is $5 per worker, what price level do workers expect? What price level actually prevails?

4. In the previous problem, what money wage will workers bargain for in the next round of negotiations (i.e., next year), assuming there is no change in the level of GDP?

5. Derive the aggregate supply curve for this economy. Graph the AS curve for three successive years when the level of GDP remains at $95 per year.

6. Use the AS curve from the previous problem to determine the price level when the price level last year was $6.25 per unit and the level of GDP is $92 per year. Explain the significance of your answer in light of problem 2.

7. Use the statistical appendix of the *Economic Report of the President* to find data on the price level in the U.S. for the last three decades. Look for the chain-type price index that most closely corresponds to the textbook theory (remember that it must be capable of deflating the whole GDP, not just one component, like consumption goods).

Chapter 9

The AS-AD Model

The AS-AD model is a complete macroeconomic model. It describes a general equilibrium involving the product market, the money market, the bond market, and the labor market. The AS-AD model generates an important distinction between the short-run and long-run behavior of the economy. In the short run, price expectations have been decided and are not subject to revision. Each period is a short run. The long run is defined as a state of the world in which all the markets are fully adjusted and price expectations are also fully adjusted. We will see that the long-run equilibrium of the AS-AD model is the natural level of GDP and the natural rate of unemployment. When the model is out of its long-run equilibrium (assuming one exists), it moves toward it through a sequence of short-run equilibria. The main dynamic factor that propels it is the cycle of price expectations, wage setting, and price setting that we studied in the previous chapter.

9.1 Dynamic adjustment in the AS-AD model

Before we can comfortably undertake a comparative equilibrium analysis of the AS-AD model, we need to be certain that the equilibrium is stable. In this analysis, we will assume, somewhat arbitrarily, that the economy achieves IS-LM equilibrium instantaneously. This means we will continuously achieve a short-run equilibrium position on the AD curve—the mirror of the IS-LM system. Similarly, we assume there are no lags between wage and price setting, so that the economy is always operating on the AS curve. The dynamic path of the economy will be described by the points of intersection

117

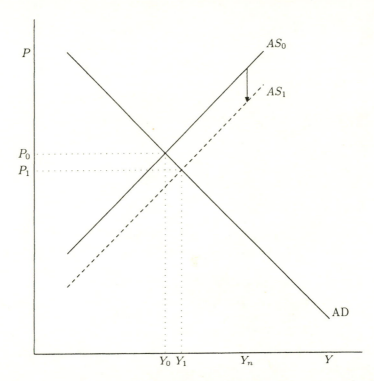

Figure 9.1: When the economy lies below the natural level of output, the AS curve shifts down. The arrow shows the change in price expectations that repositions the AS curve. As prices fall, the economy moves along the AD curve to a higher level of GDP. This process continues until the economy reaches the natural level of GDP where price stability prevails. In this theory, recessions are self-correcting.

between the AS and AD curves over time.

Consider a level of GDP lying below the natural level of output, such as Y_0 in Figure 9.1. At this level of output, the actual price level falls short of the expected price level. Workers receive a higher real wage than befits their weak bargaining position; employers will insist upon pay cuts. As workers revise their expectations downward and accept pay cuts, the AS curve shifts downward. This shift will cause prices to fall, but falling prices stimulate aggregate demand through the Keynes effect and initiate movement down the AD curve. The economy automatically travels through a sequence of short-run equilibria that take it to the natural level of GDP. A similar argument, starting from a level of GDP above the natural level of output, demonstrates

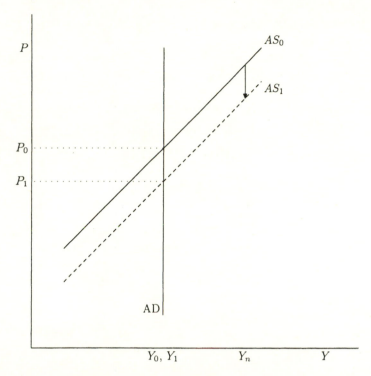

Figure 9.2: When the AD curve is vertical (or just very steep), the economy may remain below the natural level of output despite falling prices.

that the natural level of output represents a stable long-run equilibrium.

Before we leave this topic, it should be pointed out that Keynes himself denied that falling prices would guarantee that the economy would be able to recover when the level of GDP is depressed. His argument, illustrated by Figure 9.2, was that in deep recessions, the AD curve is vertical (or very nearly so), either because investment spending is insensitive to interest rates or because the economy is in a liquidity trap. In either case, no amount of deflation will suffice to bring about an economic recovery. Keynes argued that fiscal policy would be indispensable in achieving recovery. This position was controversial because it denies that a market economy is self-regulating. Modern macroeconomic theory tends to ignore Keynes's skepticism about the self-regulating properties of market economies, although it is not yet clear that this stance is well justified. For example, as we have seen, Japan in the

1990s experienced falling prices and economic stagnation, which is consistent with Keynes's position.

We will proceed under the assumption that investment spending is sufficiently interest-sensitive to rule out the possibility illustrated by Figure 9.2, but this should be taken as a pedagogical strategy rather than an endorsement of the self-regulating properties of the capitalist economy.

9.2   Economic policy in the short and long run

Since both fiscal and monetary policy affect the position of the AD curve, they have similar representations in the AS-AD model. A comparative equilibrium analysis of economic policy concerns two distinct moments, the short run and the long run. To conduct such an analysis, we must begin in a long-run equilibrium at the natural level of GDP so we have a basis for comparison. For example, as shown in Figure 9.3, either a stimulative fiscal policy or a stimulative monetary policy shifts the AD curve outward. In the short run, the new equilibrium level of GDP increases, as does the price level. At the new, higher level of GDP, as we have seen, the AS curve will shift upward because workers revise their price expectations, which have not foreseen the price increase that resulted from the stimulative policy. These upward shifts will continue until the system returns to the natural level of GDP and establishes a new long-run equilibrium, as we saw in the last section.

Policy changes consist of two stages: (i) First, policy affects the position of the AD curve, causing movement along the AS curve. (ii) Then, since the economy is no longer at its natural level of output, the AS curve shifts over time to restore the long-run equilibrium. The economy moves along its AD curve until it returns to the natural level of output. The distinction between fiscal and monetary policy can only be seen by looking more deeply into the behavior of the IS-LM model that underlies the AD curve.

9.3   Fiscal policy

Consider an increase in government spending. Figure 9.4 represents events using the IS-LM diagram. (For the representation using the AS-AD diagram, return to Figure 9.3.) As we saw in the previous section, the AD curve shifts

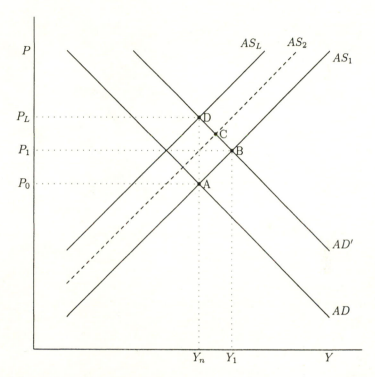

Figure 9.3: Starting from the original long-run equilibrium (A), a stimulative policy (fiscal or monetary) shifts the AD curve outward, raising the level of prices and output in the short run (B). Since GDP now lies above its natural level, the AS curve will shift upward because workers will revise their price expectations, which repositions the AS curve and moves the economy along the new AD curve. The first such shift is shown by the dashed AS curve, AS_2 and position (C). The upward spiral of wages and prices moves the economy along the AD curve until a new long-run equilibrium (D) is re-established at the natural level of output.

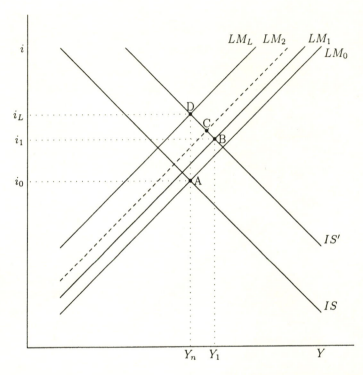

Figure 9.4: A stimulative fiscal policy shifts the IS curve out. The position of the LM curve depends on the real money supply, M/P. Even in the short run (B), the LM curve shifts upward since $M/P_1 < M/P_0$. As the price level rises, it erodes the real money supply further and continues to shift the LM curve upward(C). The first such shift is shown by the dashed LM curve. Eventually, the LM curve reaches its long-run position (D), shown by LM_L. The positions labeled A, B, C, and D correspond to their counterparts in Figure 9.3.

out. The new short-run equilibrium occurs at a higher level of output and a higher price level. In the IS-LM diagram, we can see that the increased level of government spending has shifted the IS curve outward. The LM curve shifts inward in the short run because of the Keynes effect induced by the price increase from P_0 to P_1. In subsequent periods, price increases continue to reduce the real money supply and shift the LM curve to the left. When the system reaches the natural level of GDP, price stability sets in and the LM curve will have achieved its new long-run position.

This verifies the conclusion reached through the "pure" IS-LM model with fixed prices: fiscal policy is an effective instrument for controlling the level of demand in the short-run, and could be used for stabilization purposes. What has the AS-AD analysis added? Now we can see that prices are likely to rise in the short run. Because this price increase reduces the real money supply, it will reduce somewhat the stimulus from fiscal policy. Since this effect probably is small in practice, the IS-LM model turns out to be a good approximation for short-run analysis, even though it ignores prices.

In the long run, output returns to its natural level. Fiscal policy does not change the level of output, but it does change its composition in the long run. We can see this by referring to the income-expenditure identity, $Y = C + I + G$. Since Y has not changed, C will not change. Investment spending has declined in order to make room for the increase in G; complete crowding out prevails in the long-run. The mechanism is the increase in the interest rate from i_0 to i_L, its new long-run value.

The trajectory that brings the system back to its natural level lies along the new AD curve. In each year, changes in price expectations will shift up the AS curve, pushing up the price level and initiating a Keynes effect that reduces the level of aggregate demand. Rising prices reduce the real money supply, which raises interest rates, providing the mechanism by which crowding out eventually prevails. In the short-run, our earlier conclusion using the IS-LM model with fixed prices that crowding in and crowding out are theoretically possible remains valid. But in the long-run, no ambiguity surrounds crowding out in the AS-AD model[1].

In real economies with income taxes and other automatic stabilizers, the government's fiscal surplus depends on the level of GDP. When GDP falls

---

[1]There is an exception to this statement. When no equilibrium at the natural level of GDP exists, because the AD curve is vertical or very steep, an increase in government spending can crowd-in investment.

during a recessionary period, the level of tax collections automatically falls and when GDP rises, more tax receipts come in. But this means that the fiscal surplus reflects both changes in actual taxing and spending policies and changes in the level of GDP caused by the business cycle. To separate these effects, economists focus attention on estimates of the *structural* or *high-employment* fiscal surplus that would prevail if GDP were at its natural level. The structural surplus is the most reliable indicator of the true character of the fiscal policies in place. A structural deficit is considered to be a stimulative policy, while a structural surplus is contractionary. An economy with a structural fiscal surplus but an actual deficit is in a recession, and it could stand the stimulus from a structural deficit (meaning an even larger actual deficit) to speed up the recovery to its long-run equilibrium. Once prosperity has returned, policy can return to a fiscally neutral stance.

9.4   Monetary policy

An increase in the money supply similarly shifts the AD curve outward, and we can analyze what happens using the IS-LM diagram as in Figure 9.5. In this case, of course, the IS curve remains fixed while the LM curve shifts out in the short run. Once again, we can see that both the level of output and price level rise in the short run. The prediction of the IS-LM model, that monetary policy can generally be counted on to stimulate output, remains qualitatively valid, even if it might modestly overestimate the size of the stimulus. Monetary policy remains a valuable instrument for macroeconomic stabilization in the short run.

In the long run, however, the monetary stimulus dissipates in rising prices. In Figure 9.5, we can see this in the movement along the new IS curve that takes the system back to its natural level of output.

By referring to the IS-LM diagram, we can see that while monetary policy shifts the LM curve out in the short run, the Keynes effect from rising prices returns the LM curve to its original position in the long run. Since the position of the LM curve is defined by the real money supply, it is clear that the real money supply has returned to its original level because the price level has risen by the same proportion as the nominal money supply. Indeed, it is clear that no real variable has been affected in the long run by the increase in the nominal money supply. This property is called the *neutrality of money*. In the AS-AD model, money is neutral in the long run.

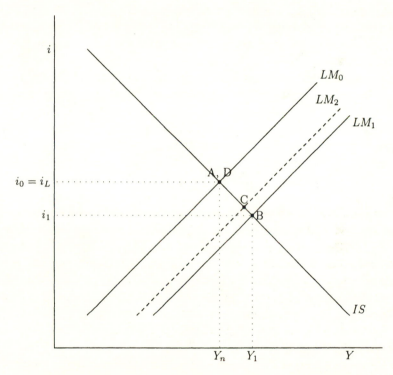

Figure 9.5: Increasing the money supply from M to M' in the AS-AD system shifts the LM curve out in the short run (B), but price inflation eventually reduces the real money supply back to its original level (A, D). Here, the position of the LM curve shifts with the real money supply, from M/P_0 to M'/P_1 and then back to M'/P_L. The dashed curve shows the position of the LM curve after one period. The positions labeled A, B, C, and D correspond to their counterparts in Figure 9.3.

The neutrality of money is an important part of the traditional monetarist claim that excessive money creation by irresponsible central banks is the cause of inflation. Monetarist economists subscribe to the *quantity theory of money*, which interprets Equation (1.7), the equation of exchange, causally. If money is neutral, it does not affect the level of output or the velocity of money (determined by the interest rate and the level of output). Thus, in the equation of exchange, $MV = PY$, any increase in M must cause an equal proportionate increase in P. It would be more accurate to call this the "quantity-of-money theory of prices."

The equation of exchange shows the three requirements for the quantity theory of money to be valid. First, the level of output must not be affected by the quantity of money; this requirement is met when there is a unique natural rate of unemployment. Second, the velocity of money must not be affected by the quantity of money; this requires that the demand for money be a stable function of interest rates and income levels, and that these variables are unaffected by the quantity of money. And third, the quantity of money must in some sense be an exogenous variable, capable of being manipulated by the policy makers. This requirement would fail to be satisfied if money were endogenous, as it is thought to be by some monetary theories. Endogenous money is created by the monetization (transformation into money) of private credit instruments. Debates about the validity of the quantity theory have focused on one or more of these three requirements.

Modern macroeconomic theory resolves the conflict between Keynesian and monetarist theory by recognizing the former as valid in the short run while the latter describes the long run. This is true whether we speak of monetary or fiscal policy.

9.5   Monetary policy under perfect foresight

In order to get some insight into the theoretical implications of rational expectations, we will briefly consider the extreme case of monetary policy under perfect foresight. Suppose that workers anticipate that the money supply is going to increase. Furthermore, suppose that they understand the structure of the economy and can predict the new price level. What price level will they predict? Clearly it must be the new long-run price level, P_L, in Figure 9.3. If it were any other price level, that would imply, as we have seen repeatedly, that the expected price is not equal to the actual price, which would contradict our assumption of perfect foresight.

If the expected price after an increase in the money supply is equal to its long-run level, that means the AS curve will shift immediately to its new long-run position. Even though the AD curve has shifted out, the AS curve has shifted up by just the right amount to prevent the increase in AD from affecting the level of output. In terms of Figure 9.3, the economy moves directly from point A to point D. The remarkable conclusion is that under perfect foresight, an anticipated monetary policy will have no real effects in the short run. The only way to escape this outcome would be to surprise workers with an unanticipated monetary policy.

Macroeconomic models that assume rational expectations and price flexibility tend to share this character. Only surprises, such as unanticipated monetary shocks or random changes in prices, have real consequences. Money in such models is neutral in both the short and long runs. However, these models remain controversial because they exaggerate the flexibility of prices[2]. For example, they ignore the stickiness of wages caused by institutional features such as multi-year contracts. As a result, while these models may be of interest to academic economists, they are less important for policy analysis than models like ours, in which money is not neutral in the short run.

9.6 Paradox of thrift

Finally, consider the effect an increase in desired saving on the part of households has in the AS-AD model. In the short run, a decrease in autonomous consumption shifts the AD curve down, or to the left. The level of output falls as it would in the basic fixed-price IS-LM model, but not quite as much because the price level falls also, creating a Keynes effect that cushions the blow. Thus, in the short run, the paradox of thrift continues to hold, with some modification, depending on the steepness of the AS curve.

In the long run, however, the economy returns to the natural level of activity, so there is no paradox of thrift in terms of output levels. In terms of saving and investment, the Keynes effect that drives the economy back to its long-run equilibrium operates by lowering interest rates and stimulating investment. We can easily deduce, from the investment-saving identity

---

[2]Rational expectations models with price flexibility are associated with the New Classical economists, and they are often criticized by the New Keynesian economists who subscribe to a model with sticky wages and prices like that in the text.

$I = S + (T - G)$, that investment in the long run must have increased *pari passu* with private saving. By assumption, government saving is unchanged. Private saving is a function of disposable income, which has returned to its original level, so it is clear that in the long run private saving has increased by the desired amount. The paradox of thrift appears to be a purely short-run phenomenon from the vantage point of a well-behaved AS-AD model.

One should keep in mind, however, that in the badly behaved AS-AD model in which Keynes believed, the paradox of thrift would indeed be a long-run possibility. Keynes denied that the Keynes effect could be counted on to restore prosperity, either because investment would not respond to lower interest rates or because the liquidity trap would stop rates from falling sufficiently. Even if Keynes's position is technically wrong, the adjustment process may be so slow and painful that it is right for all practical purposes.

9.7   Strengths and limitations of the AS-AD model

The AS-AD model is the basic framework for the analysis of stabilization policy directed at combating the stubborn tendency of modern economies to slip into recessions. It gives policy makers a powerful understanding of how monetary and fiscal policies can be used to stimulate the economy in the short run. It also cautions policy makers to avoid trying to create growth beyond the natural level of output, since this creates inflationary pressure. It does not tell us, however, what the natural level of output actually is, and many disagreements among economists ultimately turn on differences of opinion about this question.

From the perspective of the AS-AD model, the fluctuations we see in real economies are either caused by exogenous demand shocks, supply shocks, or both. We discussed the types of demand shocks in connection with the IS-LM model. An example of a demand shock might be the recession in Japan during the 1990s, caused by a financial crisis that led to a sharp decline in business investment.

A supply shock affects the position or slope of the AS curve by changing the natural rate of unemployment, the responsiveness of wages to unemployment, or both. An example of a supply shock might be the boom in the U.S. during the 1990s that some economists have attributed to a drop in oil prices, a resurgence of technological change, or both. These shocks could have increased the price-determined real wage, lowering the natural rate of unemployment, and shifting the AS curve outward.

A common belief among economists is that there is symmetry between favorable and unfavorable shocks, so that the economy tends to cycle around its natural level. In this case, policy should be stabilizing, easing when the economy is in a slump, but putting on the brakes during an excessive boom. However, many economists continue to agree with Keynes that capitalist economies generate more negative shocks than positive shocks, requiring that policy makers pay more attention to filling the gap between the actual level of GDP and the potential or natural level.

The AS-AD model in this chapter predicts that once the economy reaches long-run equilibrium, prices stabilize. In real economies for the last half-century, prices have risen more or less continuously, even with a few exceptions in recessions. To understand the policy dilemma of inflation and unemployment, we need to extend the AS-AD model so it can project a more realistic picture of inflation.

Problems for Chapter 9

1. Draw the AS-AD and IS-LM diagrams that describe a tax cut. Identify the new short-run position and the new long-run equilibrium on each diagram. Be sure to label each important landmark on your diagrams.

2. In the previous problem, describe the short-run and long-run effects of the policy on each term in the income-expenditure identity and each term in the investment-saving identity.

3. Draw the AS-AD and IS-LM diagrams that describe a contraction in the money supply. Identify the new short-run position and the new long-run equilibrium on each diagram. Be sure to label each important landmark on your diagrams.

4. In the previous problem, describe the short-run and long-run effects of the policy on each term in the income-expenditure identity and each term in the investment-saving identity. Discuss the neutrality of money in this case.

5. Use the statistical appendix of the *Economic Report of the President* to find data on the price level in the U.S. (You can use the same data suggested in the problems from Chapter 8.) Make a graph showing the movements of prices over time. Does it support the AS-AD theory that there is a stable long-run equilibrium price?

Chapter 10

Inflation and Unemployment

Inflation is defined as a continuous increase in the price level, measured by the rate of growth of prices or

$$\pi_t = \frac{P_t - P_{t-1}}{P_{t-1}}$$

Again, we will usually leave the t subscript implicit and write, for example, $\pi = (P - P_{-1})/P_{-1}$. In the AS-AD model, the focus is on the price level, P. But the same basic model extends easily to the analysis of inflation.

10.1 The AS curve and inflation

It is customary to focus on the relationship between inflation and unemployment rather than between inflation and the level of output. That is why we start with the AS curve written out in terms of the unemployment rate, using Equation (8.1):

$$P = P^e(1 + \mu)[n_0 - n_1 u]$$

We can simplify the algebra without losing any important content by assuming that $n_0 = 1$. Dividing both sides by P_{-1} gives us

$$\frac{P}{P_{-1}} = \frac{P^e}{P_{-1}}(1 + \mu)[1 - n_1 u]$$

The expected rate of inflation is defined by

$$\pi^e = \frac{P^e - P_{-1}}{P_{-1}}$$

When we substitute the definitions of inflation and expected inflation into the AS curve, a nearly linear inverse relationship between inflation and unemployment emerges. Since π and u are generally small percentages, which are even smaller when they multiply each other, we can drop all the product terms and obtain the following linear approximation (defining the consolidating parameter $\alpha = n_1(1 + \mu)$):

$$\pi = \pi^e + \mu - \alpha u \qquad (10.1)$$

This equation is called the *expectations-augmented Phillips curve.*

The Phillips curve is an extension of the AS curve, expressed in terms of inflation and unemployment. The difference between the AS curve and the modern theory of the Phillips curve lies in the treatment of expectations. In the AS-AD model, we assumed that the expected price level would equal the lagged value of the price level, or $P^e = P_{-1}$. But this means that the expected rate of inflation in the AS model is always zero, because people anticipate that prices will remain constant. In this case, the Phillips curve reduces to

$$\pi = \mu - \alpha u$$

We know that the equilibrium rate of inflation in the AS-AD model is zero, because the system achieves a long-run price equilibrium when it reaches the natural rate of unemployment. Setting π to zero and solving for u gives us

$$u_n = \mu/\alpha$$

so that the Phillips curve associated with the AS curve assumption that $\pi^e = 0$ is

$$\pi = -\alpha(u - u_n)$$

This was the form first studied by A.W. Phillips (1958). Subsequent research convinced economists (Friedman, 1968) that it made no sense to assume that the expected rate of inflation was always zero, and they developed the expectations-augmented Phillips curve.

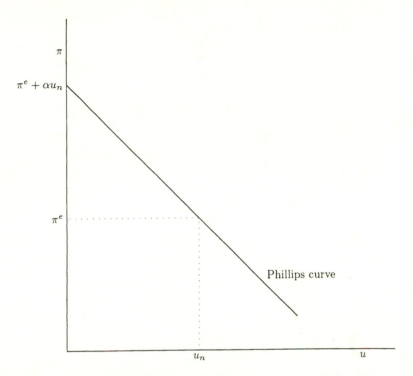

Figure 10.1: The expectations-augmented Phillips curve is an extension of the AS curve. When the unemployment rate achieves its natural level, the expected inflation rate will be exactly equal to the actual inflation rate. We use this landmark to position the Phillips curve.

10.2 Expectations-augmented Phillips curve

Similarly, when we allow for inflation expectations, we can simplify Equation (10.1) by setting $\pi^e = \pi$ and solving for $u_n = \mu/\alpha$. Substituting back into the original equation gives us a good general-form equation for the expectations-augmented Phillips curve:

$$\pi = \pi^e - \alpha(u - u_n) \tag{10.2}$$

Recall that with mark-up pricing the rate of price inflation depends on (and is equal to) the rate of growth of wages. The right-hand side of this equation states that the rate of growth of wages will be equal to the expected rate of inflation plus the size of the gap between the bargained real wage and the price-determined real wage. This gap is measured by the term $-\alpha(u-u_n)$. For example, if workers expect the inflation rate to be 2 per cent, and if the wage gap is 1 per cent, they will demand pay increases equal to 3 per cent—2 per cent just to keep up with inflation plus 1 per cent more to bring their real wage up to the bargained real wage.

The expectations-augmented Phillips curve shown in Figure 10.1 graphs Equation (10.2). The Phillips curve describes the inflation-unemployment trade-off for a given expected inflation rate.

If workers have adaptive expectations of inflation, they will base their forecast of the inflation rate on past observations of inflation. A simple version of adaptive expectations is

$$\pi^e = \pi_{-1}$$

We can write the expectations-augmented Phillips curve specialized for this treatment of adaptive expectations as

$$\pi = \pi_{-1} - \alpha(u - u_n) \tag{10.3}$$

We will concentrate on using this specific form of the Phillips curve.

When the unemployment rate is equal to the natural rate of unemployment, the inflation rate will be equal to the expected inflation rate. This fact can always be used to locate the position of the Phillips curve in dynamic analyses. Maintaining the simple version of adaptive expectations shown above, the expected inflation rate will always be the actual inflation rate one period earlier.

When the unemployment rate exceeds the natural rate, the inflation rate will be lower than expected. This is directly analogous to the dynamics of prices and price expectations in the AS-AD model, and most of the reasoning developed there carries over. With unemployment high, the bargained real wage is below the actual, price-determined real wage, because workers have overestimated the inflation rate and the price level. A deflationary gap, or more precisely a *disinflationary* gap, prevails[1]. Workers will revise their forecast in the next period. The expected rate of inflation will decline. This decline will shift the Phillips curve downward, much as the AS curve shifted in similar circumstances. Figure 10.3 illustrates.

---

[1]Deflation refers to a decline in the price level. Disinflation refers to a decline in the inflation rate, or slower growth of prices.

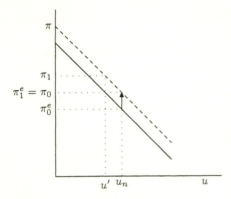

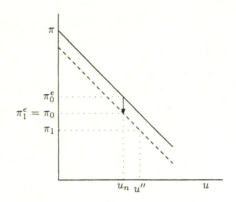

Figure 10.2: At low unemployment rates, $u < u_n$, the expected rate of inflation always falls short of actual inflation. The Phillips curve shifts up in each period as inflation expectations change. The arrow shows how the change in expectations re-positions the Phillips curve, assuming that $\pi^e = \pi_{-1}$.

Figure 10.3: At high unemployment rates, $u > u_n$, the expected rate of inflation exceeds the actual rate of inflation. The Phillips curve shifts down in each period as inflation expectations change. Under adaptive expectations, expected inflation chases after actual inflation.

When the unemployment rate is below the natural rate, the inflation rate will exceed the expected rate of inflation. With unemployment low, workers have underestimated inflation and the bargained real wage will exceed the actual real wage. An inflationary gap prevails. Workers will revise their forecast of inflation upward, shifting the Phillips curve upward in the next period. Figure 10.2 illustrates.

Figures 10.2 and 10.3 make it clear that when unemployment is not at its natural rate the Phillips curve must shift. But the Phillips curve alone does not tell us what the unemployment rate will be, any more than the AS curve alone tells us the level of output. We need to consult the AD relationship for a complete picture. In the AS-AD model, price changes create a Keynes effect that moves the economy along its AD curve, changing the level of output and the unemployment rate. To see this in the context of inflation, we need to reformulate the AD curve in more dynamic terms.

10.3   The dynamic aggregate demand curve

Recall that the reduced form of the IS-LM model is the aggregate demand curve showing that the level of aggregate demand is an inverse function of the price level, or[2]

$$Y = a_4 + a_5 \frac{M}{P}$$

To move from this static AD equation to a dynamic equation that accommodates inflation and monetary growth, we need to define the growth rate of output, g_Y, and the growth rate of money, g_M. The growth rate of the price level has already been defined to be π, the inflation rate. Thus, we define:

$$g_Y = \frac{Y - Y_{-1}}{Y_{-1}}$$

$$g_M = \frac{M - M_{-1}}{M_{-1}}$$

We can come reasonably close to the dynamic aggregate demand equation by making some simplifying assumptions. First, let us take the consolidating parameter a_4 to be zero. Second, we make use of a handy math fact: the growth rate of a ratio of two variables is approximately equal to the difference between the growth rates of the variables, and we can reasonably take this to be an exact equality[3]. Applying these assumptions, we obtain the dynamic AD equation:

$$g_Y = g_M - \pi \tag{10.4}$$

This dynamic AD equation states that the growth of demand is equal to the growth of the real money supply, which makes good sense based on what we know about the static AD curve. In economic terms, the growth rate of aggregate demand, the left hand side of Equation (10.4), tells us how fast the economy is moving along its static AD curve. The right side of Equation

---

[2]Here, by the way, we will see why we have kept M separate from the consolidating parameters defined in earlier chapters.

[3]This math fact can be proved by taking logarithms of the ratio, differentiating with respect to time, and recognizing that the time derivative of a logged variable is equal to the exponential growth rate of the variable. The discrete-form growth rates in this text are closely approximated by exponential growth rates for small, realistic values.

(10.4) measures the rate of growth of the real money supply, which tells us how rapidly the LM curve is shifting.

The growth rate of the nominal money supply is set by monetary policy. We continue to assume that monetary policy is passive: the central bank sets a constant growth rate for the money supply and lets the economy adjust. Up to this point, we have taken the monetary growth rate to be zero, but we are now prepared to let g_M assume any value. For a zero monetary growth rate, Equation (10.4) tells us that the faster prices are rising, the more inflation reduces the real money supply, and the faster the economy contracts, moving back along its static AD curve. For a positive monetary growth rate, the dynamic AD curve tells us that when inflation exceeds the growth of money it will erode the real money supply and the Keynes effect will result in movement back along the static AD curve. For inflation below the monetary growth rate, the Keynes effect is stimulative, generating movement down the static AD curve.

10.4 Output, unemployment, Okun's Law

To establish the link between the dynamic AD curve and the Phillips curve, we need to link up the unemployment rate and the growth of output. This time we are reformulating the static production function into a more dynamic equation. The production function we adopted was simply $Y = N$. The definition of the unemployment rate is $u = (L - N)/L$. Substitute the production function and difference this equation to produce:

$$\Delta u = \frac{-1}{L}\Delta Y = \frac{-Y}{L}g_Y$$

If the economy were to achieve full employment, so that $Y = N = L$, this relationship would simply be $\Delta u = -g_Y$. Ordinarily, the economy lies below full employment, so let us use a linear approximation. This gives us an equation that was first used for policy analysis by Arthur Okun when he chaired the Council of Economic Advisors for President Kennedy. The equation, called *Okun's Law*, is written:

$$\Delta u = -\beta g_Y \tag{10.5}$$

where $\beta < 1$ is a parameter[4].

---

[4]This derivation has assumed a constant labor force, L, consistent with the rest of the

Okun's Law states that when output is stable, the unemployment rate will remain constant. Unemployment declines during periods of positive growth and increases during periods of negative growth. Estimates suggest that the parameter β has a value of around .4 in the U.S. Each 1 percentage point of growth brings the unemployment rate down by .4 percentage points. Put another way, it takes about 2.5 percentage points of growth to bring the unemployment rate down by a full percentage point in one year[5].

10.5   The Phillips curve model

We now have completed the Phillips curve model. It is really a dynamic version of the AS-AD model. There are three unknowns: the unemployment rate, the inflation rate, and the growth rate of output. These three unknowns (or endogenous variables) are determined by three relationships, Equations (10.3), (10.4), and (10.5). When an economic model contains enough independent relationships to determine its endogenous variables, it is said to be *closed* or fully determined. We could say that Okun's Law has been used to close the Phillips curve model, since the Phillips curve and the AD equation were not sufficient.

10.5.1   Difference form

By writing the main equations in difference form, we can represent the whole model concisely. With the assumption of adaptive expectations, $\pi^e = \pi_{-1}$, the *Phillips curve in difference form* is written $\Delta\pi = -\alpha(u - u_n)$. The whole Phillips curve model in difference form is

$$\Delta\pi = -\alpha(u - u_n) \tag{10.6}$$
$$\Delta u = -\beta g_Y \tag{10.7}$$
$$g_Y = g_M - \pi \tag{10.8}$$

book and with the Marshallian short-run approach. We can relax this assumption in the interests of greater realism by assuming that there is some underlying trend rate of growth of the labor force, $\bar{g}$, making Okun's equation $\Delta u = -\beta(g_Y - \bar{g})$.

[5]To be more precise, it takes 2.5 percentage points of growth *above the trend growth rate* (which is around 2-3 per cent per year) to lower the unemployment rate by one percentage point. The trend growth rate is the rate of labor force growth plus the rate of productivity growth.

This model can be reduced even further by substituting the third equation into the second equation. Since the growth rate of the money supply is exogenous (being determined by the monetary authority), this leaves just two equations with two unknowns. But because the unknowns are changes in the unemployment rate and the inflation rate, this representation is not very transparent. It is easy to write the model out in level form, however.

10.5.2 Level form

Since $\Delta\pi = \pi - \pi_{-1}$ and $\Delta u = u - u_{-1}$, the Phillips curve model in level form is written:

$$\pi = \pi_{-1} - \alpha(u - u_n) \tag{10.9}$$

$$u = u_{-1} - \beta g_Y \tag{10.10}$$

$$g_Y = g_M - \pi \tag{10.11}$$

It is important to realize that this is a dynamic model that describes the temporary equilibrium of the economy in each period over some stretch of time. In each period, the previous values of π and u are known, which makes them predetermined variables.

Once again, we can reduce the model further by substituting the third equation into the second, which gives us:

$$\pi = \pi_{-1} - \alpha(u - u_n)$$

$$u = u_{-1} - \beta(g_M - \pi)$$

The Phillips curve model predicts the value of the endogenous variables, π and u, in each period on the basis of the given exogenous parameters, α, β, u_n, and g_M, and the predetermined variables, π_{-1} and u_{-1}. Such a dynamical system can be solved sequentially, or period-by-period, for its trajectory over time. This is called the *recursive solution* of the system. It can also be solved in closed form, which means each variable is expressed as a function of time and the initial conditions, although that is more challenging mathematically.

This particular model can be shown to be stable. Starting from any initial conditions, the trajectory will converge on a stable long-run equilibrium. However, unlike previous dynamic models we have seen, the Phillips curve model generates a cyclical trajectory because it will *overshoot* its long-run equilibrium repeatedly. Overshooting is best understood through a physical analogy with a pendulum. If you start a pendulum away from its rest point, it will descend to the rest point and keep on going, thus overshooting its long-run equilibrium (the rest point). In the Phillips curve model, the lagged response of inflation expectations to actual inflation generates overshooting.

10.6 Long-run equilibrium

When we use the expression "long run" in economics, it means that the system is fully adjusted along some dimensions. In the Phillips curve model, the long-run is defined by attainment of the natural rate of unemployment and by equality between the inflation rate and the expected inflation rate. The term long-run is also used in other contexts in economics to describe an equilibrium in which the capital stock has had time to adjust fully to economic forces. Some writers have begun using the term "medium run" to describe the former state, devoting long-run to the latter.

The long-run equilibrium in the Phillips curve occurs when the inflation and unemployment rates have converged on stable, constant values. We can easily solve for those values by substituting zeroes into the Phillips curve model in difference form. The solution is

$$
\begin{aligned}
\Delta u &= 0 \\
\Delta \pi &= 0 \\
g_Y &= 0 \\
\pi &= g_m \\
u &= u_n
\end{aligned}
$$

This is a long-run equilibrium because the system is fully adjusted in its two important dimensions. The inflation rate has settled down to the long-run value that generates no changes in the unemployment rate. The unemployment rate has settled down to the natural rate, at which the expected inflation rate equals the actual inflation rate. Thus, there are no further shifts in the Phillips curve caused by revisions in inflation expectations, or further changes in the unemployment rate, caused by changes in the

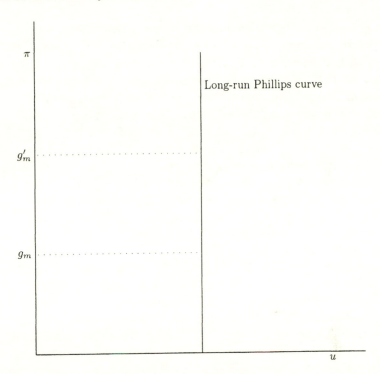

Figure 10.4: The long-run Phillips curve is vertical when there is a unique natural rate of unemployment. The central bank can effectively choose the long-run inflation rate by selecting the right growth rate for the money supply. A higher monetary growth rate, g'_m, leads to more inflation in the long run.

real money supply. This characterization of the long run will become clearer in the next section.

The long-run inflation rate is equal to the growth rate of the money supply. This illustrates the quantity theory of money (or if you prefer, the quantity of money theory of prices). Figure 10.4 shows that different choices by the central bank of monetary growth rates have no effect on the long-run unemployment rate, which remains the natural rate of unemployment. When money growth has no real effects on the economy—when it only affects the inflation rate—money is said to be *superneutral*. The vertical long-run Phillips curve shown in Figure 10.4 illustrates the superneutrality of money. One implication of superneutrality is that any policy effort to lower the unemployment rate below its natural rate (i.e., force the economy to operate to the left of the long-run Phillips curve) can only be effective if the inflation rate is constantly rising. This is called the *accelerationist hypothesis*. Proponents of the accelerationist hypothesis coined the frequently used term "non-accelerating inflation rate of unemployment" or NAIRU to describe the natural rate of unemployment.

It is important to remember that the long-run Phillips curve is vertical only when there is a unique natural rate of unemployment. If there are multiple natural rates of unemployment, for example because of hysteresis effects, the long-run Phillips curve may be downward sloping. The long-run Phillips curve will still be steeper than the short-run Phillips curve in this case, but not vertical. We will concentrate on the accelerationist model for expositional purposes.

10.7   Dynamics of the Phillips curve model

Subject the Phillips curve model to some shock, such as a change in monetary policy, and it undergoes a cyclical dynamic adjustment process that returns it to its long-run equilibrium. Understanding the dynamic behavior of the economy through the Phillips curve model is a bit like learning to play the piano with both hands. There are two things going on at once. First, the expected rate of inflation will be changing in each period because the expected inflation rate will generally not be validated by the actual inflation rate. Second, the real money supply will generally be changing, causing Keynes effects that alter the level of aggregate demand and the unemployment rate, because the inflation rate will generally not equal the growth rate of the money supply.

The first dynamic process is illustrated in Figures 10.1—10.3. In Figure 10.1, it is clear that the Phillips curve is always positioned by the expected rate of inflation. Study this figure and be sure you understand how to position the Phillips curve, knowing the expected rate of inflation. Figures 10.2 and 10.3 show how adaptive expectations cause shifts in the Phillips curve over time. In each period, the expected rate of inflation will be equal to the lagged inflation rate. This fact allows us to position the Phillips curve in each period, knowing only the lagged inflation rate.

This positioning process can be summarized by a simple rule of thumb: When the unemployment rate is below (above) the natural rate, the Phillips curve must shift upward (downward). When the unemployment rate is below the natural rate, the inflation rate will exceed the expected inflation rate. In the next period, the Phillips curve must shift upward, as workers adjust their expectations to conform to their observations. When the unemployment rate exceeds the natural rate, inflation runs below the expected rate. The Phillips curve must shift downward, as workers' expectations adjust to their observations.

The second dynamic process involves the dynamic AD curve and Okun's Law. From Equation (10.4), we can see that when inflation exceeds the growth rate of the money supply, the growth of output will be negative. That is because of the Keynes effect: reductions in the real money supply are contractionary. Conversely, as inflation becomes lower than money growth, the growth of output will be positive because the Keynes effect of an increasing real money supply is stimulative.

Okun's Law translates these statements about output growth into statements about the unemployment rate. By substituting Okun's Law, Equation (10.5), into the dynamic AD curve, Equation (10.4), we derive

$$\Delta u = -\beta(g_M - \pi)$$

from which it is clear that unemployment is rising whenever the inflation rate exceeds the growth rate of the money supply, g_M, and falling whenever the inflation rate is less than money growth.

We can put these two dynamic processes together to describe conceptually the recursive solution of the model in the aftermath of a monetary or fiscal policy shock, using the Phillips curve and IS-LM diagrams.

10.7.1 Monetary policy

Consider what happens when the central bank raises the rate of monetary growth once and for all (e.g., from 5 per cent to 6 per cent for all subsequent periods). Because we will want to conduct a comparative equilibrium analysis, we must begin in a long-run equilibrium position.

Figure 10.5 shows four key moments in the long-run trajectory: the initial equilibrium, the impact of the policy in its first year, the impact in its second year, and the ultimate new long-run equilibrium.

In its first period, the policy moves the economy along its existing Phillips curve. Since workers follow adaptive expectations, they believe that the inflation rate will remain at its original level (the old long-run equilibrium inflation rate).

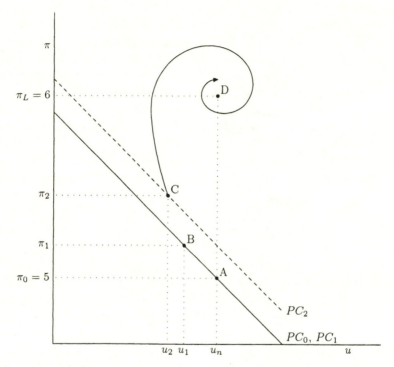

Figure 10.5: Starting from a long-run equilibrium (A), an increase in the rate of growth of the money supply from 5 per cent per year to 6 per cent per year causes the system to move along its Phillips curve in the short run (B). Because inflation expectations chase after actual inflation, next year's equilibrium lies on the new Phillips curve (C). Ultimately, the system will achieve the new long-run equilibrium (D). The arrow shows the path taken when the model has a stable focus, which involves overshooting the equilibrium.

In its second period, the policy works through both dynamic processes we described above. The Phillips curve shifts upward because the expected rate of inflation, which positions the Phillips curve, chases after the actual rate of inflation, which rose in the first year. The unemployment rate in Figure 10.5 has continued to decline, because the inflation rate is still below the new growth rate of the money supply set by the central bank.

At some point in time, the economy will reach a *turning point* where the unemployment rate will cease dropping and begin to rise. This will occur when the inflation rate rises above the growth rate of the money supply. The Phillips curve will then be shifting upward and the unemployment rate will be rising, so that inflation and unemployment increase simultaneously, a phenomenon known as *stagflation*. The ability of the expectations-augmented Phillips curve to explain the stagflation of the 1970s played a major role in its acceptance by the economics profession.

Another turning point is reached when the unemployment rate rises above the natural rate of unemployment. As we have seen, in this configuration the Phillips curve shifts downward over time because inflation expectations overestimate inflation, and are being revised downward. The economy experiences falling inflation and rising unemployment until the next turning point is reached.

This dynamic process describes the behavior of an economic model with a stable focus, which means that its trajectory spirals inward, converging on the equilibrium as the trajectory passes through a sequence of turning points. It can be shown using formal mathematical analysis that this particular model is indeed stable, meaning that the trajectory does converge on the long-run equilibrium. Further discussion of this point is presented in the Appendix. With a minor change in how inflation expectations are modeled, the Phillips curve model can generate a stable node, in which case the trajectory converges monotonically on the equilibrium, without any spirals[6].

The analysis of Figure 10.5 shows the logic of the accelerationist hypothesis. If the monetary authorities wanted to prevent the unemployment rate from returning to the natural rate, they would have to raise the monetary growth rate repeatedly. The result would be a continual increase in the inflation rate. Since technically speaking, this represents an acceleration of the

---

[6]The minor change is to work with an error-correction treatment of adaptive expectations in the form $\Delta \pi^e = \lambda(\pi_{-1} - \pi^e_{-1})$ where $0 < \lambda \leq 1$. This reduces to our assumption that $\pi^e = \pi_{-1}$ when $\lambda = 1$.

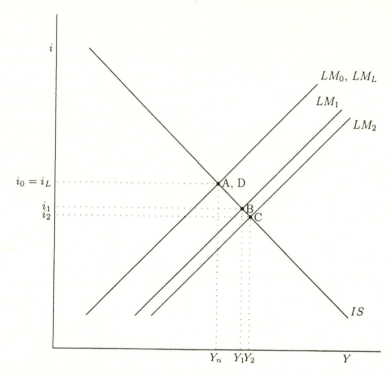

Figure 10.6: The increase in the growth rate of the money supply shown in Figure 10.5 initially shifts the LM curve out. But eventually, when inflation exceeds money growth, the LM curve shifts back. In the Phillips curve model with a stable focus, the LM curve repeatedly overshoots its long-run position, LM_L, by smaller and smaller amounts.

price level rather than the inflation rate, the term "non-accelerating inflation rate of unemployment" is not very precise, but it has achieved acceptance nonetheless. (Inflation is to prices as velocity is to distance, so an increase in inflation represents an acceleration of the price level.)

To get a deeper understanding of what is happening in Figure 10.5, we turn to our old friend, the IS-LM diagram, in Figure 10.6. The monetary policy shifts out the LM curve in the first year. In the second year, the LM curve continues to shift out since inflation has not yet risen to the rate of money growth. When the inflation rises to the rate of money growth, the LM curve will stop shifting out and begin shifting in; this is the turning point. In the long run, the LM curve returns to its original position, which illustrates the superneutrality of money.

This thought experiment started out in a long-run equilibrium in order to apply the comparative equilibrium method, but a stimulative monetary policy would be hard to justify if the economy were running at the natural rate of unemployment. In practice, when unemployment rises above the natural rate, stimulative monetary policy is justified as an instrument for speeding the recovery process, and our analysis suggests it will be effective in that role.

10.7.2   Fiscal policy

A stimulative fiscal policy (e.g., an increase in government purchases) shifts the IS curve outward, and generates the dynamic effects shown in Figure 10.7. Once again, we start in full long-run equilibrium for comparative purposes and identify four key moments in the dynamic trajectory.

In the first period, the fiscal policy lowers the unemployment rate and the economy moves along its original Phillips curve. Workers believe inflation will continue at its old level because they are using adaptive expectations.

In the second period, the two dynamic processes operate simultaneously. The Phillips curve shifts upward because the expected inflation rate chases after the actual inflation rate as it rises. The unemployment rate will rise in the second period because inflation now lies above the growth rate of the money supply, which the monetary authority has not changed; the Keynes effect is contractionary.

In the long run, the inflation and unemployment rates return to their original values, since the monetary policy has not changed. A stimulative fiscal policy has a short-run inflationary effect, but no long-run effect on inflation.

To understand the real effects of the fiscal policy, we need to turn to the IS-LM diagram. Refer back to Figure 9.4 in Chapter 9. In the long run, the increase in government purchases results in a higher interest rate, with no change in the level of output. The higher interest rate will crowd-out private investment spending. Since the level of output has not changed, the crowding out will be complete. This is exactly what we decided would happen using the simpler AS-AD model, which is not surprising since the Phillips curve model is just a dynamic version of the AS-AD model.

In practice, a stimulative fiscal policy would be justified as an instrument of stabilization policy when the unemployment rate exceeds the natural rate.

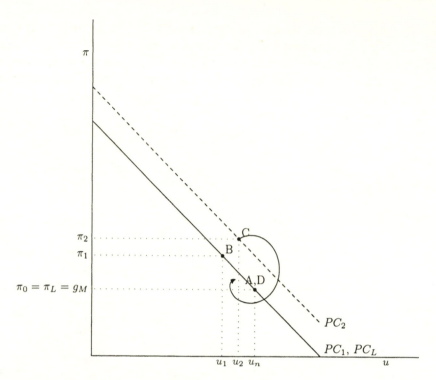

Figure 10.7: A fiscal expansion lowers unemployment and raises inflation temporarily (B). In the Phillips curve model with a stable focus, the trajectory, shown by the arrow, eventually brings the system back to its long-run equililbrium (D), exactly where it started (A). The inflation rate in the long run is determined solely by monetary growth.

Our analysis shows that such a policy can indeed speed up the recovery to the natural rate.

10.8   Disinflation and monetary policy

The Phillips curve model plays an important role in the conduct of monetary policy in most advanced countries today. Monetary policy makers have been preoccupied with reducing inflation since the 1970s, when inflation rates spiked up because of the OPEC oil price shocks. The Phillips curve model conveys the bad news that the only way to reduce inflation is to put the economy through a period of above-normal unemployment. The *sacrifice ratio* measures how much excess unemployment it takes to reduce the inflation rate by 1 percentage point. Consider a period of time from $t = 0$, when disinflation starts, to $t = T$, when the economy achieves a new long-run equilibrium. The inflation rate declines from π_0 to π_T. Formally, the sacrifice ratio is defined as

$$\frac{\sum_0^T (u_t - u_n)}{\pi_0 - \pi_T}$$

The numerator of the sacrifice ratio measures the cost of reducing inflation in point-years of excess unemployment. (To reckon in point-years, multiply percentage points of unemployment by duration in years.) To squeeze 1 percentage point of inflation out of the system, it may take one year with the unemployment rate 2 percentage points above the natural rate, or two years with the unemployment rate 1 percentage point above the natural rate, or four years with the unemployment rate .5 percentage point above the natural rate, or some other combination. In any case, if the sacrifice ratio is 2, it will take two point-years of unemployment to bring inflation down 1 percentage point.

This point is illustrated in Figure 10.8, which shows the Phillips curve in difference form. The difference form is handy because it remains in the same position over time during the dynamic trajectory of the model. Policy makers can view this curve as a menu of possible policy choices. The two that are illustrated might be thought of as "gradualism" versus "cold turkey" disinflation. No matter how the policy is timed, the sacrifice associated with reducing inflation by a given amount will always be the same, measured in point-years of excess unemployment, because the sacrifice ratio is property of the Phillips curve.

In fact, in our Phillips curve model, with adaptive expectations of the form $\pi^e = \pi_{-1}$, the sacrifice ratio is the reciprocal of the slope of the Phillips curve[7],

$$\frac{\sum_0^T (u_t - u_n)}{\pi_0 - \pi_T} = \frac{1}{\alpha}$$

Estimates of the Phillips curve in the U.S. often place the value of α between .5 and 1, making the sacrifice ratio between 1 and 2. The bad news is that

---

[7]With the more general error-correction treatment (see previous footnote) of expectations, $\Delta\pi^e = \lambda(\pi_{-1} - \pi^e_{-1})$, the sacrifice ratio will be $1/(\alpha\lambda)$.

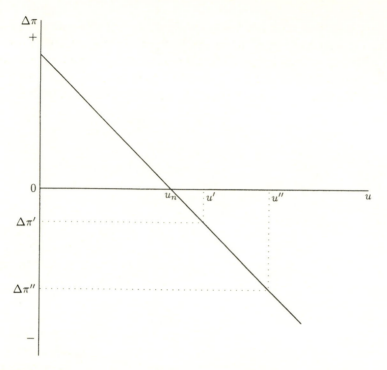

Figure 10.8: The Phillips curve in difference form illustrates well the policy options. To reduce inflation by a given amount, the central bank can choose to raise the unemployment rate a small amount for many years, lowering the inflation rate a small amount in each year (u' and $\Delta\pi'$) or it can choose to raise the unemployment rate a large amount for only one or a few years, getting rid of the same total amount of inflation in a short time (u'' and $\Delta\pi''$). But the sacrifice, measured in point-years of excess unemployment, is always the same.

reducing inflation is painful. It requires sacrifices on the part of many millions of workers to get rid of each percentage point of inflation.

The good news is that the U.S. inflation rate does not increase very much when unemployment is below the natural rate. A high sacrifice ratio, in other words, implies a shallow Phillips curve and indicates that the economy is not very inflation-prone. If α is .5, the economy can operate 1 percentage point below the natural rate with only a .5 percentage point increase in inflation each year. Ten years of such prosperity (for workers otherwise unemployed) results in only 5 additional percentage points of inflation. Obviously, such a policy could not continue indefinitely. But the true value of the natural rate of unemployment is not known with any precision, and in fact is the subject of much controversy. If the sacrifice ratio is high, this recommends a monetary policy of "testing the water" by letting the unemployment rate fall until inflation begins to occur. In this case, there is little danger of creating excessive inflation but great benefit in the form of high employment and output levels.

10.9 Limitations of the Phillips curve model

Sharp public debates on precisely how to conduct monetary policy take place within the Phillips curve framework, making this an important and practical topic. Many of these debates are basically disagreements about the parameters of the Phillips curve such as the sacrifice ratio and the natural rate of unemployment, whose values are surrounded by uncertainty. Another source of controversy is disagreement about the underlying costs of inflation and unemployment.

The Phillips curve model as presented here lacks realism in its representation of monetary policy. In practice, central banks rarely follow the passive policy of targeting the money supply growth rate as we have assumed here. Instead, they actively manage the level of aggregate demand in response to unemployment and inflation rates. The next chapter extends the Phillips curve model to encompass such an active monetary policy. Unlike previous extensions in this book, this one actually reduces the level of complexity, in this case by getting rid of dynamic oscillations that don't seem very realistic.

Another weakness of this chapter is that we have implicitly assumed that firms succumb to money illusion in their investment decisions by responding to the nominal interest rate without adjusting for inflation. That assumption eliminates some mathematical complexity but is obviously unsatisfactory, and we will rectify this weakness in the next chapter.

Problems for Chapter 10

Where indicated, these problems refer to a hypothetical economy described by the following:

$$\pi = \pi^e - .5(u - 4)$$

$$\Delta u = -.4 g_Y$$

$$g_Y = g_M - \pi$$

$$\pi^e = \pi_{-1}$$

Note that we have used a percentage for the natural rate of unemployment (4%), so for consistency we must do likewise for all the percentage terms.

1. In year 0, the monetary growth rate is 5% per year and the economy is in long-run equilibrium. The central bank changes the growth rate of money to 10% per year in year 1 and all subsequent years. Draw the Phillips curve and IS-LM diagrams, and identify the position of the economy in years 0, 1, and 2, as well as in its new long-run equilibrium. Label all landmarks carefully.

2. Using the previous problem, calculate the inflation and unemployment rates in years 0, 1, and 2 as well as in the new long-run equilibrium.

3. In the previous problem, calculate the total amount of excess unemployment that would result from the monetary stimulus from year 0 until the economy achieves its new long-run equilibrium. Be careful about signs.

4. In year 0, the monetary growth rate is 10% per year and the economy is in long-run equilibrium. The central bank decides to reduce inflation to 4% per year in three equal steps. Their target path for inflation is 10%, 8%, 6%, 4%, 4% and 4% for years 0, 1, 2, 3, 4 and 5. Calculate the monetary growth rates in years 1, 2, 3, 4 and 5 that generate the desired path. How many point-years of excess unemployment are required?

5. Use the data in problem 1, construct a spreadsheet model for this hypothetical economy and use it to solve recursively for the path taken by the unemployment and inflation rates for 25 years. Make a graph of this path with inflation on the vertical and unemployment on the horizontal axis.

6. Prove that the sacrifice ratio is $1/\alpha$.

7. Using the statistical appendix of the *Economic Report of the President*, gather data on the price level and the unemployment rate over a time

period of your choice. (You can use price data suggested in the problems for Chapter 8.) Calculate the inflation rate and the change in the
inflation rate. (i). Make a scatter plot of the inflation rate against the
unemployment rate. Try to explain the pattern using the expectations-
augmented Phillips curve model. (ii). Make a scatter plot of the *change*
in inflation against the unemployment rate, and fit a curve to the data.
What is your estimate of the slope of the Phillips curve, the sacrifice
ratio and the natural rate of unemployment for the U.S. economy?

Chapter 11

A Model with Active Monetary Policy

Central banks in modern advanced countries try to manage the money supply and interest rates so that unemployment rates and inflation rates remain under control. There is considerable debate about how central banks should conduct monetary policy, as well as about how they actually do operate, but there is little reason to think that central banks target the growth of the money supply as rigidly as we have assumed. It is more reasonable to think that the U.S. Federal Reserve Board and other central banks "lean against the wind": they raise interest rates to combat rising inflation, and lower interest rates to combat rising unemployment. With this assumption about monetary policy, we will take the Phillips curve model a step closer to reality[1].

11.1   The real interest rate

Up to this point, we have ignored the effects of inflation on the cost of borrowing. Having gotten this much macroeconomic theory under our belts, we can afford to emend the analysis by distinguishing between the real and nominal interest rates, just as households and firms do in practice.

The real interest rate is the nominal interest rate adjusted for inflation. It shows the return to an investor, or the cost to a borrower, measured in goods

---

[1]The pedagogical approach of this chapter was suggested by Romer (2000), who calls it "macroeconomics without the LM curve."

rather than in money. Consider the purchase of a bond worth the equivalent of one good at the current price, P. After one year, this investment returns $(1 + i)P$. How much does it return measured in goods? The price that the investor expects to prevail in one year is $P^e_{+1} = (1 + \pi^e)P$. Therefore, the return measured in goods, which is the real rate of interest, r, is

$$1 + r = \frac{(1 + i)P}{P^e_{+1}} = \frac{1 + i}{1 + \pi^e}$$

For reasonably low rates of inflation, we can solve this expression for r and approximate the result closely with the standard equation for the real rate of interest, which is known as the *Fisher equation* in honor of the pioneering work of Irving Fisher :

$$r = i - \pi^e \tag{11.1}$$

It is the real, rather than the nominal, rate of interest that central banks are most concerned with, since it affects investment spending when decision-makers do not suffer from money illusion.

11.2   The central bank reaction function

We have already learned that the central bank can influence the interest rate by changing the money supply through open market operations or other policies. Rather than continuing to focus on the money supply itself, then, let us refocus on the interest rate, and in particular, the real interest rate. We will assume that the central bank responds to inflation and unemployment through the *central bank reaction function*[2], which we write

$$r = h_0 + h_1\pi - h_2u \tag{11.2}$$

where h_1 and h_2 are parameters that reflect the central bank's sensitivity to inflation and unemployment. For example, we model a central bank that loathes an increase in inflation through a high value of h_1. The intercept term, h_0, reflects the central bank's long-run inflation goals, as explained below.

---

[2]For estimates of the Fed reaction function in the context of a medium-scale econometric model of the U.S. economy, see Fair (1994).

We will see that these parameters determine the inflation rate allowed by monetary policy in the long run.

The reaction function (RF) replaces the traditional LM curve. The theory is that given an unemployment rate and an inflation rate, the central bank responds by choosing the money supply that generates the desired real interest rate, as described by Equation (11.2). Clearly, the central bank must have fairly precise knowledge of the structure of the asset markets in order to operate this way. This theory works well under adaptive expectations where there are no offsetting changes in the expected inflation rate that cancel out the changes in the nominal interest rate. Since it describes market clearing in the asset markets, the reaction function can be regarded as a replacement for the LM curve[3].

11.3 The AD curve and the IS-RF model

Replacing the traditional LM curve with the central bank reaction function requires that we replace the traditional AD curve with a version of the AD curve that shows how aggregate demand responds to different inflation rates, rather than different price levels. This can be easily accomplished by combining the IS curve and the reaction function (RF), calling the result the IS-RF model.

11.3.1 The IS-RF model

Since the reaction function replaces the LM curve, it can easily be combined with the IS curve to describe the equilibrium level of aggregate demand. Recall that the IS curve is based on the inverse relationship between the interest rate and investment spending. Clearly, the real, rather than nominal, rate of interest determines investment spending since it represents the true cost of capital funds. If businesses or households expect a higher inflation rate, all else equal, they should recognize that this makes borrowing less costly since they will be paying back their loans with inflated dollars. The investment function in the presence of expected inflation should be re-written

---

[3]The traditional LM curve, based on a fixed money supply, does not depend on the real interest rate and is unaffected by changes in the expected rate of inflation. This makes the IS-LM apparatus somewhat awkward in the presence of expected inflation, and we will not attempt to explain it.

$I = I(Y,r)$. This means that the IS curve, too, should be written out in terms of the real interest rate. Recalling from Chapter 4 that a_0 and a_1 are consolidating parameters that depend on the underlying behavior of consumption, investment, and government spending, we will write the IS curve as follows:

$$Y = a_0 - a_1 r \tag{11.3}$$

In order to translate the IS curve from its original form into a statement about the interest rate and unemployment, we use the definition $u = (L - Y)/L$ to replace Y with $(1-u)L$. Rearranging, we obtain the IS curve written out in terms of the unemployment rate:

$$u = (1 - \frac{a_0}{L}) + \frac{a_1}{L} r \tag{11.4}$$

The central bank reaction function (RF), Equation (11.2), and the IS curve, Equation (11.4), constitute a model of short-run equilibrium just like the IS-LM model. Given an inflation rate, which positions the RF curve, the short-run equilibrium will be given by the intersection of the IS and RF functions, as can be seen in the lower panel of Figure 11.1. When the inflation rate is low (such as π_0 in the Figure), the central bank will be willing to allow a low real interest rate and low unemployment rate. When the inflation rate is high (such as π_1 in the Figure), the central bank raises the interest rate, resulting in a higher unemployment rate. We can call this the IS-RF model.

11.3.2   The dynamic AD curve

By substituting Equation (11.2) into Equation (11.4), we obtain a type of AD curve that relates the rate of inflation (rather than the price level) to aggregate demand. Using consolidating parameters[4] to reduce clutter, this *dynamic AD curve* is

$$\pi = a_6 + a_7 u \tag{11.5}$$

The dynamic aggregate demand curve makes a natural companion to the Phillips curve because both are expressed in terms of the rates of unemployment and inflation. We have written it out with π on the left-hand side to

---

[4]The consolidating parameters are $a_6 = (a_0 - L - a_1 h_0)/(a_1 h_1)$ and $a_7 = (L + a_1 h_2)/(a_1 h_1)$.

make it easier to visualize the aggregate demand curve on the Phillips curve diagram. But from a theoretical standpoint, causation runs from inflation to unemployment. Given an inflation rate, the central bank responds by choosing a real interest rate. The real interest rate determines the unemployment rate, through the IS curve. The economy is on its dynamic AD curve when the central bank has chosen a real interest rate that generates an unemployment rate consistent with the reaction function for that inflation rate. The assumption is that the central bank has good knowledge of the IS curve, so that it can make fairly precise decisions.

11.3.3 Visualizing the dynamic AD curve

The theory behind the dynamic aggregate demand curve involves active monetary policy rather than the Keynes effect that generated the static AD curve. We can visualize the dynamic AD curve in Figure 11.1, which shows the central bank reaction function for two different inflation rates. The IS curve here is Equation (11.4), since we are working with unemployment rather than output. The upper panel shows the dynamic AD curve, and the lower panel shows the IS-RF model from which it is derived.

When inflation is high, the central bank responds with high interest rates to increase unemployment, leaning against the inflation wind. The position of the central bank reaction function reflects this tighter monetary policy. In practice, the central bank would reduce the money supply in order to raise interest rates. High interest rates choke off investment and reduce aggregate demand, which raises the unemployment rate. When inflation is low, the central bank loosens up on the money supply to let interest rates fall and lower the unemployment rate. In this theory, the central bank basically chooses a position along the IS curve, depending on how much inflation prevails.

With respect to policy initiatives, the dynamic AD curve with active monetary policy behaves much like the static AD curve. Fiscal policy, or any parameter change that shifts the IS curve, results in shifts in the dynamic AD curve. A stimulative fiscal policy will shift the dynamic AD curve to the left, or inward, since it will lead to lower unemployment. A fundamental change in the monetary regime also shifts the dynamic AD curve. For example, if the central bank decided to get tough on inflation, we might model that as an increase in the parameters h_0 or h_1. The dynamic AD curve would shift to the right, signifying monetary tightening.

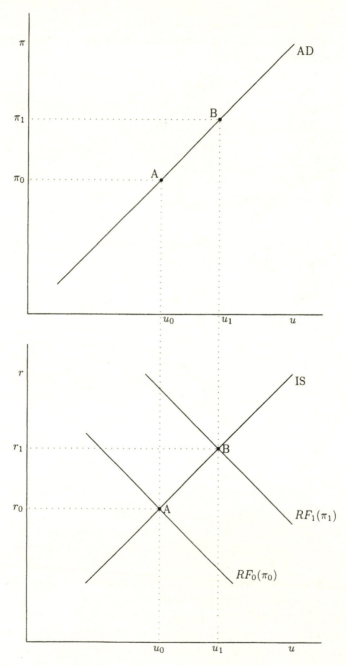

Figure 11.1: The dynamic aggregate demand curve arises from active monetary policy. When the central bank responds to inflation and unemployment through its reaction function (RF), higher rates of inflation induce tighter monetary policy and result in higher unemployment rates. Note that the IS curve is positively sloped here because the unemployment rate is on the horizontal axis.

This theory is both easier to understand and more realistic than the theory of the static AD curve. It describes well the drama of monetary policy as it is played out in public.

11.4 Target inflation and policy rules

We can use Equations (11.2 and 11.3) to determine the long-run equilibrium values of the interest rate and the long-run equilibrium rate of inflation.

11.4.1 The natural rate of interest

By substituting Y_n into Equation (11.3), we can see that the long-run value of the real interest rate is:

$$r_n = \frac{a_0 - Y_n}{a_1}$$

Here the n subscript is mnemonic for the *natural rate of interest*, which is another term for the long-run equilibrium real rate of interest. The natural rate of interest is unaffected by monetary policy. However, it is capable of being changed by fiscal policy, since it depends on the parameters of the IS curve. For example, an increase in government spending will shift the IS curve outward by increasing the parameter a_0. The natural rate of interest will increase as well.

11.4.2 The target inflation rate

The long-run inflation rate is obtained by assuming that the unemployment rate has achieved its natural rate, substituting r_n into the reaction function, and solving for the long-run inflation rate, which we will denote π^*:

$$\pi^* = \frac{r_n + h_2 u_n - h_0}{h_1}$$

The long-run inflation rate depends on the natural rates of interest and unemployment, and the parameters of the reaction function. It is clear that central bankers can target the long-run inflation rate by choosing appropriate parameters in the reaction function. Indeed, we can now interpret these parameters (h_0, h_1, and h_2) as a reflection of the central bank's choice of long-run inflation rate, or its *target inflation rate*. For example, if the central bank wants to wipe out inflation altogether, it will set h_0 equal to $r_n + h_2 u_n$.

Finally, the long-run nominal interest rate is obtained from the definition of the real interest rate, Equation (11.1). In the long-run, the expected inflation rate will be equal to the actual inflation rate, making the long-run nominal interest rate

$$i^* = r_n + \pi^*$$

This application of the Fisher equation helps explain many puzzling features of the way financial markets respond to news about changes in monetary policy.

11.4.3   Monetary policy rules

The central bank reaction function captures some important aspects of modern monetary policy. A similar approach to monetary policy has been proposed by John Taylor, who calls for a policy rule consisting of changing the nominal interest rate in response to deviations of inflation from its target value and to deviations of unemployment from its natural level. If we take the long-run rate of inflation to represent the target rate of inflation, we can replace h_0 with $r_n + h_2 u_n - h_1 \pi^*$ in the reaction function, Equation (11.2). Using the definition of the real rate of interest, we can easily derive a version of the *Taylor rule* from the reaction function itself[5]:

$$i = \pi^e + r_n + h_1(\pi - \pi^*) - h_2(u - u_n)$$

Taylor argues that the coefficients on the inflation gap and the output gap in his equation should be set equal to around .5 for optimal macroeconomic performance. While he proposed this rule as a guide to what the central bank should do, some evidence suggests that it is a good approximation to what the U.S. central bank actually has done over recent decades.

Many central banks in the world have declared their goal to be the achievement of a pre-announced, target rate of inflation. When inflation exceeds this target, they tighten up on monetary policy. When inflation is

---

[5]Unlike Taylor's formulation (Taylor, 1999), this version includes expected inflation rather than actual inflation on the right hand side. Also, Taylor uses the percentage deviation between output and the natural level of output rather than the gap between unemployment and the natural rate of unemployment.

lower than the target, they ease up. One could interpret the reaction function as a formalization of this behavior, which is called *inflation targeting*[6].

11.5 The Phillips curve–IS-RF model

We can combine the dynamic aggregate demand curve generated by the IS-RF model with the Phillips curve (which is really a dynamic aggregate supply curve). This gives us a simple yet powerful tool for analyzing inflation and unemployment. The dynamic AD curve, Equation (11.5), and the Phillips curve, Equation (10.3), together fully determine the two unknowns, π and u in each period, with lagged inflation, π_{-1}, functioning as a pre-determined variable. They form the dynamic system:

$$\pi = a_6 + a_7 u$$

$$\pi = \pi_{-1} - \alpha(u - u_n)$$

The solution to this system involves a first-order difference equation, which cannot produce the kind of oscillations we observed in the previous chapter[7].

We can visualize the long-run equilibrium of this model by means of the Phillips curve diagram in Figure 11.2. Here the dynamic AD curve and the Phillips curve intersect at the long-run equilibrium position. The inflation rate at this point is the target rate of inflation, π^*. This model can be effectively used to analyze monetary policy, fiscal policy, and various supply-side disturbances.

---

[6]Inflation targeting is a form of nominal targeting, in which a nominal variable such as the money supply, nominal GDP, or inflation is chosen to be the policy anchor. In this spirit, it might be better modelled under the special assumption that $h_2 = 0$, making policy indifferent to the unemployment rate.

[7]The recursive solution is obtained by substitution to get

$$\pi = \frac{\alpha(u_n - a_6)}{1 + \alpha a_7} + \frac{1}{1 + \alpha a_7}\pi_{-1}$$

and the solution for u in each period can then be found by substituting into Equation (11.5). The recursive solution describes the trajectory of the model in transit to its long-run equilibrium, and derives its name from the procedure of solving each period by looking back at the previous period.

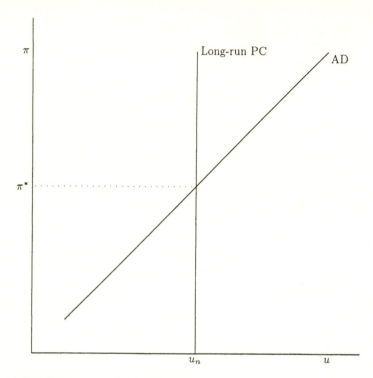

Figure 11.2: When monetary policy responds to unemployment and inflation by changing the interest rate, the AD curve arises as a stable relationship between inflation and unemployment. At low inflation rates, monetary policy eases, resulting in high demand and low unemployment. At high inflation rates, monetary policy tightens. The long-run equilibrium is achieved where the AD curve intersects the long-run Phillips curve.

11.6   Monetary policy

A disinflationary monetary policy in this model is considerably more controlled and realistic than in the model of the previous chapter. A central bank decision to lower its inflation target can be represented as an increase in the value of h_0. Such a contractionary policy will shift the dynamic AD curve down in (u,π) space, since it involves raising the interest rate for every level of inflation, and this will raise the unemployment rate. The short-run effect of the policy can be seen in Figure 11.3. Obviously (and intuitively), tighter monetary policy induces a recession. In the new short-run equilibrium, inflation is lower and unemployment higher than in the original position.

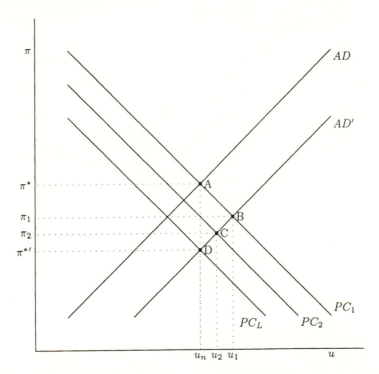

Figure 11.3: A disinflationary monetary policy shifts the AD curve downward as the central bank switches to a lower inflation target. The short-run effect raises the unemployment rate (B), but the central bank then controls the trajectory so that it stays on the new AD curve. The Phillips curve shifts down as inflation expectations adjust over time.

We know from the previous chapter that the Phillips curve shifts down whenever the unemployment rate lies above the natural rate of unemployment because in this case workers have overestimated inflation and will subsequently reduce their inflation expectations. The position of the Phillips curve is determined by the expected rate of inflation. Thus, the inflation rate continues to decline, as shown in Figure 11.3, and this is effected through *shifts* in the Phillips curve rather than through movements along the Phillips curve. As the Phillips curve shifts downward, the economy moves along its AD curve until it reaches the new long-run equilibrium. Note that the economy does not overshoot this equilibrium, basically because the central bank is conducting an active stabilization policy.

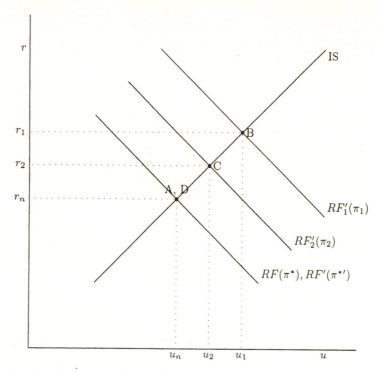

Figure 11.4: A disinflationary monetary policy shifts the RF curve outward as the central bank switches to a lower inflation target, raising the real interest rate in the short run. As inflation declines, the central bank allows the interest rate to fall, bringing the economy back to the natural rates of unemployment and interest in the long run. Points A-D correspond to positions A-D in Figure 11.3.

We can gain additional insight into this scenario by considering the underlying IS-RF diagram shown in Figure 11.4. The shift to a new, tighter monetary reaction function (RF') pushes the real rate of interest up sharply in the short run. But having done the job of creating unemployment and initiating disinflation, the central bank allows the real interest rate to decline as inflation comes down. Ultimately, the economy returns to the same long-run position on the IS-RF diagram. This reflects the superneutrality of money.

It is interesting to contemplate the path travelled by nominal interest rates in this experiment. When monetary policy tightens, obviously it raises nominal rates. But over time, the contraction in economic activity reduces the inflation rate. The expected rate of inflation chases after the actual inflation rate, under adaptive expectations, so it too declines. In the asset markets, this reduction in inflation expectations will eventually predominate over tight money, causing the nominal interest rate to decline to a level *below* its original level. Thus, the nominal interest rate will first increase, and then decrease below its original level.

This behavior explains why central bank tightening often produces conflicting opinions in the media from financial experts. There are many interest rates in real economies, and the central bank can control only the short-term rate on interbank borrowing. What effect does Fed tightening have on other, longer-term rates? Some experts are thinking of the short run when they predict that a Fed tightening will raise interest rates. But others focus on the long-run effects on inflation expectations when they predict that a Fed tightening will lower interest rates. There are naturally disagreements about the speed with which inflation expectations will change.

11.7 Fiscal policy

An increase in government purchases of goods and services will also shift the AD curve, as shown in Figure 11.5. A fiscal stimulus will increase the level of output and lower unemployment in the short run.

With the unemployment rate below the natural rate, inflation expectations will begin to increase, shifting the Phillips curve upward. These shifts will move the economy along its new AD curve until it reaches its new long-run equilibrium as shown in Figure 11.5. Notice that the long-run inflation rate has risen because the central bank has permitted its target rate of inflation to rise in recognition of the new fiscal policy and it is allowing more monetary growth in the long run. Underlying this increase in the target inflation rate is the increased long-run or natural interest rate generated by the fiscal policy. (Recall that the long-run inflation rate equals $[r_n + h_2 u_n - h_0]/h_1$.)

We can get a deeper understanding of the increase in the natural rate of interest by studying Figure 11.6, which shows the same fiscal stimulus from the perspective of the IS-RF diagram. Notice that the RF curve has shifted in the short run, in response to the increase in inflation that we observed in Figure 11.5.

Under strict inflation targeting, the central bank may be reluctant to permit its target rate of inflation to rise in this way. It may choose to resist the demand stimulus by re-evaluating the parameters of its reaction function.

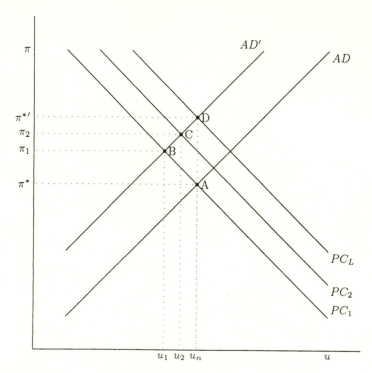

Figure 11.5: A fiscal expansion shifts the AD curve upward, assuming no change in the central bank reaction function. In the short run, unemployment declines and inflation increases. Since this policy raises the long-run real interest rate, it will raise the long-run rate of inflation.

11.8   Supply shocks

Another useful exercise concerns supply shocks. We will consider the effects of a permanent supply shock, such as a reduction in the natural rate of unemployment. As shown in Figure 11.7, a reduction in the natural rate of unemployment has a disinflationary effect on the economy, which on impact finds itself above the new natural rate. The Phillips curve shifts down, since its position depends on the expected rate of inflation, which has not yet changed, and the natural rate of unemployment, which has fallen.

Over time the inflation rate declines because of changes in inflation expectations, and the economy marches down along the AD curve, driven by shifts in the Phillips curve. Ultimately, it achieves the new equilibrium with

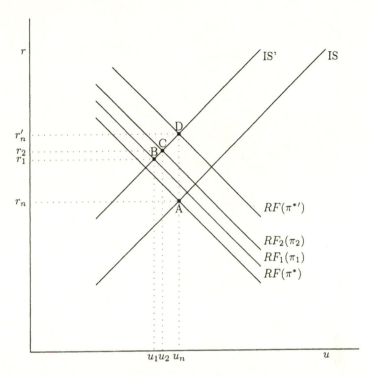

Figure 11.6: A fiscal expansion shifts the IS curve upward. In the short run, the RF curve shifts out as the central bank responds to the increase in the inflation rate. Continued increases in inflation result in further shifts in RF, until the new long-run equilibrium is achieved at a higher natural rate of interest. Points A-D correspond to positions A-D in Figure 11.5.

lower inflation and lower unemployment. The central bank can afford to let the real interest rate decline because the natural level of GDP is now higher than before, and this decline translates into a lower target rate of inflation. Many observers believe the U.S. economy went through such a process of declining inflation and unemployment during the 1990s.

An inflationary shock that raises the natural rate of unemployment would obviously create the opposite pattern of events. The Phillips curve would shift outward until the new long-run equilibrium is achieved with higher unemployment and inflation. The most famous example of an inflationary shock occurred in the 1970s, when the Organization of Petroleum Exporting Countries (OPEC) succeeded in raising the price of crude oil sharply. As predicted

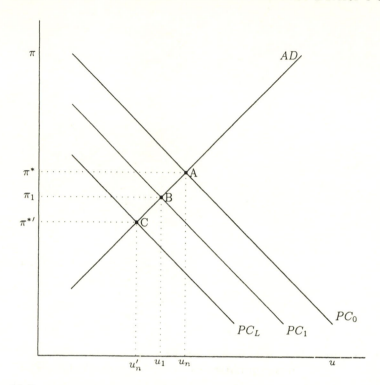

Figure 11.7: A favorable supply shock that reduces the natural rate of unemployment generates a burst of economic growth with declining inflation.

by the model, inflation and unemployment rates rose simultaneously in most advanced industrial countries.

11.9   Political economy of the AD curve

An inflationary supply shock serves to illustrate the political economy of the reaction function, by showing the implication of differences in the central bank's responsiveness to inflation and unemployment. The reaction function reflects the central bank's attitude toward the costs of inflation and unemployment. A central bank that regards inflation as relatively harmless but unemployment as socially wasteful would assign a relatively small value to h_1 and a large value to h_2 when faced with an inflation shock. Generally speaking, labor unions and political parties that represent the working class

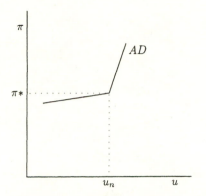

Figure 11.8: A populist central bank that is more concerned with high unemployment will be more accommodating to inflationary shocks than to disinflationary shocks. The AD curve will be kinked and convex as a reflection of this kind of reaction function.

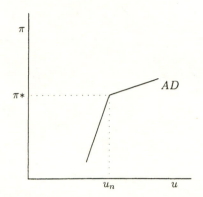

Figure 11.9: A conservative central bank that is more concerned with high inflation will be less accommodating to inflationary shocks than to disinflationary shocks. The AD curve will be kinked and concave as a reflection of this kind of reaction function.

advocate this kind of monetary policy because the costs of inflation are much less important to working people than are the costs of unemployment. A central bank that values low, stable inflation and is willing to tolerate substantial unemployment would make the opposite assignment. Generally speaking, financial interests (banks and wealthy investors) have a vested interest in this approach because they suffer losses on their financial investments when inflation increases unexpectedly, causing the real rate of interest they receive to fall below the rate they had anticipated.

This identification between a steep AD curve and a "populist" central bank breaks down when we consider a disinflationary shock. A favorable shock that shifts the Phillips curve inward would lower the inflation and unemployment rates. A steep AD curve implies that the central bank has chosen to absorb the shock mainly through lower inflation. But this would probably be the path chosen by a central bank oriented toward the financial interests who benefit most from lower inflation. A populist central bank would have no objection to lowering the unemployment rate, since unemployment is involuntary and wasteful. We might model this idea by specifying the reaction function for a populist central bank so that the response parameter h_2 becomes smaller when $u < u_n$. This would put a kink in the AD curve,

which would be steep when $u > u_n$ and flat when $u < u_n$. Similar considerations apply to a conservative central bank, which might be more sensitive
to inflation above its target rate[8]. In this case, the AD curve would be flat
when $u > u_n$ and steep when $u < u_n$. These two possibilities are illustrated
in Figures 11.8 and 11.9. To use this approach to analyze a supply shock,
we need to recognize that the kink in the AD curve occurs at the perceived
natural rate of unemployment, which inevitably adjusts to changes in the
natural rate with a lag.

If the long-run Phillips curve is not vertical, this comparison between
a populist and conservative central bank assumes even greater significance.
A populist central bank would be willing to reduce the unemployment rate
even at the expense of relatively high inflation. A conservative central bank
would strive to keep inflation low, even at the expense of relatively high
unemployment. Since we do not know if the Phillips curve is vertical, it may
well be the case that the type of monetary policy in place determines the
long-run unemployment rate toward which the economy gravitates.

Monetary policy in most democratic countries is supposed to be established through democratic processes, at least in principle. The ability to
choose wisely among competing approaches to monetary policy is one of the
most important reasons to study macroeconomics. Rather than viewing the
AD curve developed in this chapter as a natural fixture of macroeconomics,
we should recognize the role that we can play as citizens in the political
processes that establish its shape and position.

The model developed in this chapter is probably the most realistic and
useful example of macroeconomic theory that we have developed in this book.
However, it vastly overstates the amount of control that central banks can
exercise in practice. For example, key parameters like the natural rates of
unemployment or interest cannot be estimated precisely. These key parameters are at the center of many spirited public debates about macroeconomic
policy, including fiscal policy, monetary policy and the appropriate response
to supply shocks.

---

[8]Formally, we could express these ideas through the reaction function

$$r = h_0 + h_{11} \min[\pi^* - \pi, 0] + h_{12} \min[\pi - \pi^*, 0] - h_{21} \min[u^* - u, 0] - h_{22} \min[u - u^*, 0]$$

where the asterisks identify the perceived target rate of inflation and natural rate of
unemployment. The populist central bank would set $h_{11} = h_{12}$ and $h_{21} > h_{22}$ while the
conservative central bank would set $h_{21} = h_{22}$ and $h_{11} > h_{12}$.

Since the model rests upon a rich foundation that runs from the IS-LM theory of aggregate demand to the conflict theory of wage and price setting, it is a keystone of these lectures on macroeconomic theory. One major omission is that the model remains closed, while real economies are embedded in an increasingly global system of trade and capital flows.

Problems for Chapter 11

These problems make use of the following data for a hypothetical economy:

$$\text{Reaction function:} \quad r = 3 + .5\pi - .5u$$

$$\text{AD curve:} \quad \pi = 1.7 + 1.075u$$

$$\text{Phillips curve:} \quad \pi = \pi_{-1} - .5(u - 4)$$

$$r_n = 4$$

Note that we have used percentages for the natural rate of unemployment and interest (both are 4%), and must do likewise with other variables for consistency.

1. Calculate the central bank's target rate of inflation. Calculate the nominal rate of interest in long-run equilibrium. Why does it differ from the natural rate of interest?

2. The central bank has decided to get tougher on inflation. The reaction function shifts to $r = 3 + 1.5\,\pi - .5\,u$ and the AD curve becomes $\pi = .566 + .358\,u$. Assuming we start in year 0 from the long-run equilibrium given in the previous problem, what will be the unemployment and inflation rates in year 1, when this policy goes into effect? What will they be in year 2? What will they be in the long run?

3. Calculate the real and nominal rate of interest in years 0, 1, 2, and in the long run in the previous problem. Explain the pattern you observe.

4. Start from the original data. Consider a fiscal contraction that shifts the AD curve to $\pi = -.311 + 1.075\,u$. Calculate the effect of the policy on inflation and unemployment in short run (in year 1) and in the long run. Calculate the new natural rate of interest.

5. Draw the Phillips curve diagram and the IS-RF diagram describing problem 2. Draw the diagrams describing problem 4.

6. Use the Phillips curve and IS-RF diagrams to analyze the behavior of the economy after an increase in the natural rate of unemployment.

7. Compare the responses of a populist central bank and a conservative central bank after a negative demand shock that shifts the IS curve inward. Use the kinked AD curves developed in the text.

8. Use the statistical appendix of the *Economic Report of the President* to find data on the interest (federal funds) rate, the inflation rate and unemployment in the U.S. Make a graph showing the movements of the real and nominal interest rates over the last three decades, assuming adaptive inflation expectations. Evaluate the evidence for a central bank reaction function. Look for periods when high inflation results in a high real interest rate, or when high unemployment results in a low real interest rate.

Chapter 12

Open Economy Basics

Globalization has raised awareness among millions of people of the forces unleashed when an economy is opened up to trade and world capital markets. No survey of macroeconomic theory would be complete without some coverage of open economy macroeconomics. This is a vast field. In order to get a grasp on it, we will concentrate on the open economy version of the IS-LM model of short-run equilibrium[1]. This means we must backtrack a bit, by returning to the assumption of fixed wages and prices.

12.1   The exchange rate

Before any agent can import a good or invest in a foreign capital market, she must obtain the foreign exchange that will be accepted there. Exchange rates are the prices of foreign currencies. We will simplify by lumping the rest of the world into one category so we can speak of "the" exchange rate[2]. For purely illustrative purposes, we will use the euro (€) to exemplify the foreign currency and the US dollar ($) to represent the home currency.

The exchange rate, e, could be measured as $/€ or as €/$. Since we have measured all other prices in dollars, we will stick with that convention and define the dimension of the exchange rate as the dollar price of the euro:

---

[1]For more in-depth treatment of the open economy, Dernburg (1989) is an excellent source.

[2]Statisticians accomplish this by calculating a weighted average of a country's bilateral exchange rates, often using trade shares as weights.

$$\dim [e] = \frac{\$}{€}$$

Many foreign exchange rates are traded using the opposite convention, whether for convenience or tradition. The Japanese yen is usually quoted as ¥/$ for convenience, for example, to avoid awkwardly small decimals.

There are two pure systems for setting exchange rates. Under *fixed exchange rates*, the central bank posts the price at which it is willing to buy or sell foreign currencies, and then tries to maintain those rates administratively. Under a *flexible or floating exchange rate* system, on the other hand, rates are established in the private markets for foreign currencies, which central banks may influence but do not control. In practice, many arrangements fall between these two extremes.

From the end of World War II until 1973, the major currencies of the world were fixed under the system set up by the Bretton Woods agreements. This system fell apart, largely because Europeans were no longer willing to accept large amounts of U.S. dollars, and the major currencies have been determined in the private markets for foreign exchange ever since. Nonetheless, significant parts of the world operate fixed exchange rate regimes and thus we will want to understand the macroeconomic theory covering both systems.

When the exchange rate rises, using our convention, the dollar is said to *depreciate* under a system of flexible exchange rates or to be *devalued* under a system of fixed exchange rates. When the exchange rate falls using our convention, the dollar *appreciates* under flexible rates or is *revalued* under fixed rates. Technically, usage should conform to the type of exchange rate regime, but the terms *devaluation* and *depreciation* have converged as synonyms in common usage. With our convention, there is a potential for confusion because, for example, when rates go up they depreciate, which sounds odd. For this reason, economists often switch to the opposite convention when they are focusing a lot on exchange rate movements. But in macroeconomic theory, our convention is widely accepted, so we must adjust to it, and we will see that there are actually some advantages in this.

The exchange rate is a nominal price. Adjusting for differences in price levels in the two countries gives us the *real exchange rate*, or

$$\frac{eP^*}{P}$$

where P^* is the foreign price level (e.g., euros per unit of European goods). We are going to return to the fixed-price assumption used in the first six chapters of this book, and ignore the role of inflation in open economy macroeconomics. It will do no harm to assume further that P and P^* are equal. In this case, we can interpret the exchange rate as both nominal and real, and save on notation.

There is a theory in international economics that in the long run, under some conditions, the real exchange rate should gravitate toward 1. The nominal exchange rate that makes the real exchange rate unity is called *purchasing power parity* or PPP for short. This theory treats the open economy macroeconomic model we are surveying as a short-run deviation from PPP. In our case, the PPP rate would be 1. The basic idea here is that the same good should cost the same, in dollars, no matter where on the globe it is purchased. An amusing example is the Big Mac (yes, the hamburger) index of PPP published by the *Economist* magazine.

Regardless of the exchange rate system, it makes sense to consider the market for foreign currency in terms of supply and demand, as in Figure 12.1. The supply of euros comes from Europeans who want to buy US exports or who want to invest capital in the US asset markets (e.g., buy a U.S. bond). The demand for euros comes from US citizens who wish to import European goods and services or who want to invest their capital in the European asset markets (e.g., buy a Eurobond). In real exchange markets, a third kind of agent—the speculators—plays an enormously important role, for good or ill, but including them in any serious way is best left for a more advanced treatment.

Under flexible exchange rates, familiar forces of supply and demand determine the rate that clears the market for foreign exchange. This is shown by the point of intersection of the D and S functions in Figure 12.1. Note that an event that increases the demand for euros, such as an increase in the desire to import or a movement of capital to Europe in response to attractive returns there, will shift the demand curve out and cause a depreciation of the dollar ($e \uparrow$). The opposite events cause an appreciation of the dollar. Similarly, an event that increases the supply of euros, such as an increase in exports to Europe or a flow of capital into the US in response to an attractive US interest rate, shifts the supply curve out and triggers an appreciation of the dollar. Specialists in international economics would cringe at this simplistic analysis, but it will serve us tolerably well in figuring out the short-run effects of economic policies.

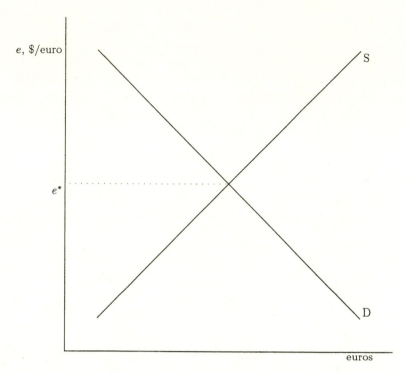

Figure 12.1: Under a regime of flexible or floating exchange rates, supply and demand in the market for foreign currency determine the equilibrium exchange rate. Supply comes from foreigners purchasing exports or investing in the home country capital market. Demand comes from home country imports or investments in foreign capital markets.

Under fixed exchange rates, the central bank stands ready to buy or sell foreign currency at its posted rate, $\bar{e}$. Only if by some fluke this happens to be the market-clearing exchange rate will the central bank be off the hook. Generally, $\bar{e}$ will be too high (as shown in Figure 12.2) or too low. When it is too high, there is an excess supply of euros, shown by an arrow in Figure 12.2. In a flexible regime, the exchange rate would simply appreciate to eliminate this excess of euros, but under fixed rates that is not an option. Instead, the central bank buys up the excess euros (or, looked at another way, sells dollars to Europeans). In the opposite case of an exchange rate that is too low, the central bank accomodates an excess demand for foreign exchange by selling euros.

These forced interventions into the foreign exchange market by the central

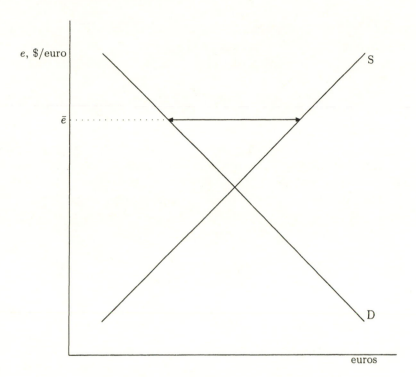

Figure 12.2: Under a regime of fixed exchange rates, the central bank posts the rate at which it stands willing to buy or sell foreign exchange. When there is an excess supply of foreign exchange, as illustrated by the arrows, the central bank buys up the surplus. This asset purchase will increase the nation's money supply.

bank are not without consequence for the domestic economy. As we learned in Chapter 1, any purchase or sale of an asset by the central bank creates a corresponding change in high-powered money, in the form of bank reserves and domestic currency. We can see this by recalling the T-account for the central bank when it buys euros:

Central Bank

ΔAssets	ΔLiabilities
+€	+Reserves
	+Currency

We also know that an infusion of high-powered money creates an increase in the money supply proper (demand deposits plus currency) through the

money multiplier process. Thus, when the central bank is forced to defend
a fixed exchange rate by purchasing foreign exchange, that will increase the
money supply. Obviously, when the central bank is selling euros, the money
supply will contract. This effect was discovered in the 18th century by David
Hume, who called it the *specie flow* mechanism since precious metal coins
(specie) were the basis of the monetary systems of the period.

There is one possible alternative open to the central bank if it does not
want its foreign exchange transactions to affect the money supply, and that is
sterilization. A sterilization is an open-market operation specifically designed
to insulate the money supply from the foreign exchange market. For example,
if the central bank were to sell bonds at the same time it buys euros, this
combination would leave unaffected the high-powered money that determines
the money supply. A T-account representation makes this plain:

Central Bank

ΔAssets	ΔLiabilities
+€	
−Bonds	

There are clearly limits to sterilization. For example, the central bank
must have an arsenal of bonds and other financial assets to sustain the sterilization illustrated above. In the opposite case in which an excess demand
for euros requires the central bank to sell off its foreign exchange, it must
clearly have ample supplies of these on hand. But for short periods of time,
sterilization is often a practical option.

Under flexible exchange rates, central banks use sterilization operations
when they want to intervene in the foreign exchange market, for example to
prevent a rapid depreciation by buying up their own currency, yet do not
want the interventions to affect their domestic money supplies.

Finally, we should not overlook the difficulties presented by a speculative
attack on a fixed exchange rate. When, like troops massed on a border,
currency speculators are convinced that a devaluation is imminent, they will
increase the demand for foreign currency as they try to close out their positions in the home currency. In this case, the excess demand for foreign
currency can quickly overwhelm the central bank, whose reserves of foreign
currency are, after all, limited. The only option available may be to shift
demand back to the home currency by raising interest rates, but the rates
required to satisfy the speculators are often so high as to be surreal. This

is no more than a temporary holding action, since such high rates are burdensome to the domestic economy. The scenario described here has played itself out on many occasions recently, such as in the UK, Italy, and Sweden in 1992 or in Thailand and other Asian nations in 1997.

12.2 The trade balance

We have already defined the trade balance as the difference between exports and imports, or net exports. But exports and imports are, strictly speaking, incommensurable because the former are domestic goods while the latter are foreign goods, which must differ or else they would be perfect substitutes. To measure imports in the same units (volume of domestic goods) as exports, we need to multiply by the real exchange rate, which by assumption is here equal to the exchange rate, e. A dimensional analysis clarifies:

$$
\dim\left(\frac{eP^*}{P}\right)Q = \dim e\left(\frac{\dim P^*}{\dim P}\right)\dim Q
$$

$$
= \left(\frac{\$}{€}\right)\left(\frac{€}{\text{European goods}}\right)\left(\frac{\text{US goods}}{\$}\right)\left(\frac{\text{European goods}}{\text{year}}\right)
$$

$$
= \frac{\text{US goods}}{\text{year}}
$$

Armed with this insight, we define net exports by $NX = X - eQ$ (recalling that we set $P^* = P$ by assumption).

12.2.1 The net export function

A nation's exports depend on two key factors, their price and the ability of foreign buyers to pay (i.e., the income of the rest of the world). Under our assumptions, the effective price of exports is determined by the exchange rate. We expect that a depreciation or devaluation should reduce the price of exports and raise their volume, and conversely for an appreciation or revaluation. An increase or decrease in foreign income should be directly reflected in export volumes.

A nation's imports similarly depend on the exchange rate and domestic income. A depreciation (or devaluation) makes foreign goods more expensive, which discourages imports. An appreciation (or revaluation) has the opposite effect. An increase in national income raises expenditure on goods of all kinds, including imported goods, just as a slump in income reduces such spending. This is an important fact, especially for understanding the short-run behavior of net exports. An economic boom, for example, sucks in imports and automatically pushes net exports downward, toward a trade deficit. Much of the short-term movement in the trade deficit reflects prosperity and depression in the home economy.

We will formalize these ideas in order to extend our existing IS-LM model into the open economy by using linear export and import functions:

$$X \;=\; x_0 Y^* + x_1 e \tag{12.1}$$
$$Q \;=\; q_0 Y - q_1 e \tag{12.2}$$

Here, $x_0 < 1$ and $q_0 < 1$ represent the *marginal propensities to import* of the foreign country and the home country. The sensitivity of exports and imports to the real exchange rate is given by x_1 and q_1. We use the asterisk (*) to denote a foreign variable.

With the export and import equations and our definition of net exports, we can write one consolidated equation for net exports:

$$\text{NX} = (x_0 Y^* + x_1 e + q_1 e^2) - e q_0 Y \tag{12.3}$$

The placement of the parenthetical expression is designed to make it clear that the net export function is yet another linear equation, assuming a constant level of foreign GDP and a constant exchange rate.

12.2.2   Balance of trade

When net exports are zero, neither a trade deficit nor surplus prevails, so we have a balance of trade. Equation 12.3 makes it clear that there will be one unique level of GDP at which a balance of trade is achieved, which we can call Y_{BT}. Algebraically,

$$Y_{BT} = \frac{(x_0 Y^* + x_1 e + q_1 e^2)}{e q_0} \tag{12.4}$$

We can visualize the behavior of net exports and the level of GDP with balanced trade in Figure 12.3. This figure shows clearly that the trade deficit widens during economic expansions.

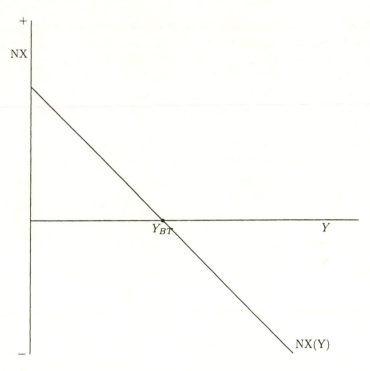

Figure 12.3: An increase in output generates an increased demand for imports, which reduces net exports. There is one level of output, Y_{BT}, at which trade is balanced. At higher levels of output than this, the economy experiences a trade deficit; at lower levels, it runs a trade surplus.

12.2.3   The Marshall-Lerner condition

Despite the fact that a depreciation increases the volume of exports and decreases the volume of imports, it is not clear from Equation 12.3 that a depreciation will necessarily lead to an improvement in a nation's trade balance. The reason is that a depreciation makes a given level of imports more expensive, in terms of the domestic output that must be swapped for it. If exports and imports are not price-sensitive, and their volumes stay constant, the country will have to pay out more of its own output for a given volume of imported goods when its currency depreciates. That is why in principle a depreciation could worsen the nation's trade deficit. Obviously, there is some critical level of price-sensitivity for exports and imports that is sufficient to ensure that depreciation leads to a higher level of net exports. As it happens, when the sum of the import and export price elasticities equals or exceeds unity in absolute value, a depreciation will increase net exports. This is called the Marshall-Lerner condition, after Alfred Marshall and Abba Lerner, who first studied this issue. We will assume that this condition prevails unambiguously[3]. In practice, there may be lags in behavior so that it may not prevail in the very short run, which means that a country may have to wait patiently before it will see the desired improvement in the trade deficit after a depreciation or devaluation.

The Marshall-Lerner condition also guarantees that a depreciation or devaluation will cause Y_{BT} to increase.

12.3   The balance of payments

The *balance of payments* surplus measures the net flow of funds into a country from all sources, which are divided into two distinct accounting categories. Funds that originate in transactions involving flows of goods or services are entered in the *current account*. These consist of funds that arise from trade and funds that arise because of investment income on the net foreign assets of the country. We will simplify by ignoring these latter, identifying the current account surplus with the trade surplus or net exports. Funds that originate in transactions involving assets are entered in the *capital account*. For example, the purchase of a US bond by a European bank involves an inflow of capital. A country that attracts a net inflow of capital is running a capital account surplus, and conversely for a capital account deficit. Thus, the capital account surplus is equivalent to net capital flows. A capital account deficit is equivalent to net foreign investment, or NFI.

The balance of payments surplus takes the form of an increase in the foreign exchange holdings of a country. Let us write F to represent foreign exchange, so that ΔF stands for the change in foreign exchange. Then we can say that

$$\Delta F = NX - NFI$$

Under fixed exchange rates, this equation describes the change in foreign exchange holdings of the central bank. As we have seen, unless the bank

---

[3]In terms of Equation (12.3), we must assume that $\partial NX/\partial e > 0$, which will be true for all $e > 1/(2q_1)(q_0 Y - x_1)$.

sterilizes a balance of payments surplus or deficit, this change in its assets will be reflected in a change in the money supply.

In balance of payments equilibrium,

$$\Delta F = 0 = \text{NX} - \text{NFI} \tag{12.5}$$

Balance of payments equilibrium is achieved under flexible exchange rates by movements in the exchange rate or in the interest rate. The requirement that the balance of payments must achieve equilibrium justifies our identification of the trade surplus with net foreign investment and the trade deficit, $-\text{NX}$, with net foreign borrowing, $-\text{NFI}$.

This identification of the trade deficit with net foreign borrowing helps us interpret the open economy version of the investment-saving identity. Recall that this identity is written

$$I = S + (T - G) - NX$$

Since the term $S + (T - G)$ represents national saving, it is now clear that a nation's investment must be equal to the national saving it generates on its own plus the financial resources made available from the rest of the world through net foreign borrowing. Foreign borrowing represents a flow of capital into the nation.

12.4 Capital mobility

The flows recorded in the capital account are purchases and sales of assets such as bonds, equities, real estate, or physical capital equipment. We simplify by assuming that the only assets are domestic bonds and foreign bonds (e.g., Eurobonds). Why would a US agent purchase a foreign bond? Obviously she does so for the return it offers. In point of fact, the world capital markets are highly sensitive to interest rate differentials, with huge amounts of financial capital ready to be dispatched globally at electronic speeds.

If domestic and foreign bonds were perfect substitutes, alike in every important respect such as risk, clearly the market would enforce equality in the expected return on these two assets. This illustrates the principle of *arbitrage*: two identical assets should have the same return because otherwise there are pure profit opportunities available that cannot survive in a competitive market. Part of the return to an investment in foreign bonds comes from the interest rate offered. Another part, however, comes from the expected change in exchange rates. If the dollar depreciates over the holding period, when the bond matures the investor gets back the return in euros plus the added bonus that comes from the appreciation of the euro. The arbitrage principle applied to domestic and foreign bonds leads to *uncovered interest parity*, the condition that the interest differential should equal the expected depreciation of the dollar.

If we write e_{+1}^E to represent the expected exchange rate in period $t + 1$ and i^* to represent the foreign interest rate, the uncovered interest parity condition is[4]

$$i = i^* + \frac{e_{+1}^E - e}{e}$$

The best way to understand this condition is to see it as an equality between two otherwise-equivalent investments. The left-hand side shows the expected return on a dollar invested in U.S. bonds. The right-hand side shows the return on the same dollar invested in Eurobonds, which is equal to the interest rate in Europe plus any expected appreciation of the euro. (Note that if the dollar depreciates, by definition the euro appreciates.)

The interest parity condition suggests that starting from a position of equality between interest rates, an increase in the domestic interest rate will cause a decline in the exchange rate. In order to maintain the same anticipated return between dollar-denominated and euro-denominated investments, the markets must expect a future depreciation of the dollar (i.e., an increase in the exchange rate). This will only happen if the current exchange rate declines as a result of the influence of capital attracted by the temporarily high return on U.S. assets (assuming constant exchange rate expectations). This is the same conclusion we reached earlier, using informal supply-and-demand reasoning. The exchange rate must rise in this way until the expected depreciation just equals the interest differential.

When domestic and foreign assets are perfect substitutes, *perfect capital mobility* prevails. This is not likely to happen in real economies, where capital is *imperfectly mobile*. In this case, there will generally be some difference

---

[4] *Covered interest parity* is a weaker condition, in which foreign and domestic returns are equalized through the purchase of a forward contract in foreign currency. Instead of speculating about the future exchange rate, an investor can lock one in through a forward contract.

in the net return on foreign investment that reflects the added risk and uncertainty attached to ownership of an unfamiliar asset. In the extreme case of *zero capital mobility*, no interest rate on foreign assets will entice domestic investors to move capital abroad, either because they are unwilling or, more likely, unable due to government restrictions on the movement of capital.

We formalize these ideas by assuming that there is a linear relationship (using f as a parameter measuring its strength) between net foreign investment and the differential between the interest rate and the foreign interest rate, i^*:

$$\text{NFI} = f(i^* - i) = fi^* - fi \tag{12.6}$$

As f approaches ∞, we approach perfect capital mobility. Under perfect capital mobility, net foreign investment can assume any value because foreigners stand ready to lend or borrow without limit. As a result, the domestic interest rate cannot stray from the foreign interest rate, and we have $i = i^*$. At the other extreme, zero capital mobility is a special case in which $f = 0$ and NFI $= 0$ for any interest differential.

The balance of payments equilibrium condition can now be written out explicitly by substituting Equations 12.6 and 12.3, giving us

$$i = i^* - \frac{x_0 Y^* + x_1 e + q_1 e^2}{f} + \left(\frac{eq_0}{f}\right) Y$$

With the help of the definition of Y_{BT}, this can be reduced to:

$$i = i^* + \frac{eq_0}{f}(Y - Y_{BT}) \tag{12.7}$$

We call the graph of this equation the *BP curve*. The BP curve is illustrated in Figure 12.4. It is no accident that the axes of Figure 12.4 are in the same units as the IS-LM system, for the BP curve is designed to work on this familiar turf. There are two useful facts illustrated in Figure 12.4. First, when the domestic and world interest rates coincide, the level of GDP on the BP curve is that for which trade is balanced, Y_{BT}. Second, points above and to the left of the BP curve represent balance of payments surpluses, while points below and to the right of the BP curve represent balance of payments deficits. Controlling for the effects of output on the current account, a balance of payments surplus is associated with a high interest rate that is attracting lots of foreign capital, while a deficit is associated with low rates that are

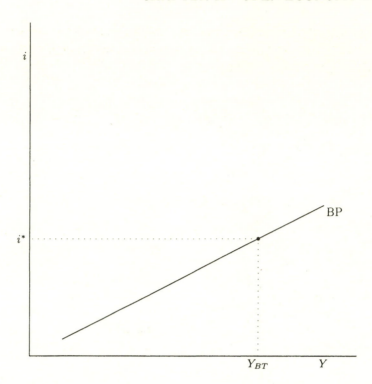

Figure 12.4: The balance of payments curve shows positions for which the overall balance of payments—the current account and capital account—are equilibrium. Higher interest rates attract an inflow of capital that can finance a greater trade deficit. At the world interest rate, i^*, capital flows are zero so the economy must run a trade balance. Points above the BP curve represent positions with a balance of payments surplus.

causing a flight of capital toward the global capital markets where returns are higher. Zero capital mobility would be represented by the vertical line, $Y = Y_{BT}$. Perfect capital mobility would be represented by the horizontal line, $i = i^*$.

Between the extremes of zero and perfect capital mobility, we will want to distinguish between *relatively immobile capital*, when the BP curve is steeper than the LM curve, and *relatively mobile capital*, when the LM curve is steeper than the BP curve. These distinctions will prove useful in understanding the effects of fiscal policy in the open economy.

The position of the BP curve depends on the exchange rate. An increase in the exchange rate (i.e., a depreciation) shifts the BP curve outward, to the right, while a decline (appreciation) shifts the BP curve inward, to the left. Here is where our dimensional convention for the exchange rate actually affords some advantage.

12.5   The open economy IS curve

Mercifully, the LM curve requires no modification in the open economy. It still represents positions in which the asset markets for money and domestic bonds are in equilibrium. The IS curve, on the other hand, does change in the open economy because net exports are expenditures on domestically produced output.

However, it is relatively easy to incorporate open economy considerations into the IS curve. The derivation for the IS curve starts with the same equilibrium condition, $Y = Z$, but now we must expand Z to include net exports, or $Z = C(Y,T) + I(Y,i) + NX(Y,e)$. Substituting Equation 12.3 and solving for GDP gives us the open economy IS curve:

$$Y = a_8 - a_9 i \qquad (12.8)$$

where

$$a_8 = \frac{1}{1 - c_1 - b_1 + eq_1}(c_0 - c_1 T + b_0 + G + x_0 Y^* + x_1 e + q_1 e^2)$$

$$= \gamma(c_0 - c_1 T + b_0 + G + x_0 Y^* + x_1 e + q_1 e^2)$$

$$a_9 = \frac{b_2}{1 - c_1 - b_1 + eq_1} = \gamma b_2$$

The open economy IS curve differs from its closed economy counterpart in two respects. First, it is affected by changes in the exchange rate[5]. An increase in the exchange rate (i.e., depreciation) increases the intercept term, which is the consolidating parameter a_8, shifting the IS curve to the right or outward. A decrease in the exchange rate (i.e., appreciation) shifts the

---

[5]Some writers choose to include the exchange rate within the IS curve, so that changes in the interest rate bring on movements along the IS curve that are caused partly by changes in the exchange rate. This works particularly well as a modeling strategy under perfect capital mobility, when the uncovered interest parity condition links the interest and exchange rates, but less well in more general cases.

IS curve to the left or inward. Again, our dimensional convention for the exchange rate pays off.

Second, the open-economy multiplier (a key determinant of the slope of the IS curve) differs from its closed economy counterpart by the addition of the marginal propensity to import, q_1, in the denominator. Obviously, from a mathematical standpoint the multiplier is smaller in an open economy than in a closed economy. From an economic standpoint, that is because an increase in output in an open economy sucks in imports. Thus, during the multiplier process, some of the demand generated by each round of the process leaks out into imports without feeding back and stimulating domestic production. The result is that the multiplier effect is less dramatic because some of the demand increase is felt by the trading partners of the home country rather than by its domestic producers.

These conceptual differences do not change the overall picture that equilibrium in the goods market leads to higher levels of GDP when the interest rate declines. The open economy IS curve slopes downward in (Y, i) space just like its closed economy sister.

12.6   Economies large and small

Before we can plunge into the open economy IS-LM model itself, we need to make it clear that even though we use the US dollar and the euro to illustrate the issues, we are not assuming that there are only two countries (the US and Europe) in the world. Models that assume two (or some small number of) countries are able to identify the interdependencies between their economies, at the expense of somewhat greater complexity. These models do not assume that the endogenous variables in the foreign country, such as Y^* and i^* in our case, are constant. They assume that each country is large enough to have a distinct impact on the levels of income, interest rates, and other variables of its trading partners. For obvious reasons, these are called *large country models*.

The IS-LM model we develop in the next two chapters assumes that the home country is small enough that changes there do not have any effect on the level of income, Y^* or interest rate, i^*, in the rest of the world. Obviously, this is not true of big economies such as that of the US or Europe. The main rationalization for using such a *small country model* is that it is simpler to work with and, if this is any consolation, does convey most of the main qualitative results that emerge from more sophisticated treatments.

Problems for Chapter 12

1. Construct the T-accounts for the central bank showing the effects of a balance of payments deficit.

2. The interest rate in the U.S. is 6% while the interest rate in Europe is 8%. The euro is currently trading for $.95. Calculate the exchange rate that financial markets expect in one year assuming perfect capital mobility prevails. Is this an expected appreciation or depreciation of the dollar?

3. Draw the balance of payments schedule and the IS curve on the same diagram. Identify the level of GDP at which net exports are zero.

4. Use the statistical appendix of the *Economic Report of the President* to find data on the current account and the trade balance in the U.S. Evaluate our practice of using the trade balance to measure the current account. Discuss the relationship between net exports and the current account in the most recent years.

Chapter 13

Fixed Exchange Rates

Under fixed exchange rates, the central bank stands ready to buy or sell foreign exchange when the balance of payments is in surplus or deficit. As we have seen, this automatically ties the money supply to the balance of payments, unless the central bank chooses to sterilize. A balance of payments surplus implies that the central bank is buying an equivalent amount of foreign exchange, which raises the nation's money supply accordingly, while a balance of payments deficit reduces the money supply. Thus, under fixed exchange rates, balance of payments equilibrium is achieved through shifts in the LM curve.

Before we proceed, it is worth spending a moment to remind ourselves that we have returned to the assumption maintained in the first six chapters: wages and prices are fixed and do not change. Extending the full model of price setting and inflation to an open economy setting is complex and there is really no consensus model yet. With no inflation in the model to give meaning to the central bank reaction function, we also return to our earlier approach toward monetary policy.

13.1   IS-LM-BP model with fixed rates

We can gather together the main results from previous chapter to assemble an open economy IS-LM-BP model. First, the LM curve from Chapter 5 continues to apply in an open economy setting with no modification. Second, the balance of payments equilibrium condition from the previous chapter and the open economy IS curve complete the model:

$$[\text{LM curve}] \quad i \;=\; -a_2(M/P) + a_3Y \tag{13.1}$$

$$[\text{IS curve}] \quad Y \;=\; a_8 - a_9i \tag{13.2}$$

$$[\text{BP curve}] \quad i \;=\; i^* + \frac{eq_0}{f}(Y - Y_{BT}) \tag{13.3}$$

These three equations uniquely determine the three endogenous variables in the open economy with fixed exchange rates: Y, i, and M. Note that M has become an endogenous variable by virtue of the specie-flow mechanism: balance of payments deficits drain money out of the economy, while surpluses draw money into the economy. For some purposes, it may be useful to work with these equations, going back to previous chapters where the consolidating parameters are described. But for most purposes we can gain a satisfactory understanding of the open economy IS-LM-BP model through figures, without excessive formal analysis.

The basic diagram is laid out in Figure 13.1. The equilibrium occurs at the intersection of the IS, LM, and BP curves. While it is not essential, it helps to further assume that an initial equilibrium involves a trade balance at Y_{BT}. That way, it is easy to determine how a particular policy change affects net exports. We will want to work out the effects of monetary policy, fiscal policy, and exchange rate policy (e.g., devaluation) under a variety of assumptions about the degree of capital mobility, which is reflected in the slope of the BP curve.

13.2   Monetary policy

13.2.1   Without sterilization

An increase in the money supply shifts out the LM curve, just as it would in a closed economy. Because a monetary expansion tends to lower interest rates and raise GDP, it will push the economy into the balance of payments deficit region, below the BP curve. (If there is zero capital mobility, the BP curve is vertical and we will be to the right of it.) Figure 13.2 shows a monetary expansion. The important thing to see is that emergence of a balance of payments deficit forces the central bank to undo its original monetary expansion, since it must now sell off foreign exchange in the amount of the payments deficit. These sales of foreign exchange automatically reduce

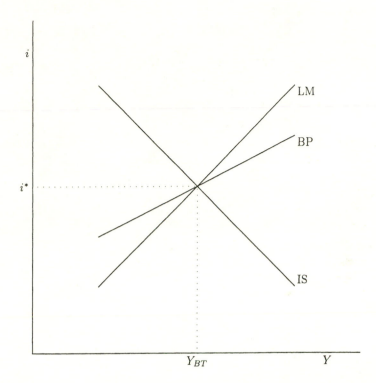

Figure 13.1: The intersection of the IS, LM and BP curves identifies an equilibrium in the open economy with fixed exchange rates. It is useful to begin any comparative equilibrium exercise at the world interest rate and the balanced trade level of GDP.

the money supply, shifting the LM curve back to its original position—the specie flow mechanism. Remarkably, the conclusion we must reach, that a monetary expansion is ineffective as a tool for stabilization, remains valid for any degree of capital mobility. This conclusion assumes that the central bank has chosen not to sterilize its purchases or sales of foreign exchange.

13.2.2 With sterilization

Affairs are quite different if the central bank chooses to sterilize its purchases or sales of foreign exchange. In this case, it can make the shift in the LM curve stick under most conditions. Figure 13.2 illustrates a monetary expansion that is effective at increasing GDP, but at the expense of a balance of

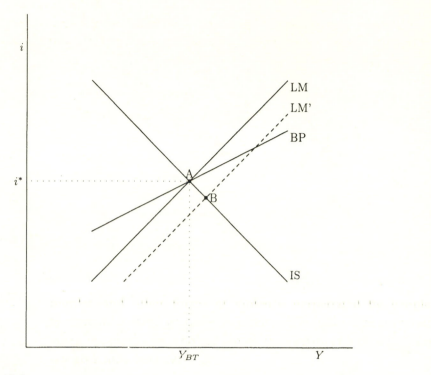

Figure 13.2: An expansion of the money supply shifts the LM curve to the right, as long as capital is not perfectly mobile. Without sterilization (A), the resulting balance of payments deficit forces the central bank to sell foreign exchange, reducing the money supply so that the economy returns to its original position. With sterilization (B), however, the central bank can simultaneously buy bonds and sell foreign exchange, preventing the money supply from declining.

payments deficit that must be sterilized. In this case, the central bank must buy bonds as it sells off foreign exchange in order to insulate the domestic money supply from the specie-flow mechanism. Obviously, this cannot go on forever, and our IS-LM model is evidently not describing a very permanent equilibrium. But it does describe a position that could be maintained for a significant amount of time under favorable conditions, and therefore one that represents a practical option for policy makers.

One condition that removes this option is perfect capital mobility. Sterilization is only able to work when the central bank can lower the interest rate. Under perfect capital mobility, all the capital in the country would flee lower interest rates. This infinite capital flight rules out sterilization completely, and makes monetary policy under fixed exchange rates and perfect capital mobility ineffective under any circumstances.

13.3 Fiscal policy

Fiscal policy in the open economy IS-LM model also depends critically on the degree of capital mobility. In terms of its impact on the balance of payments, there is a watershed between relatively immobile capital and relatively mobile capital. Recall that these conditions are defined by which curve, the BP or the LM, is steeper.

As shown in Figure 13.3, in the case of relatively immobile capital where the BP curve is steeper, a fiscal expansion shifts the IS curve out and temporarily places the economy in a balance of payments deficit. From an economic standpoint, the fiscal expansion raises GDP and this automatically generates a trade deficit as the booming economy sucks in imports. (Recall that we start with a trade balance for analytical convenience.) With low levels of capital mobility, the higher interest rate that has emerged as the economy moves up along its LM curve is just not sufficient to attract enough capital inflow to finance fully the trade deficit. The balance of payments deficit that ensues generates the familiar decline in the money supply through the specie-flow mechanism and this shifts the LM curve up and to the left. Ultimately, the adjustment in the money supply will restore a complete IS-LM-BP equilibrium at a higher rate of interest. Note that with immobile capital, the specie-flow mechanism effectively forces a monetary tightening that at least partially neutralizes some of the stimulative force of the fiscal expansion.

When capital is relatively mobile, as in Figure 13.4, the fiscal expansion raises interest rates by more than enough to offset the emergent trade deficit. In this case, the economy will temporarily find itself with a balance of payments surplus. With a payments surplus, the specie-flow mechanism kicks in and increases the money supply, shifting the LM curve outward. These shifts in the money supply continue until their underlying source—the payments surplus—has been overcome and the economy finds itself in a full IS-LM-BP equilibrium. With relatively mobile capital, the specie-flow mechanism effectively forces a monetary expansion that amplifies the stimulative force of the fiscal expansion.

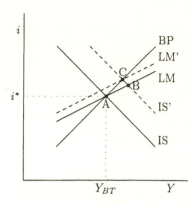

Figure 13.3: A fiscal expansion with relatively immobile capital creates a balance of payments deficit at (B). Under fixed exchange rates, the money supply declines until balance of payments equilibrium is reestablished at (C).

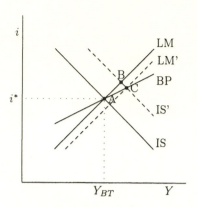

Figure 13.4: A fiscal expansion with relatively mobile capital creates a balance of payments surplus at (B). Under fixed exchange rates, the money supply increases until balance of payments equilibrium is reestablished at (C).

Thus, the higher the degree of capital mobility, the more effective will fiscal policy be as a stabilization policy. In the limiting case of perfect capital mobility, a fiscal expansion will always generate its full multiplier effect, with no retarding crowding out from higher interest rates, because the interest rate remains at its world level at all times.

On the other hand, when zero capital mobility prevails, fiscal policy cannot do much about the level of GDP, since the specie-flow mechanism forces a return to the vertical BP curve. An expansionary fiscal policy would succeed in raising interest rates by so much that it generates full crowding out, with the level of GDP fixed at Y_{BT}. There is, however, the option of using sterilization operations to neutralize the specie-flow mechanism, in which case the expansionary policy would succeed in raising GDP as long as the sterilization can be sustained.

13.4   Devaluation and revaluation

Under fixed exchange rates, devaluation and revaluation are policy options that do not exist in the closed economy. A devaluation affects both the BP

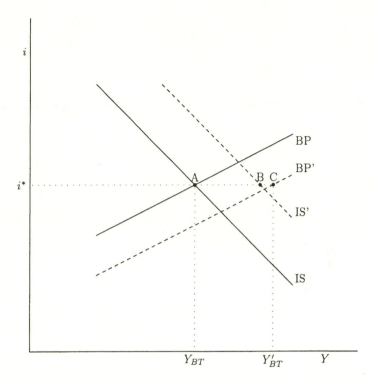

Figure 13.5: A devaluation increases net exports, assuming the Marshall-Lerner condition is satisfied, and shifts both the IS and BP curves to the right. The BP curve shifts ($\overline{AC}$) by more than the IS curve ($\overline{AB}$). (Note for future reference that a depreciation, under flexible exchange rates, would have the same effect.)

and IS curves, shifting them to the right when the Marshall-Lerner condition prevails as we assume. It also increases the level of GDP for which trade is balanced, Y_{BT}. We can visualize these shifts by referring to Figure 13.5, which shows the effects of a devaluation with an intermediate degree of capital mobility. The vertical line marks the position of Y_{BT}. Sighting horizontally along the line $i = i^*$, notice that the vertical line marking Y_{BT} has shifted by more than the IS curve.

For a full analysis of a devaluation we turn to Figure 13.6. Here it is clear that the economy will temporarily find itself in a balance of payments surplus, and this for two reasons. First, a trade surplus has emerged due to the devaluation itself, and this occurs no matter the degree of capital mobility.

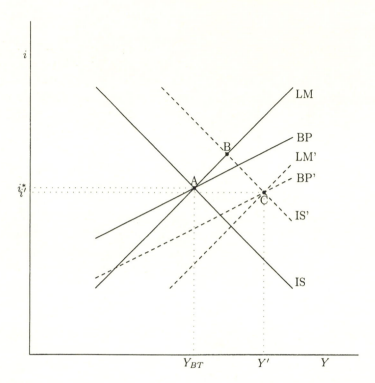

Figure 13.6: A devaluation under fixed rates initially creates a balance of payments surplus driven by the current account (B). This causes the money supply to increase, sending the LM to the right until balance of payments equilibrium is restored (C).

Second, interest rates have risen, attracting an inflow of capital. (With zero mobility, obviously the payments surplus would be entirely attributed to the current account.) Under fixed exchange rates, the specie flow mechanism now takes over and raises the domestic money supply. Ultimately, a complete IS-LM-BP equilibrium is reestablished at a lower rate of interest and higher level of GDP. Since Y_{BT} has increased by more than Y, the economy now enjoys a trade surplus owing to the devaluation, unless capital mobility is zero, in which case it must maintain a trade balance.

This conclusion that a devaluation raises the level of GDP remains valid for any degree of capital mobility. Under zero mobility, a devaluation may be the only way to permanently increase GDP, without resorting to the temporary expedient of sterilization, since the economy is strictly constrained by balance of payments considerations.

In practice, a devaluation is often forced upon a government during a currency crisis and taken to be sign of weakness. We can get some idea of the forces at work by considering perfect capital mobility, under which the uncovered interest parity condition prevails. If the financial markets come to expect a depreciation, they will move their short-term capital out of the country unless the domestic interest rate rises sufficiently. How much must domestic rates rise? The parity condition suggests they must rise by the same amount that the exchange rate is expected to depreciate. But if the interest rate is measured annually, we must annualize the expected depreciation. For example, if the currency is expected to depreciate by 5 per cent in one month, that translates into a 60 per cent increase on an annual basis (12×5). The central bank must therefore be prepared to raise the domestic interest rate to $i^* + 60$ in order to prevent the flight of capital. Clearly, no central bank can withstand such punishment for long before relenting to the pressures of the market.

13.5 The policy mix in an open economy

Just as it does in the closed economy, Tinbergen's Rule requires that a government with multiple policy objectives must have a sufficient number of policy instruments to secure its goals. In an open economy setting, the policy makers want to achieve some appropriate level of domestic output, which is called *internal balance*, together with an acceptable level of net exports, called *external balance*. For example, the government may want to achieve high employment with a balance of trade. To achieve these two goals, two instruments are needed, such as fiscal policy and the exchange rate itself. Rigorous thinking about the appropriate policy mix for a small open economy was pioneered by two Australian economists, W. Salter (1959) and Trevor Swan (1960). We can illustrate the problem by using a version of the key diagram developed by them.

The modified Salter-Swan diagram in Figure 13.7 identifies internal balance with the natural level of GDP. Here the natural level of GDP is assumed, somewhat arbitrarily, to be independent of the real exchange rate[1]. Positions

---

[1]Some theories of the natural rate of unemployment suggest that it would decrease after a real appreciation or revaluation because that would raise the price-determined real wage.

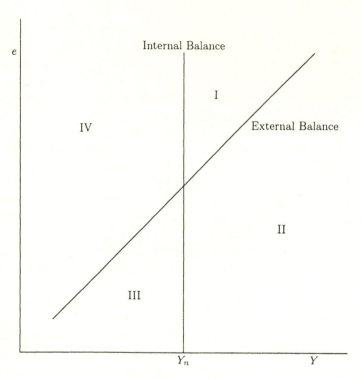

Figure 13.7: This modified Salter-Swan diagram illustrates the problem of achieving both internal and external balance. Points to the left of the internal balance schedule represent recessions, while points to the right are inflationary. External balance means a balance of trade, which can be achieved at a higher level of output as the exchange rate rises (devalues). Points above the external balance curve represent trade surpluses, while points below represent trade deficits.

to the left of Y_n represent recessions while positions to the right are economic booms that threaten to generate inflation. External balance is represented as an upward sloping function such as Equation (12.4) that shows how Y_{BT} changes as the exchange rate varies[2]. The external balance curve slopes upward because as the real exchange rate increases (a devaluation), exports tend to increase, and the country can afford to operate at a higher level of GDP without sucking in excessive imports. Positions below the external balance curve represent trade deficits, while positions above represent trade

---

[2]Technically, Equation (12.4) is a non-linear function. By assuming the Marshall-Lerner condition prevails, we restrict the range to the positively sloped part of this function.

surpluses. The target position for policy makers lies right at the intersection
of the internal and external balance curves.

The Salter-Swan diagram provides a handy analytical framework for in-
terpreting the policy options, which vary depending on which of the four
quadrants formed by the internal and external balance schedules we consider. We need to recall that a devaluation tends to stimulate aggregate
demand; therefore, a devaluation leads to movement in a northeast direction
($\nearrow$). A revaluation reduces aggregate demand; therefore, a revaluation leads
to movement in a southwest direction ($\swarrow$). A fiscal expansion at the existing
exchange rate leads to movement to the east ($\rightarrow$) while a contraction leads
to movement to the west ($\leftarrow$).

Suppose we find ourselves in quadrant III, with a recession and a trade
deficit. Clearly, we need stimulus, but what kind? A fiscal stimulus combats
the recession, but makes the trade deficit worse. A policy instrument in this
position is said to be in a *conflict* or *dilemma* situation. The appropriate
setting for a policy instrument in conflict can be ambiguous. For example,
unless we know the precise structure of the economy, it will be difficult to
tell in advance whether the right fiscal policy in quadrant III is expansionary
or contractionary. A devaluation, on the other hand, is not in a conflict
situation in quadrant III. Raising the exchange rate both improves the trade
balance and generates needed growth. It might be the case that devaluation
provides enough stimulus on its own through its effects on net exports to
bring the economy to internal balance before it wipes out the trade deficit.
If that is the case, then further devaluation will push output into the inflation
zone. The appropriate policy at this point becomes one of fiscal restraint,
combined with continued devaluation. On the other hand, if devaluation
succeeds in achieving external balance before the natural level of output is
reached, then continued devaluation joined by fiscal expansion will be needed
to complete the task.

In quadrant IV, the economy is mired in recession but it enjoys a trade
surplus. Here the exchange rate is in conflict, and the appropriate policy is
ambiguous. A revaluation reduces the trade surplus but worsens the recession. Better to use an expansionary fiscal policy to increase demand and soak
up some of the trade surplus. If the economy achieves internal balance and
still has a trade surplus, that signals the need for a revaluation to complete
the operation. But if it achieves a balance of trade before it has internal
balance, that signals the need for a devaluation to achieve the policy goals.

This reasoning can easily be extended to cover quadrants I and II. In either case, the authorities need to select the policy instrument that is not in a conflict situation to initiate the stabilization program. Then, when internal or external balance is achieved, policy makers can determine what the right setting is for the instrument that was in a conflict situation.

13.6   Pitfalls of devaluation

There are two significant problems with devaluation as a stabilization policy, both of which reach beyond the simplifying assumptions we have made. First, our analysis focuses on a small open economy and understates the effects of devaluation on the rest of the world. This exaggerates the beneficial aspects of devaluation, which seems to be an unquestionably good way to stimulate an underutilized economy. The harmful aspects of devaluations are felt by the trading partners, who experience a revaluation in their bilateral exchange rates with the home country. A revaluation delivers a contractionary demand shock to the recipient country, which is likely to be unwelcome. If so, a retaliation, in the form of a defensive devaluation by the trading partner is likely to follow in short order. Many economists have argued that such *competitive devaluations* contributed to the severity of the Great Depression of the 1930s, and fear of such counterproductive policy games has been cited as one reason for the establishment of the euro among countries of the European Union.

Second, by ignoring the effects on wage and price setting, we may have grossly exaggerated the effectiveness of devaluations to stimulate the home economy itself. A devaluation raises the price of imported goods. This will raise the consumer price level, which is directly inflationary. Moreover, the increase in the consumer price level reduces the price-determined real wage that workers actually receive. We have seen that a reduction in the PRW is indirectly inflationary, because it creates a wage-price spiral according to the conflict theory of inflation. This wage-price spiral can partially or fully undo the stimulative effect of the original devaluation, by causing the *real* exchange rate to return partially or fully to its original level. This effect, called *real wage resistance*, explains why modern governments are often less than enthusiastic about using devaluation as a policy tool, whether they are right or not. (Real wage resistance is a problem when the economy is at its natural level, but not when there is excess unemployment and a devaluation might really make good sense.)

Devaluation and revaluation are a natural bridge to the study of open economy macroeconomic theory under flexible exchange rates, since changes in the exchange rate play the central role there in reestablishing balance of payments equilibrium.

Problems for Chapter 13

1. Draw the IS-LM-BP diagram for a small open economy with relatively mobile capital under fixed exchange rates whose central bank has reduced the domestic money supply (i) without sterilization (ii) with sterilization. Describe the sterilization using the T-account of the central bank.

2. Draw the IS-LM-BP diagram for a small open economy under fixed exchange rates whose government has reduced its spending (i) with zero capital mobility and no sterilization and (ii) with perfect capital mobility. In each case, determine the effect of the policy on each term in the income-expenditure and investment-saving identities, and interpret.

3. Draw the IS-LM-BP diagram for a small open economy with relatively mobile capital that has revalued its currency. Determine the effect on each term in the income-expenditure and investment-saving identities and interpret.

4. Use the Salter-Swan framework to construct a policy program for a small open economy with an inflationary level of GDP and a trade surplus.

Chapter 14

Flexible Exchange Rates

Under flexible exchange rates, the central bank does not administer the price of foreign exchange. This restores control over the money supply to the central bank. The exchange rate is determined in the private market. It will adjust so that in equilibrium there is a balance of payments equilibrium. Thus, while in the fixed exchange rate model the money supply and LM curve do the equilibrating, in the flexible exchange rate this role is taken over by the exchange rate and the IS curve.

14.1   IS-LM-BP with flexible exchange rates

Again, we can gather together the basic results from previous chapters to assemble a formal IS-LM-BP model with flexible rates. As with fixed rates, the LM curve from the closed economy carries over without modifications. The BP curve, too, needs no further elaboration. Since equilibration under flexible rates takes place through changes in the exchange rate, it helps to write out fully the consolidating parameter, a_8, in order to reveal plainly the dependence of the IS curve on the exchange rate. The whole model is:

$$[\text{LM curve}] \quad i = -a_2(M/P) + a_3Y$$

$$[\text{IS curve}] \quad Y = \gamma(c_0 - c_1T + b_0 + G + x_0Y^* + x_1e + q_1e^2) - a_9i$$

$$[\text{BP curve}] \quad i = i^* + \frac{eq_0}{f}(Y - Y_{BT})$$

These three equations uniquely determine the three unknowns in the open economy with flexible exchange rates: Y, i, and e. It is worth reminding ourselves that an increase in the exchange rate (in this context, a depreciation) must shift both the IS curve and the BP curve to the right. A depreciation also increases Y_{BT}; in fact, as we learned in the previous chapter, it does so by more than it shifts the IS curve.

Once again, we will conduct the analysis of this model at an informal level, using the IS-LM-BP diagram to gain insight into the model's features.

14.2   Monetary policy

One of the main arguments in favor of flexible exchange rates has traditionally been that it restores sovereignty to the central bank, giving a country some control over its monetary destiny. There is no better way to see this than to study the two extreme cases in terms of capital mobility.

14.2.1   Zero capital mobility

With no capital mobility, a country cannot borrow or lend to the rest of the world to finance a trade deficit or surplus. It must always operate with a balance of trade, and the exchange rate will adjust in order to enforce this restriction. With zero mobility, the BP curve is the vertical function, $Y = Y_{BT}$, as shown in Figure 14.1. An increase in the money supply shifts the LM curve to the right, as always. In the absence of trade, this would lower the interest rate and bring about an economic expansion. With trade, however, this movement, were it possible at the given exchange rate, would push the economy into a balance of payments deficit. Since we know that a payments surplus or deficit cannot survive because the exchange rate adjusts, we will call this an *incipient* deficit to emphasize that it is a hypothetical position before equilibrium has been achieved. In this case, the incipient deficit arises because of the deficit in the current account.

With an incipient deficit, the exchange rate will depreciate. The increase in the exchange rate shifts the BP and IS curves to the right, as shown in Figure 14.1, until a new IS-LM-BP equilibrium has been established. At the new equilibrium, the interest rate is lower (so investment will increase), the exchange rate is higher (so the country now enjoys higher exports), and the level of GDP has gone up (pulling in more imports). It is not hard to see the

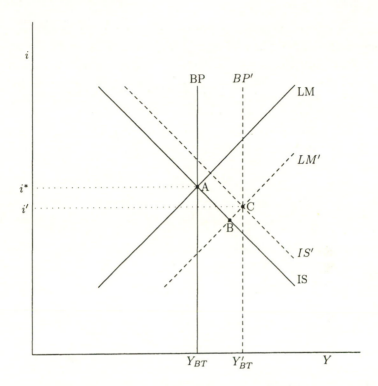

Figure 14.1: Under flexible exchange rates and zero capital mobility, a monetary expansion stimulates an economic boom that generates an incipient balance of payments deficit (B). The currency depreciates, shifting the IS and BP curves to the right until balance of payments equilibrium is achieved (C).

attraction of flexible exchange rates for a small economy having very little ability to borrow or lend in global capital markets.

14.2.2 Perfect capital mobility

At the other extreme, when a country can borrow or lend in unlimited quantities at the world rate of interest, it can finance a trade deficit or surplus of any size. As Figure 14.2 reminds us, the BP curve for such a country is the horizontal line $i = i^*$. A depreciation or appreciation has no effect on the position of the BP curve, which is totally dependent on the capital account.

An increase in the money supply shifts the LM curve to the right, as

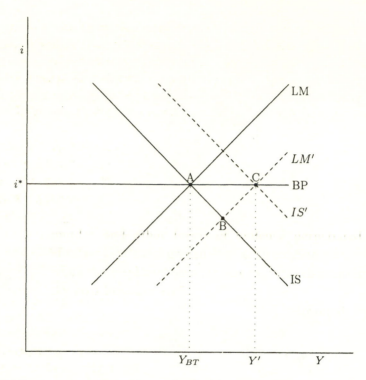

Figure 14.2: A monetary expansion under flexible exchange rates and perfect capital mobility generates an incipient balance of payments deficit (B), both by stimulating economic growth and by lowering interest rates, which would initiate an outflow of capital. Thus, the currency depreciates, sending the IS curve to the right until balance of payments equilibrium is achieved at the world interest rate. Note that Y_{BT} also shifts to the right (not shown), creating a trade surplus in the new equilibrium.

always. The increased money supply creates an incipient deficit. In this case, the incipient deficit arises because of an outflow of capital, driven by low domestic interest rates. This outflow causes a depreciation of the exchange rate, which shifts the IS curve to the right as before. The exchange rate must depreciate sufficiently so that the new IS-LM equilibrium occurs at the world rate of interest, on the (unchanged) BP curve.

Interestingly, at the new equilibrium, a trade surplus must prevail. We know this because we know (from the previous chapter) that a depreciation shifts out Y_{BT} by more than it shifts the IS curve. Another way to demonstrate this fact is to ask why GDP has risen here. Round up the usual suspects by writing out the income-expenditure identity: $Y = C(Y,T) + I(Y,i) + G + \text{NX}(Y,e)$. Consumption has risen, but only as the result of expanded income, not as a prime cause. Investment has risen, but also as the result of expanded income and not as a prime cause, since the interest rate has not changed. Government spending is constant by assumption. By a process of elimination, the expansion must have been fundamentally caused by an increase in net exports.

Once again, we find that flexible exchange rates not only restore sovereignty to the monetary authority, they introduce a new source of leverage over demand in the form of the exchange rate. A monetary expansion tends to depreciate the currency, which stimulates exports. The leverage over aggregate demand prevails under all degrees of capital mobility, but it is more pronounced the greater the degree of capital mobility.

There is an important difference, however, between the economic expansions we have just considered. Under zero mobility, the expansion was balanced in terms of imports and exports, both of which increased by the same amount. This means that the trading partners of the domestic country experience a gentle shock delivered through their current account. Under perfect mobility, on the other hand, the expansion was driven by an increase in exports that exceeded the increase in imports. The trading partners would experience a more violent shock delivered through their capital account by an inflow of capital and subsequent change in exchange rates, and a contractionary shock delivered through their current account in the form of a trade deficit. It is sometimes said that a monetary expansion under flexible exchange rates and high capital mobility amounts to the export of the domestic country's unemployment problems. Joan Robinson (1937) calls this the *beggar thy neighbor* effect, after a British children's game.

Thus, once high degrees of capital mobility prevail, the argument in favor of flexible over fixed exchange rates quickly weakens, because it becomes possible for a large country to destabilize its neighbors in unwelcome ways. This lesson has been brought home repeatedly during the recent historical experience with flexible exchange rates.

14.3   Fiscal policy

A fiscal expansion initially shifts out the IS curve. Whether that creates an incipient balance of payments deficit or surplus depends on the degree of capital mobility.

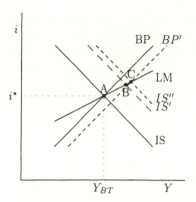

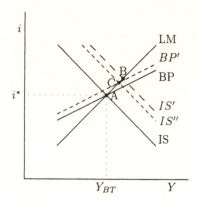

Figure 14.3: Under flexible exchange rates, a fiscal expansion with relatively immobile capital creates an incipient balance of payments deficit (B). Thus, the currency depreciates, shifting the IS curve further until balance of payments equilibrium is achieved (C).

Figure 14.4: A fiscal expansion with relatively mobile capital creates an incipient balance of payments surplus (B). Thus, the currency appreciates, shifting the IS curve back until balance of payments equilibrium is achieved (C).

With relatively immobile capital, shown in Figure 14.3, a fiscal expansion creates an incipient deficit. In this case, the increase in the trade deficit caused by the booming economy cannot be financed from the capital account, because the interest rate has not risen enough to attract sufficient capital inflows. The incipient deficit leads to a depreciation of the currency, which shifts out both the IS and BP curves until a complete IS-LM-BP equilibrium is re-established. Thus, the exchange rate effect actually reinforces the original fiscal stimulus. The fiscal stimulus has increased GDP and interest rates, raising consumption levels but having an ambiguous effect on investment spending. Even though a depreciation has occurred, GDP will have expanded sufficiently that a trade deficit now prevails, with the economy running above its new level of Y_{BT}. This example can help explain why many governments in the world express the fear that a fiscal expansion will create a depreciation of their currency, because their countries do not enjoy unlimited credit on global capital markets.

With relatively mobile capital, shown in Figure 14.4, a fiscal expansion creates an incipient surplus. In this case, the increase in the interest rate has attracted more than enough capital inflow to finance the current account deficit created by the booming economy. The incipient surplus leads to an appreciation of the currency, which shifts both the IS and BP curves to the left until a complete IS-LM-BP equilibrium is re-established. Thus, the exchange rate effect retards the original fiscal stimulus. Again, the economy now runs a trade deficit, both because the booming economy sucks in imports as before and because the appreciation has discouraged net exports. This example can help explain the US economy in the 1980s, when large budget deficits were associated with a sharp appreciation of the dollar and quite massive trade deficits. The US economy experienced an appreciation because its ability to borrow and lend freely permitted an inflow of capital that increased demand for US dollars.

We can see that under flexible exchange rates, higher capital mobility reduces the effectiveness of fiscal policy as a tool for managing aggregate demand. In fact, when capital mobility is perfect, the negative effects of an appreciation resulting from a fiscal expansion will completely offset any positive effects from the fiscal expansion itself. In this case, neither the interest rate nor GDP will change. The increase in government spending has not caused any crowding out or -in of investment spending, but it has led to a decline in net exports. Economists sometimes say that in this circumstance a fiscal expansion crowds-out net exports.

There is some evidence that the fiscal expansions in the US in the 1980s crowded out net exports but not investment, which is consistent with the open economy IS-LM model with a high degree of capital mobility.

It would be wrong to think that a fiscal expansion has no effect on aggregate demand when capital mobility is high. More correctly, a fiscal expansion affects aggregate demand in the wrong place. By triggering a sharp appreciation and collapse of net exports, a fiscal expansion delivers a stimulative shock to other countries, which experience depreciations in their own currencies and trade-led expansions in demand. If they are already operating near full capacity, such shocks may not be welcome.

14.4 Fixed versus flexible regimes

The properties of the IS-LM model under perfect capital mobility were first explored by Robert Mundell (1963) and J. Marcus Fleming (1962) working independently in the 1960s. In their honor, the open economy IS-LM model under perfect mobility is often called the Mundell-Fleming model. The Mundell-Fleming model permits a particularly clear comparison between the effects of monetary and fiscal policy under the two polar extremes, fixed and flexible exchange rate regimes. The following table uses a + to represent policy effectiveness and a 0 to represent policy ineffectiveness in regulating the level of GDP.

	Fixed	Flexible
Fiscal	+	0
Monetary	0	+

The essence of the Mundell-Fleming model, as far as policy effectiveness goes, is that a fiscal expansion works well under fixed exchange rates, in terms of increasing GDP, but not at all under flexible rates. A monetary expansion works well under flexible exchange rates, but not at all under fixed rates.

As always when dealing with open economy issues, it is important not to lose sight of the rest of the world when evaluating policy effectiveness. This is particularly important under flexible exchange rates and a high degree of capital mobility. Because shocks are transmitted so quickly through the markets for capital and foreign exchange, we must be careful about the impact of any policy on our trading partners. One suggestion would be to adjust the policy mix to avoid sharp changes in interest rates, which might initiate unwelcome changes in exchange rates. Thomas Dernburg (1989) has called this "good neighbor" macroeconomics.

14.5   Comments on Mundell-Fleming

There are several well-known problems associated with the Mundell-Fleming model, or indeed, with any of the open economy IS-LM models we have surveyed. Nonetheless, these models continue to serve policy analysts well, because despite their deficiencies they deliver good qualitative predictions about the short-run effects of stabilization policies. One complaint, for example, is that the Mundell-Fleming model treats foreign and domestic asset markets inconsistently. The domestic asset markets, portrayed by the LM curve, are in a stock equilibrium, while the balance of payments condition is a flow equilibrium. A country that runs a trade deficit financed by a capital inflow is accumulating a debt to the rest of the world. Ultimately, the portfolios of foreign investors will become saturated with these debt instruments, and the capital flows will dry up. But more sophisticated models that incorporate these portfolio decisions often wind up delivering similar predictions about the short-run effects of stabilization policy.

A more serious complaint has already been raised in the previous chapter. By maintaining the assumption of constant wages and prices, the Mundell-Fleming model must ignore the effects of inflation in the open economy. Unfortunately, there is no simple, consensus model of inflation in the open economy on a par with the AS-AD model of the closed economy. One problem is that the natural rate of unemployment depends on the price-determined real wage, and the PRW may be determined by the real exchange rate. We have already discussed this in connection with real wage resistance to a devaluation, and that discussion applies with equal force to depreciations under flexible exchange rates. A real apppreciation or revaluation, for instance, raises the PRW and relaxes the inflation constraints on aggregate demand by raising the natural level of GDP. Some models suggest that for this reason, an open economy operates along a horizontal long-run Phillips curve. Yet other models, often published in textbooks, continue to assume that there is one unique natural rate of unemployment, even in an open economy.

There is one generalization about inflation and open economy macroeconomic theory that seems safe. When prices are free to vary, the distinction between the real and the nominal exchange rate blurs considerably. This can cloud up the Mundell-Fleming typology of policy effectiveness described above, because when prices are flexible, the real exchange rate can never be fixed even when the nominal rate is administered effectively. Pursuing this point, however, would take us into more advanced topics and defeat one of the purposes of this book, which has been to survey modern macroeconomic theory at its most basic and most practical level.

Problems for Chapter 14

1. Draw the IS-LM-BP diagram for a small open economy under flexible exchange rates whose government has reduced spending under (i) relatively immobile capital (ii) perfect capital mobility. In each case, determine the effect on the exchange rate.

2. In the previous question, for each case analyze the effects of this policy on each term in the income-expenditure and investment-saving identities for an open economy. Explain and interpret your findings.

3. Draw the IS-LM-BP diagram for a small open economy under flexible exchange rates whose central bank has reduced the money supply (i)

with zero capital mobility (ii) with perfect capital mobility. Describe
the effects on the country's trading partners.

4. Use the statistical appendix of the *Economic Report of the President*
   to gather data on the percentage composition of GDP, including net
   exports and the fiscal surplus of the government sector. Evaluate the
   effects of fiscal policy on net exports in the 1980s. Did the large U.S.
   budget deficits of the 1980s crowd out net exports? Did they crowd-out
   or crowd-in investment?

Chapter 15

The Classical Growth Model

In all the previous models we have surveyed, the economy achieves a stable equilibrium *level* of output. But real economies frequently enjoy steady growth interrupted by relatively brief recessions. To develop the tools to understand and interpret economic growth requires that we focus on the accumulation of capital and the increase of the labor force, which are (along with technological change) the mainsprings of growth. Like people who wear bifocals, viewing distant objects through a different lens than they use for reading, economists switch from the static models we have studied in previous chapters to growth models with quite a distinctive character to address these issues.

Growth theory has returned to macroeconomics, after a brief disappearance in the 1970s and 1980s, because of new developments in the theory and because the fiscal policy debates of the last two decades have raised practical issues. In particular, as we have seen in previous chapters, under some circumstances large fiscal deficits can crowd-out private investment spending. But in the standard AS-AD framework, crowding out does not affect the level of output—it merely changes its composition. To understand the consequences of reducing the resources a nation devotes to investment requires that we slip the bonds of the static macroeconomic model, since it explicitly abstracts from growth of the capital stock.

This chapter presents a simplified model of growth in the Classical tradition of Adam Smith, David Ricardo, and Karl Marx[1]. Two features that distinguish this model from similar efforts in the neoclassical tradition (pre-

---

[1]See Foley and Michl (1999) or Marglin (1984) for a more detailed introduction to Classical and neoclassical growth theory.

sented in the next chapter) are its attention to the class structure of saving, and its recognition that capital, not labor, may be the chief constraint on long-run growth. Partly because of its austere character, growth theory provides us an excellent opportunity to understand the underlying differences between two important schools of thought or paradigms in economic theory, the Classical and neoclassical traditions.

15.1   The production function

Previously, we assumed a very simple production function, of the form $Y = N$. Implicitly, we were assuming the existence of plenty of excess capacity so that the capital stock, K, would not constrain the firms' ability to produce output. When we switch to the growth lens, it would seem more appropriate to assume that the economy is operating at full capacity. We can formalize this using the *Leontief production function*, named after Wassily Leontief:

$$Y = \min[\rho K, yN]$$

where $\rho = Y/K$ is the output-capital ratio at full capacity, and $y = Y/N$ is the output-labor ratio or the productivity of labor at full capacity. We will also make extensive use of the capital-labor ratio, $k = K/N$.

The $\min[.,.]$ function always takes the value of the smaller of the two numbers. Thus, when we are operating below the capacity, ρK, defined by a given capital stock, $\bar{K}$, output will always be yN. (This was what we have been assuming to this point, with $y = 1$.)

The Leontief production function models a technology that combines capital goods and labor in a fixed ratio. A familiar example might be a lawnmower that is operated by one worker. Capital goods and labor are pure complements in production under this kind of technology. This has an important implication, for as long as there are no technical changes that affect the productivity of capital or labor, the growth rate of employment will be equal to the growth rate of the capital stock. Using the definition[2] $g_x = (x_{+1} - x)/x$ for the growth rate of any variable, x, we write:

$$g_N = g_K \tag{15.1}$$

---

[2]Note that this definition represents a slight change from how we previously defined the inflation rate and growth rate of output.

As the capital stock grows, it generates demand for additional workers in order to keep production at full capacity levels. The economic interpretation is that the growth rate of labor demand, g_N, is determined by the rate of capital accumulation, g_K.

Most growth models recognize that the capital stock depreciates through physical deterioration or obsolescence, and indeed, depreciation or capital consumption constitutes a substantial part of the gross product of modern economies. However, since it plays a passive role in growth theory we will ignore depreciation and assume somewhat fancifully that capital goods last forever.

15.2 Wages and profits

We have already seen that the GDP can be divided between wages and profits, the constituents of value-added. We will use the lower-case w to represent the real wage, W/P, and Π to represent total profits. We will be particularly interested in the *rate of profit*, or $v = \Pi/K$, because this measures the rate of return on invested capital. With these definitions, the national income identity between output and income is written

$$Y = wN + vK$$

Dividing the national income identity by N and rearranging produces a handy version of the national income identity, the *wage-profit curve*:

$$w = y - vk \qquad (15.2)$$

The wage-profit curve shows the fundamental trade-off in a capitalist economy between labor and capital income when the economy operates at full capacity, as defined by its available capital stock.

15.3 Saving and investment

While we have hitherto been content to disregard differences in saving out of wages and profits, the Classical economists typically regarded the profits of capitalists as the chief source of saving, investment, and capital accumulation. We will assume that workers do no saving at all, so that all saving originates in profit incomes. We further assume that capitalists save a constant fraction, s_c, of their income, making overall saving

$$S = s_c \Pi$$

This is the Classical theory of consumption. Obviously, the capitalist propensity to consume is $(1 - s_c)$ and the worker propensity to consume is unity.

As the paradox of thrift illustrated in earlier chapters, there is no guarantee that saving will be translated into investment in new capital goods. We also learned that under some conditions, the paradox of thrift resolves itself in the long run. It is a standard feature of both the Classical and the neoclassical growth models that they assume Say's Law, which is an automatic identification of saving with planned investment:

$$I^p = S$$

Since there can be no difference between planned and actual investment, we will drop the superscript. Investment represents new additions to the nation's capital stock, which we can express through the stock-flow identity that $K_{+1} = K + I$ or $I = K_{+1} - K$. Thus, the growth rate of capital or the *rate of accumulation* is simply the ratio of investment to capital, or $g_K = I/K$. Using Say's Law, the rate of accumulation can be written in terms of the capitalist saving rate and the profit rate:

$$g_K = s_c v \tag{15.3}$$

We call this the *Cambridge saving equation* in honor of the Cantabrigian economists such as Nicholas Kaldor and Joan Robinson who have kept the Classical tradition alive in macroeconomics. Pasinetti (1974) provides a good introduction to this tradition.

15.4   Labor market

With Equations (15.1)–(15.3), we are well on our way to completing the Classical growth model. In order to close the model, we must specify two more determining equations. The Classical tradition suggests two quite different possibilities. The first option takes the real wage to be determined exogenously, and regards the supply of labor as endogenous. The second option takes the supply of labor as exogenous, and regards the real wage as endogenously determined.

15.4.1 Endogenous labor supply

We have already seen that in a model with imperfectly competitive product markets, the mark-up pricing equation determines the real wage, which we called the price-determined real wage. The Classical economists did not adopt this explanation, however. Instead, they proposed a subsistence wage theory. Because this theory defined subsistence to include a cultural and moral element, we will call it the conventional wage theory. In this approach, social, political, and institutional factors determine the conventional real wage, $\bar{w}$. We can formalize the conventional wage theory thus:

$$w = \bar{w} \tag{15.4}$$

The supply of labor in the Classical model responds in the long run to the demand for labor. The earliest Classical economists thought that demographic forces would generate such a response. For example, an increase in the demand for labor might cause a temporarily high wage, which would reduce premature deaths and encourage child-bearing, causing the wage to return to its conventional level as the labor force grew to accommodate the increased demand for labor. Later Marx argued that capitalist economies operate in a larger historical and social context that gives them access to a latent reserve army of labor, such as agricultural communities largely outside the market economy. In a global context, the rich countries today do seem to have access to the world's labor surpluses through immigration.

We can visualize the Classical theory with an endogenous supply of labor in Figure 15.1, which shows that the economy can attract an unlimited number of workers at the prevailing real wage. In other words, the labor force, which previously was taken to be fixed, will respond in the long run to the demands of the economy. We will simply abstract from any long-run unemployment[3], setting $L = N$ in order to express the idea that the labor

---

[3]Alternatively, assume the economy operates at the natural rate of unemployment, so that $N = (1 - u_n)L$ and $L = N/(1 - u_n)$. In this case, any given demand for labor induces a surplus of workers to appear, for example, because workers recognize they will have to wait until a job opening appears.

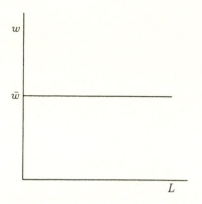

Figure 15.1: In the Classical economy with an endogenous labor supply, the supply curve for labor is perfectly elastic (horizontal) at the conventional real wage, $\bar{w}$. The number of workers in any period is determined by the number of jobs.

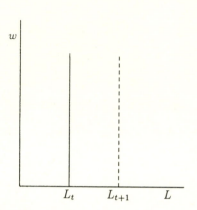

Figure 15.2: In the Classical economy with an exogenous labor supply, the supply curve for labor is perfectly inelastic (vertical) in each period. The number of workers grows at the natural rate, n, so that $L_{t+1} = (1+n)L_t$.

force is endogenously determined. Since we are working with growth rates, it is more helpful to express this idea thus:

$$g_L = g_N \tag{15.5}$$

The economic interpretation is that the growth of labor demanded determines the growth of labor supply. The assumption of endogenous labor supply implies that the economy is not constrained by the availability of labor. In this case, the main constraint on economic growth becomes the accumulation of capital.

15.4.2   Exogenous labor supply

At the other extreme, we consider an economy that has come up against the constraint of labor supply. The simplest assumption about labor supply is that it is growing at a constant rate, which is often called the *natural rate of growth*, n. We write

$$g_L = n \tag{15.6}$$

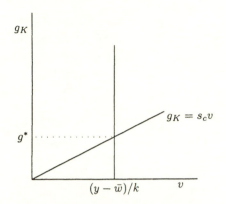

Figure 15.3: In the Classical economy with an endogenous labor supply, the steady state growth rate, g^*, is determined by the Cambridge equation and the profit rate associated with the conventional real wage.

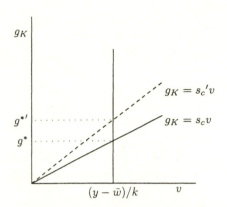

Figure 15.4: In the Classical economy with an endogenous labor supply, an increase in the capitalist saving propensity will raise the steady state growth rate without changing the rate of profit.

to formalize the assumption of exogenous labor supply. This assumption is illustrated in Figure 15.2.

We will have to drop the assumption that the wage is determined exogenously, replacing it with the full employment assumption that the wage adjusts to maintain continuous equality between the supply of labor, L, and the demand for labor, N. Formally,

$$g_N = g_L \tag{15.7}$$

captures the idea of continuous full employment succinctly. The economic interpretation is that the growth of labor supply determines the growth of labor demanded.

15.5 Classical endogenous growth

We can close the Classical model by incorporating the assumption of endogenous labor supply. Equations (15.1), (15.2), (15.3), (15.4) and (15.5) constitute a fully determined growth model. There are five endogenous variables: g_N, g_K, g_L, w, and v. The exogenous variables are y, k, s_c, and $\bar{w}$. Models in which the rate of growth is an endogenous variable that can change permanently in response to changes in exogenous parameters such as the saving rate are called *endogenous growth models*. The Classical model with endogenous labor supply is an example of an endogenous growth model.

It is immediately obvious that since the wage is determined by the conventional real wage, $\bar{w}$, the rate of profit is readily determined through (15.2), the wage-profit equation. The rate of profit will be $v = (y - \bar{w})/k$. Then the rate of accumulation can be determined through (15.3), the Cambridge equation. We can visualize the Classical model with an endogenous supply of labor in Figure 15.3, which shows how these two equations determine the equilibrium profit and growth rates. Once the rate of capital accumulation has been determined, the rate of growth of employment, g_N, and of the labor force, g_L, follow, since they must all be equal. When all the relevant variables are growing at the same rate, a growth model has achieved its *steady state*. We denote the steady state growth rate g^*.

The Classical model of endogenous growth takes the distribution of income between wages and profits to be determined exogenously, while the growth of capital and labor are determined endogenously. The Cambridge equation is a key relationship because it shows how the rate of profit determines the rate of growth.

Modern policy makers are interested in the growth effects of variations in their national saving rates. The best way to satisfy their curiosity is through a comparative equilibrium analysis. Figure 15.4 illustrates the effect of an increase in the capitalist saving propensity, s_c. Since the wage is determined exogenously and the technology has not changed, the rate of profit remains constant. Increased saving in this model raises the rate of capital accumulation, the growth rate of employment and the growth rate of the labor force.

15.6   Classical exogenous growth

We can also close the Classical model by incorporating the assumptions of exogenous labor supply. Equations (15.1), (15.2), (15.3), (15.6), and (15.7) constitute a fully determined growth model. There are five endogenous variables, as before: g_N, g_K, g_L, w, and v. The exogenous variables are y, k, s_c, and n.

It is immediately obvious that since the supply of labor grows at a constant rate and since full employment is maintained continuously, the rate of capital accumulation must also match the exogenous growth of the labor

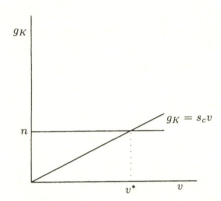

Figure 15.5: In the Classical economy with an exogenous labor supply, the steady state profit rate, v^*, is determined by the Cambridge equation and the natural rate of growth.

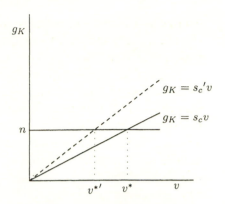

Figure 15.6: In the Classical economy with an exogenous labor supply, an increase in the capitalist saving propensity will lower the steady state profit rate without changing the rate of growth.

force through Equation (15.1). This is an example of an *exogenous growth model*. With the rate of accumulation determined in this way, the Cambridge equation specifies what steady state rate of profit is needed to generate the appropriate amount of saving, which is clearly $v^* = n/s_c$. We can visualize the Classical model of exogenous growth in Figure 15.5, which shows how these two equations determine the equilibrium profit and growth rates. Finally, the wage-profit curve tells us what wage will be associated with this rate of profit, or $w^* = y - (n/s_c)k$.

The Classical model of exogenous growth takes the growth of the labor supply and capital to be determined exogenously, while the distribution of income between wages and profits is determined endogenously. One way to understand this model is to temporarily suspend the full employment assumption. If the wage happened to be too low, the rate of profit would be so high that capital accumulation would exceed the growth rate of labor supply, implying an excess demand for labor. This excess demand should create market forces to increase the wage until the labor market clears (supply and demand are equal). Similarly, if the wage happened to be too high, the opposite chain of events would tend to bring it down. By assuming continuous full employment, we are taking a short-cut directly to the steady state equilibrium that is implied by these self-correcting tendencies. The implicit assumption is that the distribution of income between wages and profits adjusts in order to maintain just the right amount of capital accumulation to ensure full employment.

The comparative equilibrium analysis of an increase in the capitalist saving propensity in the exogenous growth model, illustrated in Figure 15.6, reaches quite a different conclusion compared to the endogenous growth model. An increase in the saving propensity cannot have any effect at all on growth. Instead, it affects the distribution of income. A higher saving rate allows the exogenous rate of accumulation to be achieved at a lower profit rate. By turning to the wage-profit equation, we can see immediately that this implies a higher wage rate.

15.7   Fiscal policy in the endogenous growth model

It is possible to incorporate the government sector in the Classical model, in order to examine the effects of a fiscal surplus, but at the cost of some complexity. We will assume that the labor supply is endogenous, in order to leave open the possibility that fiscal policy affects growth.

Let us consider a highly stylized fiscal program that has two phases. In phase one, the government collects a tax and invests the proceeds in the equity market. In real economies, governments operate funds, such as government employee pension funds, that do indeed hold the stocks and bonds of private corporations. In phase two, the government uses its wealth to fund a constant amount of government consumption spending per worker for all subsequent periods. Since the economy is growing, the government has to save some of the returns on its equity fund. This plan will illustrate how a fiscal surplus can contribute to growth. For simplicity, we will assume that phase one lasts for only one period.

We must be careful about what kind of tax we choose. For our purposes, a good choice is a *consumption tax* because this kind of tax can leave the amount of saving intact, resulting in a lower level of consumption. Since capitalist saving is not affected, the path over time of capitalist wealth will not be changed by the fiscal program. We will assume a progressive tax that falls only on capitalist income. This is not essential to the main results and it simplifies the analysis.

In the first period of this plan (call it period 0), the government collects a consumption tax, T, and saves the entire amount. Note that T represents the fiscal surplus. The capital stock in the next period is thus

$$K_1 = (1 + s_c v)K_0 + T$$

The term $(1+s_c v)K_0$ represents capitalist wealth in period 1, which continues to follow the Cambridge equation. The government's wealth in period 1 is just T since the government starts with no wealth. Clearly, the growth rate in the first period exceeds the growth rate given by the Cambridge equation, because the government is contributing to national saving[4].

In period 1, the government holds wealth equal to its fiscal surplus in period 0, or $K_1^G = T$, and (using $N_1 = K_1/k$) government wealth per worker is described by

$$\frac{K_1^G}{N_1} = k\frac{K_1^G}{K_1}$$

What fiscal policy will preserve the government's wealth on a per worker basis? Clearly, the government's wealth needs to grow at the same rate as the capitalists' wealth in order to keep the ratio on the right hand side constant. This requires that the government saves the same fraction of government profits as the capitalists save out of their profits. The government is then free to spend the rest. With this dynamic fiscal policy, the level of government spending will always be

$$G = (1 - s_c)v K^G$$

Because the government's wealth is growing at the same rate as the capitalist's wealth, the ratio of the two remains constant. This model achieves a steady state by virtue of its dynamic fiscal policy. In phase two, the growth rate returns to its original value, given by the Cambridge equation.

Thus, we can see how a fiscal surplus contributes to economic growth. Even though the fiscal surplus does not affect the steady state growth rate, the capital stock and level of employment have been permanently raised above the level that would have prevailed in the absence of the fiscal policy. Economists describe this as a *level effect* because it increases the level of activity without affecting its long-run rate of growth.

---

[4]By dividing both sides by K_0, we get $1 + g_K = 1 + s_c v + T/K_0$. Thus, the growth rate increases by the tax, expressed as a percentage of the capital stock, or T/K_0.

15.8   Fiscal policy in the exogenous growth model

If we try this plan in the model with exogenous labor supply, it will not succeed in raising the level of the capital stock because there are not enough workers to accommodate more capital. During the first period, the increased demand for workers caused by the government's saving requires that the wage rise and profit rate fall. During the subsequent periods, the government now owns some wealth, which permits it to finance some spending. Thus, the fiscal policy has distributive effects. In the first period, it affects the wage and profit rates. In subsequent periods, these rates return to their normal values, but capitalists own less wealth than they would have in the absence of the fiscal policy while the government now owns enough wealth to finance some consumption spending, which presumably benefits workers. Thus, the distribution of consumption has been permanently changed through this fiscal program.

From the point of view of economic policy making, the key issue is clearly whether the real economy is better described by the endogenous or the exogenous growth model. The Classical theory cannot decide a priori, but it does suggest that the answer might be found in close study of the underlying labor constraints on growth. It may be that the real economies lie somewhere between these two extremes. Most economists have been trained in the neoclassical tradition, which typically assumes that in the long run, full employment of an exogenously given labor force prevails. The next chapter elucidates the standard neoclassical growth model.

Problems for Chapter 15

Problems 2, 4, and 5 make use of the following parameter values: labor productivity is 100, capital per labor unit is 200, and the capitalist saving propensity is .8. (Units are constant dollars per year.)

1. In the Classical model of endogenous growth, describe the effects on all the endogenous variables of each of the following parameter changes: (a) an increase in labor productivity, holding the output-capital ratio constant (b) an increase in the capital-labor ratio, holding labor productivity constant (c) an increase in the capitalist propensity to save (d) an increase in the conventional wage.

2. Use the Classical model of endogenous growth to find the endogenous variables in an economy in which the conventional wage is 80 per labor unit.

3. In the Classical model of exogenous growth, describe the effects on all the endogenous variables of each of the following parameter changes: (a) an increase in labor productivity, holding the output-capital ratio constant (b) an increase in the capital-labor ratio, holding labor productivity constant (c) an increase in the capitalist propensity to save (d) an increase in the natural rate of growth.

4. Use the Classical model of exogenous growth to find the endogenous variables in an economy in which the natural rate of growth is 5 percent per year.

5. In the Classical model of endogenous growth, the government collects a one-period consumption tax of 15 from the capitalists in period 0, investing its fiscal surplus in capital. (Units are constant dollars.) For all subsequent periods, the government keeps constant the ratio of government-owned capital to the labor force. The conventional wage is 80 per labor unit, the amount of capitalist wealth in period 0 is 1000 and the government owns no wealth in period 0. (a) Calculate the amount of capital and level of employment in periods 1 and 2. (b) Calculate the amount of capital and level of employment that would have prevailed in periods 1 and 2 in the absence of this fiscal policy. (c) Calculate the rate of growth of capital in periods 0, 1, and 2. (d) Explain these results, using the concept of level effects.

Chapter 16

The Neoclassical Growth Model

The most influential neoclassical growth model was developed in the 1950s by Robert M. Solow and T.W. Swan and is known as the Solow-Swan growth model[1]. Like the Classical model with exogenous labor supply, this model takes the growth of the labor supply to be the main constraint on capital accumulation. But unlike the Classical model, the Solow-Swan model assumes that the saving rates out of wages and profits are equal (and in fact, it suppresses all differences between capitalists and workers). In order to ensure that the Solow-Swan model achieves a stable equilibrium, it is necessary to assume the existence of a neoclassical aggregate production function.

16.1 The neoclassical production function

The Leontief production function treats capital and labor as complements for one another. The justification is that capital equipment is engineered to be used by a fixed number of workers. The neoclassical aggregate production function treats capital and labor as continuous substitutes for one another. It assumes that it is always possible to make the technique of production a little more capital-intensive and a little more productive. The existence of a neoclassical aggregate production function has been the subject of intense debate for almost half a century. Classical economists, starting with Joan

---

[1]For elaboration of the Solow-Swan model, consult Foley and Michl (1999) or Jones (2001).

Robinson (1953), have vigorously criticized this assumption[2].

The most commonly used type of neoclassical production function is the Cobb-Douglas production function, which has the form

$$Y = AK^{\phi}N^{1-\phi}$$

where $0 < \phi < 1$ and A is a constant scale factor. This production function displays constant returns to scale, meaning that doubling all the inputs exactly doubles output. When a production function displays constant returns to scale, we can always factor out the term $1/N$ in order to express the function in per-worker terms. Thus, the Cobb-Douglas function becomes

$$y = Ak^{\phi}$$

recalling that y represents output per worker and k capital per worker.

The great advantage of the production function in per-worker form is that it permits us to represent a three-dimensional mathematical object (the production function itself) in two dimensions. Figure 16.1 illustrates the main properties of the Cobb-Douglas production function in per-worker form. As we increase the amount of capital per worker (called "substituting capital for labor"), the productivity of labor increases.

If you draw a ray through the origin to a point on the production function, as is done in Figure 16.1, its slope will be equal to the output-capital ratio for that capital-labor ratio, since $\rho = y/k$. If you pick a point farther out on the production function, with a higher capital-labor ratio, it is clear that the ray you draw will have a smaller slope. This tendency for the output-capital ratio to decline as you increase the amount of capital per worker is a manifestation of diminishing returns. Adding more and more capital, holding labor constant, results in smaller and smaller increments to output. We will see how this property leads to a steady state equilibrium in the Solow-Swan model.

Both the Leontief and the Cobb-Douglas production functions exhibit diminishing returns. In the Leontief function, the drop in returns is abrupt and discrete; when capital and labor are complements you cannot exceed the maximum feasible output per worker. In the Cobb-Douglas function, the returns diminish continuously since capital and labor are always substitutes.

---

[2]This debate was known as the "Cambridge capital controversy" because it enlisted economists from MIT in the U.S. and Cambridge University in the U.K. For more details, consult Kurz and Salvadori (1995).

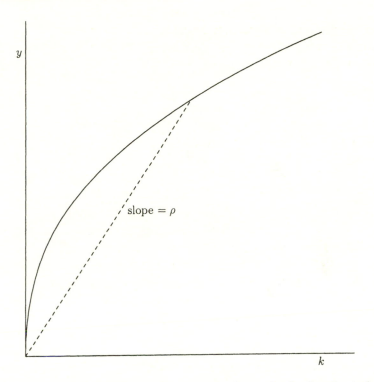

Figure 16.1: The distinctive shape of the Cobb-Douglas production function is the result of continuously diminishing returns. As the capital-labor ratio increases, the output-labor ratio increases by smaller and smaller increments. But it is always possible to increase output per worker by switching to a more capital intensive technique (i.e., with a higher capital-labor ratio). The ray through the origin has a slope equal to the output-capital ratio; as the result of diminishing returns, it decreases as the capital-labor ratio rises.

16.2 Saving and investment

The Solow-Swan model does not distinguish between the saving behavior of workers and capitalists, or between private and public consumption spending. It implicitly treats the government as an extension of the household sector, and the typical household as a combination of capital-owner and worker. The model simply assumes that a constant fraction, s, of all income is saved; we will call s the national saving propensity[3]. Thus, we have

---

[3]This is just a specialized version of the consumption and saving theory we used in the IS-LM model. We are setting $s = (1 - c_1)$ and $c_0 = 0$.

$$S = sY$$

As in the Classical model, the Solow-Swan model assumes that in the long run, all saving is invested in real capital so that Say's Law prevails, and $I^p = I = S$. We continue to define the growth rate of capital by $g_K = I/K$. Therefore, we can write the rate of capital accumulation as a function of the output-capital ratio, dividing the saving function by K to obtain

$$g_K = s\rho$$

In the Solow-Swan model, the rate of capital accumulation will be very high if the economy starts off with little capital per worker, because the output-capital ratio will be high under these circumstances, as we showed above. But as capital accumulates and the capital-labor ratio rises, that will slow growth down by reducing the output-capital ratio, again as we showed above, until it achieves its long-run equilibrium or steady state value.

16.3   The steady state equilibrium

The Solow-Swan model achieves its steady state equilibrium when the capital-labor ratio remains constant over time. We can use the math fact[4] that the growth rate of any ratio, $a = b/c$, is the growth rate of b minus the growth rate of c, or $g_a = g_b - g_c$. The growth rate of the capital-labor ratio, k, is $g_k = g_K - g_N$.

As in the Classical model with exogenous labor supply, the Solow-Swan model assumes that the labor force grows at a constant rate, n, and that full employment is maintained continuously. Substituting $g_K = s\rho$ lets us write the growth rate of the capital-labor ratio as

$$g_k = s\rho - n$$

What would it take for the capital-labor ratio to achieve a constant, steady state value (i.e., zero growth)? Clearly, we must find a position where

---

[4]This math fact applies to the exponential growth rate. For the discrete-form growth rates used in this book, it is a close approximation as long as they are small in magnitude.

$s\rho = n$. If we multiply both sides by k, (and recall that $\rho k = y$), we can see that this position implies

$$sy = nk$$

The left-hand side of this equation describes saving per worker. The right-hand side of this equation describes the amount of saving per worker that is required to equip the new workers that enter the labor force with exactly the same amount of capital as the existing workers; this is called required saving[5]. The steady state equilibrium occurs where saving per worker equals required saving per worker.

We can visualize the steady state equilibrium in Figure 16.2, which shows the production function, the required saving function, and actual saving (all in per-worker form). The steady state capital-labor ratio, k^*, occurs where the required saving function intersects the saving function. Steady state labor productivity, y^*, is the amount of output per worker associated with the steady state capital-labor ratio.

The steady state shown in Figure 16.2 is an equilibrium because if we arbitrarily start at a lower (or higher) capital-labor ratio, it is easy to see that the capital-labor ratio would increase (or decrease) over time. When $k < k^*$, for example, actual saving lies above required saving. Looking back at the equations, it is clear that in this circumstance, $g_K > n$ and $g_k > 0$. Thus, a capital-labor ratio below k^* cannot be an equilibrium, because it will be increasing over time. Similar reasoning should convince us that a capital-labor ratio above k^* cannot be an equilibrium, because it will be decreasing over time. These dynamics push the economy toward its steady state. Since they involve the transition to the steady state, they are called the *transitional dynamics* of the Solow-Swan model.

16.4   Solving for the steady state

We can derive an explicit equation for the steady state values of labor productivity and the capital-labor ratio, assuming the Cobb-Douglas production

---

[5]For example, if K=\$10,000, N=100 workers, k=\$100 per worker, and n=.05 per year, then there will be 5 new workers (.05 × 100 workers) next year. Giving them as much capital as the existing workers requires \$500 per year in total saving, or \$5 per (existing) worker per year, which is nk or (.05 per year × \$100 per worker).

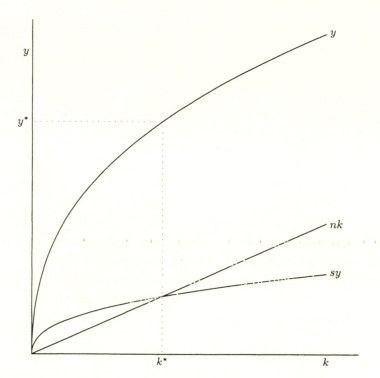

Figure 16.2: The steady state equilibrium in the Solow-Swan model occurs where saving per worker (sy) equals required saving per worker (nk). As the labor force grows at the rate n, each new worker is equipped with the same amount of capital (k^*) as all the existing workers, so the capital-labor ratio remains steady over time.

function. By substituting the production function into the steady state condition, $sy = nk$, we get $sAk^\phi = nk$, which simplifies to

$$k^* = (\frac{sA}{n})^{\frac{1}{1-\phi}}$$

Having found the steady state capital-labor ratio, it is a simple matter to substitute it into the production function to obtain

$$y^* = A^{\frac{1}{1-\phi}}(\frac{s}{n})^{\frac{\phi}{1-\phi}}$$

These explicit solutions make it easy to study the effects of parameter changes on the steady state values of the key endogenous variables of the

Solow-Swan model. But it is also possible to determine these effects by using the diagrams.

We are also interested in the growth rates of key variables. As we have already seen, in the steady state the growth rate of the capital-labor ratio goes to zero. The growth rate of labor productivity will also be equal to zero there. It follows from the mathematics of the growth rate of a ratio that the growth rate of capital and the growth rate of output must be equal to the natural rate of growth in the steady state, or

$$g_K = g_Y = n$$

This reflects the fact that the Solow-Swan model is an exogenous growth model, in which the growth of the labor supply is the ultimate constraint on capital accumulation and output growth. It is possible for capital and output growth to exceed the natural rate during the transitional dynamics, if the economy starts out with little capital per worker, but eventually these growth rates must slow down owing to the operation of diminishing returns until they achieve the natural rate of growth.

16.5 Comparative dynamics of saving

One of the most important applications of the Solow-Swan model is to the issue of how an increase in the national saving rate affects the long-run equilibrium of the economy. We have already studied this question in the previous chapter. A crucial difference here is that under the neoclassical production function, capital and labor are substitutes. An increase in the national saving rate will increase the steady state capital-labor ratio and steady state labor productivity, as can easily be seen by examining the equations in the previous section.

We can also see this by using the diagram for the Solow-Swan model, as in Figure 16.3. An increase in the saving rate shifts up the actual saving function, but it does not affect the required saving function or the production function itself. Thus, the new steady state occurs at a higher capital-labor ratio. Since each worker has more capital to work with, output per worker will also increase in the long run as the result of a higher national saving rate.

In the long run, an increased saving rate has no effect on the rate of growth of output or capital, since, as we have seen, these are determined by

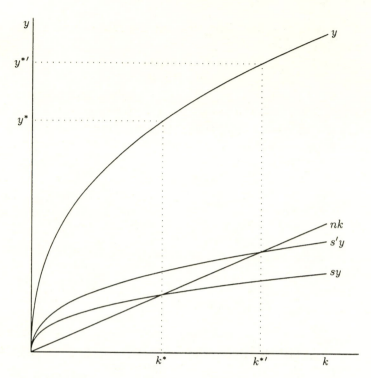

Figure 16.3: An increase in the saving rate in the Solow-Swan model results in a higher steady state capital-labor ratio and therefore a higher steady state level of labor productivity. Greater thriftiness results in higher levels of output and capital per worker in the long run, but no change in the growth rates of output and capital since these must ultimately return to the natural rate of growth.

the natural rate of growth. This conclusion, which many find to be counter-intuitive, is common to any exogenous growth model. But in the Solow-Swan model, it should be clear that the increased saving rate has a level effect on output and capital; these will achieve higher values for all subsequent periods after the increase in saving. Put another way, the growth rates of capital and output will increase, but only temporarily. When the economy reaches its new steady state, they revert to the natural rate of growth.

What effect will an increased saving rate have on the nation's standard of living, as measured by consumption per worker? We have seen that increased saving raises labor productivity, so there is more income available. But an increased saving rate by definition implies that a lower fraction of income is consumed. We can see this by writing out the expression for steady state consumption per worker:

$$c^* = (1 - s)y^*$$

Obviously, at some point a high value of s leaves little or nothing for consumption. It can be shown that there is one saving rate that maximizes the amount of consumption per worker, which is called the *golden rule* saving rate. When the saving rate is below its golden rule value, any increase in the saving rate will raise the steady state consumption per worker. There is widespread agreement that modern nations operate in just such a position[6]. That is important because it means that increases in the national saving rate lead to higher living standards, according to the Solow-Swan model.

This conclusion has been at the center of the debates about fiscal policy in the U.S. and other countries in recent decades. When opponents of fiscal deficits complain that they reduce the national saving rate, diminish the amount of capital each worker has at her disposal, and cut into the nation's living standard, they are applying the Solow-Swan growth model. From this perspective, a fiscal surplus can be welcome because it increases the national saving rate and contributes to a higher level (but not long-run growth rate) of labor productivity, consumption, capital, and output.

16.6 Visions and divisions in macroeconomic theory

The Classical and neoclassical growth models provide students with an excellent opportunity to gain insight into differences of opinion among economists. This is certainly not the only debate in the economics profession, nor perhaps the major debate, but it is one with particularly clear lines of demarcation.

Divisions among economists almost always start with a different vision of the nature of a relevant economic problem. In this case, neoclassical economic theory at a very fundamental level regards the allocation of scarce resources as the central economic problem. The neoclassical growth model

---

[6]As demonstrated in the mathematical appendix, with a Cobb-Douglas production function, the golden rule saving rate is equal to the power term ϕ. The saving rate in the U.S. is around .15 while the value of ϕ is typically estimated to lie between .25 and .6, well above the observed saving rate.

reflects that vision in its choice of an exogenous labor supply (the resource constraint) that is fully employed (scarce) at all times. The Classical vision regards the distribution of income between wages, which are mainly consumed, and profits, which are largely re-invested, as the central drama in a capitalist economy. The Classical model reflects that vision by its decision to model the class structure of saving, and by giving serious consideration to the possibility that capital, rather than labor, represents the main constraint on long-run economic growth. Thus, the Classical model includes a sub-case, with endogenous labor supply, that does not make much sense in a neoclassical approach because it does not rest on the fundamental scarcity of resources, and the neoclassical model assumes that all households are both capitalist and worker, which does not make much sense in a Classical approach because it denies the significance of the class structure of saving.

One of the great challenges to students of economic theory is to identify the underlying differences in vision among competing schools of thought, and to trace through the consequences of these differences in the structure and assumptions of the models that economists draw upon for their policy conclusions and interpretations of real economic phenomena. This book has been dedicated to completing the first step in gaining such breadth of understanding by conveying the principles that are widely recognized, drawn upon, and sometimes criticized by the rich assortment of modern macroeconomic theorists.

Problems for Chapter 16

Problems 1–4 make use of the following parameter values: The production function is $Y = K^{.4}N^{.6}$ and the natural rate of growth is .05 per year (5 percent per year). All units are constant dollars per year.

1. Suppose the national saving rate in Solovia is .15. Evaluate the steady state capital-labor ratio, labor productivity, and consumption per worker.

2. The Solovian saving rate has been raised to .4 as the result of a fiscal surplus. Evaluate the steady state capital-labor ratio, labor productivity, and consumption per worker in the new long-run equilibrium. Was the fiscal policy a success (compare with your answers in question 1)?

3. The Solovian economy in question 1 begins with a capital stock of 500 and a labor force of 100 in period 0. Construct a spreadsheet model that

calculates in each subsequent period: the labor force, capital stock, level of output, amount of saving, capital-labor ratio, labor productivity, growth rate of capital, and growth rate of output. Your spreadsheet should cover about 75 periods. Explain the behavior of the model (hint: use graphs to clarify what is happening).

4. The fiscal authorities in question 2 were so impressed with themselves that they have decided to raise the saving rate even further, to .45. Evaluate this policy.

Appendix A

Mathematical Appendix

A.1 Mark-up pricing

First, we will use the inverse demand function, $P_i = P_i(Y_i, Y) = D^{-1}(Y_i, Y)$ because a monopolist chooses the level of output and observes how it affects prices and profit. The profit function is

$$P_i(Y_i, Y)Y_i - WY_i$$

If we differentiate the profit function and set the result to zero, the solution gives us the profit maximizing condition. This technique, setting the first derivative of a function to zero, is called the *first-order condition*. The first-order condition for the profit function is

$$\frac{\partial P_i}{\partial Y_i}Y_i + P_i - W = 0$$

This expression can be rearranged to give us

$$P_i\left(1 + \frac{Y_i \partial P_i}{P_i \partial Y_i}\right) = W$$

Now we use the definition of the elasticity of product demand as the absolute value of the percentage change in the quantity demanded associated with a given percentage change in price, or

$$\eta = -\frac{\partial Y_i / Y_i}{\partial P_i / P_i}$$

243

to give us the expression for the profit-maximizing price

$$P_i = \left(\frac{1}{1 - \frac{1}{\eta}} \right) W = (1 + \mu)W$$

This expression makes clear that a smaller elasticity of demand implies a larger mark-up since $\mu = 1/(\eta - 1)$.

A.2   A dynamic Keynesian cross model

To formalize the dynamic process of adjustment in the Keynesian cross model, we need to specify a behavioral rule describing how the level of production is chosen. One simple rule is that the firms match the current level of output to the last level of demand they observe, or

$$Y = Z_{-1}$$

These are dated variables with the t subscript suppressed. The equation reads: "output at time t is equal to demand at time $t - 1$." This rule is formally equivalent to the assumption that is implicit in the text, namely that firms change output by the same amount that their inventories change in the previous period, or $\Delta Y = -(Y_{-1} - Z_{-1})$.

From the equation for aggregate demand, this assumption leads to a first-order difference equation:

$$Y - c_1 Y_{-1} = c_0 - c_1 T + \bar{I} + G$$

To achieve a closed-form solution to this equation for any arbitrary initial level of output, Y_0, we first find the particular solution, and then find the complementary solution to the homogeneous equation. The general solution is just the sum of the particular solution and the complementary solution.

The particular solution is any solution to the original difference equation. It can found by substituting the unknown Y^* into the equation, which then can be solved for Y^*. The particular solution is the equilibrium level of output, $Y^* = \gamma(c_0 - c_1 T + \bar{I} + G)$.

For the complementary solution to the homogeneous equation, $Y - c_1 Y_{-1} = 0$, we make the educated guess that the solution takes the form $Y = Ab^t$, where A is an arbitrary constant and b is a parameter to be derived. Substitute this test solution into the homogeneous equation to derive $Ab^t - c_1 Ab^{t-1} = 0$. From this it is clear that $b = c_1$ and the complementary solution is just $Y = Ac_1^t$.

The general solution is therefore

$$Y = Y^* + Ac_1^t$$

To definitize the arbitrary constant A, knowing the initial level of output, Y_0, substitute $t = 0$ into the general solution to obtain $A = Y_0 - Y^*$. The general solution can now be written

$$Y = Y^* + (Y_0 - Y^*)c_1^t$$

In other words, the level of GDP at any time is equal to the equilibrium value plus an error-adjustment term that depends on how far (and what direction) from equilibrium the economy began and how much time has elapsed. Since the marginal propensity to consume is less than unity ($c_1 < 1$), the economy will eventually converge on its equilibrium when this error-adjustment term vanishes.

One weakness of this dynamic model is that it leaves the firm indifferent to its inventory-sales ratio. A more satisfying approach would assume that firms operate with some desired inventory-sales ratio.

A.3   Matrix solution of the IS-LM Model

The solution to the IS-LM model can be obtained using Cramer's Rule by first rearranging the IS-LM model,

$$\begin{aligned} Y + a_1 i &= a_0 \\ -a_3 Y + i &= -a_2(M/P) \end{aligned}$$

and then writing it out in matrix form:

$$\begin{pmatrix} 1 & a_1 \\ -a_3 & 1 \end{pmatrix} \begin{matrix} Y \\ i \end{matrix} = \begin{matrix} a_0 \\ -a_2(M/P) \end{matrix}$$

The reduced form equations follow from applying Cramer's Rule:

$$Y^* = \frac{\begin{vmatrix} a_0 & a_1 \\ -a_2(M/P) & 1 \end{vmatrix}}{\begin{vmatrix} 1 & a_1 \\ -a_3 & 1 \end{vmatrix}} = \frac{a_0 + a_1 a_2(M/P)}{1 + a_1 a_3}$$

$$i^* = \frac{\begin{vmatrix} 1 & a_0 \\ -a_3 & -a_2(M/P) \end{vmatrix}}{\begin{vmatrix} 1 & a_1 \\ -a_3 & 1 \end{vmatrix}} = \frac{a_0 a_3 - a_2(M/P)}{1 + a_1 a_3}$$

The first of these expressions is Equation (6.1) and the second is Equation (6.2).

A.4   Comparative IS-LM equilibrium analysis

The characterizations of fiscal and monetary policy presented in the text relied on informal arguments. To prove them, we need to analyze mathematically Equations (6.1 and 6.2), the reduced form equations of the IS-LM model.

A.4.1   Fiscal policy

We can recover some sense of how the behavior of this model depends on the original structural parameters by looking at the multiplier effect of an increase in government purchases. Mathematically, we want to evaluate the dY/dG ("the derivative of Y with respect to G"), which is roughly equal to $\Delta Y/\Delta G$. We can use the following facts to arrive at a solution:

$$da_0/dG = \gamma \quad da_1/dG = 0$$
$$da_2/dG = 0 \quad da_3/dG = 0$$

From the reduced form equations, we find that:

$$dY^*/dG = \frac{\gamma}{1 + a_1 a_3}$$

This equation for the *impact multiplier for government spending* together with the definitions of the consolidating parameters, allows us to see that the multiplier effect will equal γ if either $b_2 = 0$ (which makes $a_1 = 0$) or $d_2 = \infty$ (which makes $a_3 = 0$). This verifies our earlier conclusion that fiscal policy is free of any crowding out when either the IS curve is vertical ($b_2 = 0$) or the LM curve is horizontal ($d_2 = \infty$). Be sure you understand the economic intuition behind this result.

We can determine whether investment spending will be crowded-out or crowded-in in general by studying the equilibrium value for investment, or

$$I^* = b_0 + b_1 Y^* - b_2 i^*$$

By substituting into the reduced form equations and taking derivatives, we discover that

$$dI^*/dG = \gamma(\frac{b_1 - a_3 b_2}{1 + a_1 a_3})$$

By using the definitions of the consolidating parameters, it becomes clear that

Crowding-in $\qquad dI^*/dG > 0 \Leftrightarrow b_1/b_2 > d_1/d_2$

Crowding-out $\qquad dI^*/dG < 0 \Leftrightarrow b_1/b_2 < d_1/d_2$

where the double-arrow indicates that the condition to the right is necessary and sufficient for the condition on the left. Again, we can verify our earlier conclusions that crowding out becomes more likely as the IS curve becomes shallower through a larger interest sensitivity of investment spending (b_2), or as the LM curve becomes steeper through a smaller interest sensitivity of money demand (d_2). Be sure you understand the economic intuition behind these results.

A.4.2 Monetary Policy

We proceed in the same way to find out the impact of monetary policy on equilibrium income. Using the reduced form equation, we find that

$$dY^*/dM = \frac{a_1}{(1 + a_1 a_3)P d_2}$$

With a little manipulation, we can easily see the two cases in which monetary policy becomes ineffective ("pushing on a string"). Using the right arrow to indicate that the condition on the left is sufficient for the condition on the right, we have:

$$b_2 = 0 \Rightarrow dY^*/dM = 0$$

$$d_2 = \infty \Rightarrow dY^*/dM = 0$$

The first statement verifies that monetary policy is ineffective when the IS curve is vertical because investment is insensitive to interest rates. The second statement verifies that monetary policy is ineffective when the LM curve is horizontal because the economy has fallen into a liquidity trap. Once again, be sure you understand the economic principles behind these conditions.

A.5 Analysis of the Phillips curve model

To analyze the dynamics of the Phillips curve model formally, let us generalize the model slightly by assuming that inflation expectations follow the error adjustment process $\Delta \pi^e = \lambda(\pi_{-1} - \pi^e_{-1})$, where $0 < \lambda \le 1$. According to this equation, workers change their inflation forecast by some fraction, λ, of the amount by which their previous forecast missed the mark. With this assumption, the whole Phillips curve model is written:

$$\pi = \pi^e - \alpha(u - u_n) \tag{A.1}$$
$$u = u_{-1} - \beta g_Y \tag{A.2}$$
$$\pi^e = \pi^e_{-1} + \lambda(\pi_{-1} - \pi^e_{-1}) \tag{A.3}$$
$$g_Y = g_M - \pi \tag{A.4}$$

This system can be solved by differencing Equation (A.1) and substituting Equations (A.2-A.4) to derive the difference equation for inflation:

$$\pi_{+2} - \left(\frac{2 + \alpha\beta(1-\lambda)}{1+\alpha\beta}\right)\pi_{+1} + \left(\frac{1}{1+\alpha\beta}\right)\pi = \frac{\alpha\beta\lambda}{1+\alpha\beta}(g_M) \tag{A.5}$$

This is a second-order difference equation with constant coefficients and constant term. Techniques for solving equations like this can be found in any standard textbook, such as Chiang (1984). Stability requires:

$$\frac{1}{1+\alpha\beta} < 1$$

so it can clearly be seen that the model is stable (since neither α nor β can be zero).

The equation will produce stable oscillations if:

$$\frac{1}{4}\left(\frac{2+\alpha\beta(1-\lambda)}{1+\alpha\beta}\right)^2 - \frac{1}{1+\alpha\beta} < 0$$

Notice that if $\lambda = 1$, as in the text model, $\pi^e = \pi_{-1}$, and this condition reduces to

$$\frac{1}{1+\alpha\beta}\left(\frac{1}{1+\alpha\beta}-1\right) < 0$$

Since the oscillation condition is clearly satisfied, the text model will always produce stable oscillations, no matter what parameter values are chosen. In general, however, when $\lambda < 1$, there will some range of parameter values that deliver a stable node, meaning that the trajectory converges directly to the equilibrium with no overshooting.

To solve for the path of the unemployment rate, a similar procedure yields a second-order difference equation for u that has the same coefficients as Equation (A.5) but whose constant term will be:

$$\frac{\alpha\beta\lambda}{1+\alpha\beta}u_n$$

A.6   The golden rule saving rate

To find the golden rule saving rate in the Solow-Swan growth model with a Cobb-Douglas production function, first simplify by assuming that $A=1$. This makes $k^* = (s/n)^{1/(1-\phi)}$ and $y^* = (s/n)^{\phi/(1-\phi)}$. Using the definition $c^* = (1-s)y^*$, we write

$$c^* = (1-s)(\frac{s}{n})^{\frac{\phi}{1-\phi}}$$

To find the maximum c^*, set dc^*/ds equal to zero. This is called the first-order condition because it relates to the first derivative of the function, $c^*(s)$. It identifies a point on the function that is either a maximum, a minimum, or a point of inflection. In this case, we can be sure it will be a maximum because the function is strictly concave. Implementing the first-order condition yields

$$\frac{dc^*}{ds} = (\frac{1-s}{s}\frac{\phi}{1-\phi} - 1)y^* = 0$$

It is clear from this expression that the first-order condition implies that $s = \phi$. Thus, the golden rule saving rate will be equal to the power term on capital in the Cobb-Douglas production function.

Appendix B

Answers to Selected Even Problems

Answers for Chapter 1

2. (i) Year 1: PY = 2.00(100) + 3.00(50) + 1.00(25) = $375 per year. Year 2: PY = 2.50(120) + 3.25(60) + 2.00(25) = $545 per year. (ii) Year 1: Y = 375 constant year 1 dollars. Year 2: Y = 2.00(120) + 3.00(60) + 1.00(25) = 445 constant year 1 dollars. P = PY/P = 545/445 = 1.22 (or as an index number P = 122 with base year P = 100). Percentage increase in Y = (445–375)/375 = .19 or 19%. Percentage increase in P = (1.22–1.00)/1.00 = .22 or 22%.

4. Since $Y = C + I + G$, 250 = 100 + I + 50 and I = $100 per year. Unplanned inventory change is actual investment minus planned investment or 100 – 75 = $25 per year. You can also calculate that output minus planned spending is 250 – (100 + 75 + 50) = $25 per year in unplanned inventory accumulation.

6. M $\doteq$ (1+.6)/(.2+.6) 500 = $1000. The change in M is 2(100)= $200.

Answers for Chapter 2

2. P = 1.5(5) = $7.50 per unit of output.

4. Price is still \$7.50 per unit of output. Quantity produced is $Y_i^d = 7.50^{-3}1000 = 2.37$ units of output. If the level of GDP is expected to be \$2000 per year, quantity produced will be $7.50^{-3}2000 = 4.74$ units or twice as much.

Answers for Chapter 3

2. Aggregate demand is $Z = 140 + .6(Y-150) + 200 + 150 = 400 + .6\,Y$. If $Y = 500$, $Z = 400 + .6(500) = \$700$ per year. Unplanned inventory change is $Y - Z = 500 - 700 = -200$. Firms will respond by stepping up production. If $Y = 1200$, $Z = \$1120$ per year, and $Y - Z = +80$. Firms will cut back on production.

4. The multiplier is $1/(1-.6) = 2.5$, so $\Delta Y = 2.5\Delta G$ and $\Delta G = 250/(2.5) = \$100$ per year. The required $G = 150 + 100 = \$250$ per year.

6. First calculate equilibrium GDP: $Y = 1/(1-.6-.1)(140 - .6(150) + 100 + 150) = \$1000$ per year. Then find public saving, $T-G = 150 - 150 = 0$, and private saving, $S = -140 + .4(1000 - 150) = \$200$ per year. National saving is therefore $0 + 200 = \$200$ per year. The new equilibrium GDP is $Y = 1/(1-.6-.1)(100 - .6(150) + 100 + 150) = \$866.67$ per year, so $S = -100 + .4(866.67 - 150) = \$186.67$ per year and national saving is $0 + 186.67 = \$186.67$ per year. National saving and private saving have gone down because investment spending has been reduced by the lower level of income. This illustrates the paradox of thrift.

Answers for Chapter 4

2. Start with $Y = Z$ and substitute for Z: $Y = 120 + .6(Y - 200) + 50 + .2\,Y - 2000\,i + 250$. Isolate Y on the left-hand side: $Y = 1/(1-.6-.2)(120 - .6(200) + 50 + 250) - 2000/(1-.6-.2)i$. Simplify: $Y = 1500 - 10,000\,i$.

4. The IS curve shifts in a parallel way by $\gamma\Delta G$ or $5(50)$. Therefore, at any given interest rate, such as .05 per year, output increases by \$250 per year.

6. A decrease in the interest sensitivity of investment spending means that a given interest rate change has less effect on investment and consequently less effect on GDP. A decrease in the multiplier means a change in investment caused by a given change in interest rates has less effect on GDP.

Answers for Chapter 5

2. Set money demand equal to money supply, or $1(2Y - 8000i) = 1600$, so $i = -1600/8000 + 2/8000\ Y$. Simplifying, $i = -.2 + .00025\ Y$.

4. In a pure currency system, the money multiplier is 1, and this open market sale reduces the money supply by $500. Therefore, the new LM curve is $i = -1100/8000 + 2/8000\ Y$ or $i = -.1375 + .00025\ Y$. The LM curve has parallel-shifted up by $-.1375 - (-.2) = .0625$. You can also say the LM curve has shifted to the left.

Answers for Chapter 6

2. $Y = 1/(1 - .6 - .2)(120 - .6(200) + 50 + 250) - 2000/(1 - .6 - .2)i = 1/(1 - .6 - .2)(120 - .6(200) + 50 + 250) - 2000/(1 - .6 - .2)[-1600/8000 + 2/8000\ Y]$. $Y = \$1000$ per year. $i = -1600/8000 + 2/8000\ (1000) = .05$ (or 5%) per year.

4. $Y = 1/(1 - .6 - .2)(120 - .6(200) + 50 + 250) - 2000/(1 - .6 - .2)i = 1/(1 - .6 - .2)(120 - .6(200) + 50 + 250) - 2000/(1 - .6 - .2)[-1880/8000 + 2/8000\ Y]$. $Y = \$1100$ per year. $i = -1880/8000 + 2/8000\ (1000) = .04$ (or 4%) per year.

6. Since investment is insensitive to interest rates, monetary policy has no effect on the level of GDP. Fiscal policy is very effective because crowding in prevails.

8. A fiscal policy of cutting government consumption spending or raising taxes contributes to raising public saving, but it also reduces GDP, which reduces private saving, so it must be combined with a stimulative monetary policy to preserve the level of GDP.

10. A tax cut shifts the IS curve out without changing the position of the LM curve. Using a bar to denote no change and an arrow to show direction of change, we have $Y \uparrow = C \uparrow + I \updownarrow + \bar{G}$ and $I \updownarrow = S \uparrow + (T - G) \downarrow$. The effect on investment cannot be determined without specific knowledge of the underlying parameters. Consumption and saving both increase because a tax cut raises disposable income.

Answers for Chapter 7

2. $Y = 1/(1 - .6 - .2)(120 - .6(200) + 50 + 250) - 2000/(1 - .6 - .2)i$ $= 1/(1 - .6 - .2)(120 - .6(200) + 50 + 250) - 2000/(1 - .6 - .2)[-(1600/P)(1/8000) + 2/8000 Y]$. $Y + 2.5 Y = 1500 + 2000 (1/P)$ so $Y = 1500/3.5 + 2000/3.5 (1/P) = 428.6 + 571.4 (1/P)$ is the AD curve.

Answers for Chapter 8

2. $1 - 2.5 (u_n) = .8$ so $u_n = .08$ or 8%. $.08 = (100 - Y_n)/100$ so $Y_n = 92$.

4. Call the first year (when $W = \$5$) $t = 1$. We want the wage at $t = 2$. The bargained real wage is $1 - 2.5(.05) = .875 = W_2/P_2^e$ and $P_2^e = P_{t-1} = P_1 = (1.25)(5) = \$6.25$ per unit, so $W_2 = 6.25(.875) = \$5.47$ per worker.

6. First, solve the AS curve to get $P = 6.25(-1.875 + .03125[92]) = \$6.25$ per unit. Problem 2 tells us that the natural level of GDP is $\$92$. When $Y = Y_n$, $P = P^e = P_{-1}$, which is exactly what we have just found.

Answers for Chapter 9

2. We use arrows to show direction and a bar to show no change. In the short run: $Y \uparrow = C \uparrow + I \updownarrow + \bar{G}$ and $I \updownarrow = S \uparrow + (T - G) \downarrow$. We cannot tell whether the increase in consumption spending will crowd investment out or in without detailed knowledge of the parameters. In the long run: $\bar{Y} = C \uparrow + I \downarrow + \bar{G}$ and $I \downarrow = S \uparrow + (T - G) \downarrow$. In the long run, crowding out will be complete.

4. In the short run: $Y \downarrow = C \downarrow + I \downarrow + \bar{G}$ and $I \downarrow = S \downarrow + (T - G)$. Money is not neutral in the short run, since it clearly has real effects. In the long run, no real variable is affected, since Y, C, I, and S all return to their original levels, and money is neutral.

Answers for Chapter 10

2. In year 0, $\pi = 5$ and $u = 4$. In year 1, $\pi = 5 - .5(u - 4) = 5 - .5([4 - .4g_Y] - 4) = 5 - .5([4 - .4 (10 - \pi)] - 4) = 7 - .2\,\pi$ so $\pi = 7/1.2 = 5.83\%$ per year. Then $u = 4 - .4\, g_Y = 4 - .4 (10 - 5.83) = 2.33\%$. In year 2, $\pi_{-1} = 5.83$ and $u_{-1} = 2.33$, so $\pi = 5.83 - .5(u - 4) = 5.83 - .5([2.33 - .4(10 - \pi)] - 4) = 8.66 + .2\,\pi$ so $\pi = 8.66/1.2 = 7.22\%$ per year. Then $u = 2.33 - .4(10 - 7.22) = 1.22\%$. In the long run, $\pi = g_M = 10\%$ per year and $u = u_n = 4\%$.

4. In year 1, $\Delta\pi = 8 - 10 = -2$, so $-2 = -.5(u - 4)$ and $u = 8$. $\Delta u = 8 - 4 = 4$ so $4 = -.4\, g_Y$ and $g_Y = -10$. Using $g_Y = g_M - \pi$, we see that $g_M = -10 + 8 = -2\%$ per year. In years 2, and 3, $\Delta\pi = -2$, so $u = 8$ and $\Delta u = g_Y = 0$. In year 2, $g_M = 6 + 0 = 6\%$ per year. In year 3, $g_M = 4 + 0 = 4\%$ per year. In year 4, $\pi = 4$ so $\Delta\pi = 0$, making $u = 4$ and $\Delta u = 4 - 8 = -4$. Thus, $g_Y = -2.5(-4) = 10$ and $g_M = 10 + 4 = 14\%$ per year. In year 5, $\Delta u = 0$, $g_Y = 0$, and $g_M = 0 + 4 = 4\%$ per year. This plan requires $4 + 4 + 4 = 12$ point-years of excess unemployment.

6. From the Phillips curve in its difference form, we know that $\pi_0 - \pi_T = \sum_0^T(-\Delta\pi) = \alpha \sum_0^T(u - u_n)$. Substituting into the definition of the sacrifice ratio gives us $\sum_0^T(u - u_n)/(\pi_0 - \pi_T) = 1/\alpha$.

Answers for Chapter 11

2. We know that in year 0, $\pi = 6\%$ per year and $u = 4\%$. In year 1, $\pi = .566 + .358\, u = 6 - .5(u - 4)$ so $u = 7.434/.858 = 8.66\%$ and $\pi = 6 - .5(8.66 - 4) = 3.67\%$ per year. In year 2, $\pi = .566 + .358\, u = 3.67 - .5(u - 4)$ so $u = 5.104/.858 = 5.95\%$ and $\pi = 3.67 - .5(5.95 - 4) = 2.69\%$ per year. In the long run, $u = 4\%$ and $\pi = .566 + .358(4) = 2\%$ per year.

4. In year 1, $\pi = -.311 + 1.075$ u $= 6 - .5(u - 4)$ so u $= 8.311/1.575 =$ 5.28% and $\pi = 6 - .5(5.28 - 4) = 5.36\%$ per year. In the long run, u $= 4\%$ so $\pi = -.311 + 1.075(4) = 3.99 \approx 4\%$ per year.

Answers for Chapter 12

2. Use uncovered interest parity: $.06 = .08 + (e^E - .95)/.95$ so $e^E = .95(.06 - .08) + .95 = \$.931$ per euro. This decline in the price of foreign currency is an appreciation from the point of view of the home country.

Answers for Chapter 13

2. Using a bar to denote no change, and arrows to show direction we see that (i) $\bar{Y} = \bar{C} + I \uparrow + G \downarrow + \bar{N}X$ and $\bar{S} + (T - G) \uparrow = I \uparrow + \bar{N}FI$. Lower interest rates have encouraged domestic investment, which has been financed through an increase in public saving. (ii) $Y \downarrow = C \downarrow + I \downarrow + G \downarrow + NX \uparrow$ and $S \downarrow + (T - G) \uparrow = I \downarrow + NFI \uparrow$. The increase in public saving has reduced demand, causing private saving and domestic investment to head south. But it has increased net foreign investment, which might be welcome if the country wished to reduce its foreign indebtedness. (These questions can also be answered using the investment-saving identity in the form $I = S + (T - G) - NX$.)

4. In quadrant I of the Salter-Swan diagram, revaluation should be chosen first since it is not in a conflict situation. Once either internal or external balance is achieved, it will become clear whether fiscal stimulus or restraint is appropriate.

Answers for Chapter 14

2. For case (i), $Y \downarrow = C \downarrow + I \updownarrow + G \downarrow + NX \uparrow$ and $S \downarrow + (T - G) \uparrow = I \updownarrow + NFI \uparrow$. Fiscal austerity reduces GDP, which depresses private consumption and saving. Since interest rates decline, the effect on domestic investment is ambiguous. The trade surplus has been created by the lower level of GDP, in spite of an appreciation of the currency.

For case (ii), $\bar{Y} = \bar{C} + \bar{I} + G \downarrow + NX \uparrow$ and $\bar{S} + (T - G) \uparrow = \bar{I} + NFI \uparrow$. Working entirely through a depreciation, the increase in public saving has caused an increase in net foreign investment, which might be welcome for a country worried about its foreign debt.

Answers for Chapter 15

2. The wage, w, equals the conventional wage, 80 /labor unit. Use the wage-profit equation to find the profit rate, and the Cambridge equation to find the growth rates: $v = (100 - 80)/200 = .1$ /yr. and $g_K = .8(.1) = .08$ /yr. $= g_N = g_L$.

4. The growth rates g_K, g_N, and g_L are all equal to the natural rate, .05 /yr. Use the Cambridge equation to find the profit rate and the wage-profit equation to find the wage rate: $v = .05/.8 = .0625$ /yr. and $w = 100 - (.0625)(200) = 87.5$ /labor unit.

Answers for Chapter 16

2. The new values are $k^* = (.4/.05)^{(1/[1-.4])} = 32$ per worker, $y^* = 32^{.4} = 4$ per worker, and $c^* = (1 - .4)4 = 2.4$ per worker. Since c^* has increased compared with the answer in question 1, the policy has been successful.

4. The new values are $k^* = (.45/.05)^{(1/[1-.4])} = 38.94$ per worker, $y^* = 38.94^{.4} = 4.33$ per worker, and $c^* = (1 - .45)4.33 = 2.38$ per worker. Since c^* has decreased compared with the answer in question 2, the policy has not been successful. The saving rate now exceeds the golden rule saving rate.

Bibliography

Baiman, R., Boushey, H., and Saunders, D., editors (2000). *Political Economy and Contemporary Capitalism*. M.E. Sharpe, Armonk, NY.

Barro, R. J. (1974). Are government bonds net wealth? *Journal of Political Economy*, 81(6):1095–1117.

Baumol, W. J. (1952). The transactions demand for cash: An inventory theoretic approach. *Quarterly Journal of Economics*, 66(4):545–556.

Baumol, W. J. and Preston, M. H. (1955). More on the multiplier effects of a balanced budget. *American Economic Review*, 45(1):140–148.

Bewley, T. F. (1999). *Why Wages Don't Fall During a Recession*. Harvard University Press, Cambridge, MA.

Blanchflower, D. G. and Oswald, A. J. (1994). *The Wage Curve*. MIT Press, Cambridge, MA.

Blinder, A. S. and Solow, R. M. (1973). Does fiscal policy matter? *Journal of Public Economics*, 81(2):319–337.

Bowles, S. (1985). The production process in a competitive economy: Walrasian, neo-Hobbesian, and Marxian models. *American Economic Review*, 75(1):16–36.

Carlin, W. and Soskice, D. (1990). *Macroeconomics and the Wage Bargain: A Modern Approach to Employment, Inflation and the Exchange Rate*. Oxford University Press, Oxford.

Chiang, A. C. (1984). *Fundamental Methods of Mathematical Economics*. McGraw-Hill, New York, 3d edition.

Dernburg, T. F. (1989). *Global Macroeconomics*. Harper and Row, New York.

Fair, R. C. (1994). *Testing Macroeconometric Models*. Harvard University Press, Cambridge, MA.

Fleming, J. M. (1962). Domestic financial policies under fixed and floating exchange rates. Technical report, International Monetary Fund Staff Papers, Washington, DC.

Foley, D. K. and Michl, T. R. (1999). *Growth and Distribution*. Harvard University Press, Cambridge, MA.

Friedman, M. (1956). *Studies in the Quantity Theory of Money*. University of Chicago Press, Chicago.

Friedman, M. (1968). The role of monetary policy. *American Economic Review*, 58(1):1–17.

Hicks, J. R. (1937). Mr. Keynes and the "classics"; A suggested interpretation. *Econometrica*, 5(2):147–159.

Jones, C. I. (2001). *Introduction to Economic Growth*. W. W. Norton and Company, New York, 2d edition.

Kahn, R. F. (1931). The relation of home investment to unemployment. *Economic Journal*, 41(162):173–198.

Kalecki, M. (1943). Political aspects of full employment. *Political Quarterly*, 14:322–331.

Kalecki, M. (1971). *Selected Essays on the Dynamics of the Capitalist Economy*. Cambridge University Press, Cambridge, UK.

Keynes, J. M. (1936). *The General Theory of Employment, Interest, and Money*. Harcourt, Brace, New York.

Kurz, H.-D. and Salvadori, N. (1995). *Theory of Production: A Long-Period Analysis*. Cambridge University Press, Cambridge, UK.

Layard, R., Nickell, S., and Jackman, R. (1991). *Unemployment: Macroeconomic Performance and the Labour Market*. Oxford University Press, Oxford.

Marglin, S. A. (1984). *Growth, Distribution, and Prices*. Harvard University Press, Cambridge, MA.

Minsky, H. P. (1975). *John Maynard Keynes*. Columbia University Press, New York.

Minsky, H. P. (1982). *Can 'It' Happen Again: Essays on Instability and Finance*. M.E. Sharpe, Armonk, NY.

Modigliani, F. and Brumberg, R. (1954). Utility analysis and the consumption function: An interpretation of cross-section data. In Kurihara, K. K., editor, *Post-Keynesian Economics*, pages 388–436. Rutgers University Press, New Brunswick, NJ.

Mundell, R. A. (1963). Capital mobility and stabilization policy under fixed and flexible exchange rates. *Canadian Journal of Economics and Political Science*, 29(4):475–485.

Pasinetti, L. L. (1974). *Growth and Income Distribution: Essays in Economic Theory*. Cambridge University Press, Cambridge, UK.

Patinkin, D. (1948). Price flexibility and full employment. *American Economic Review*, 38(4):543–564.

Phillips, A. W. (1958). The relation between unemployment and the rate of change of money wage rates in the United Kingdom, 1861–1957. *Economica*, 25(100):283–299.

Pigou, A. C. (1943). The classical stationary state. *Economic Journal*, 53(212):343–351.

Robinson, J. (1937). *Essays in the Theory of Employment*. Macmillan, London.

Robinson, J. (1953). The production function and the theory of capital. *Review of Economic Studies*, 21(2):81–106.

Romer, D. (2000). Keynesian macroeconomics without the LM curve. *Journal of Economic Perspectives*, 14(2):149–169.

Rowthorn, R. E. (1977). Conflict, inflation, and money. *Cambridge Journal of Economics*, 1(3):215–319.

Salter, W. (1959). Internal and external balance: The role of price and expenditure effects. *Economic Review*, 35:226–236.

Snowdon, B., Vane, H., and Wynarczyk, P. (1994). *A Modern Guide to Macroeconomics*. Edward Elgar Publishing Co., Aldershot, UK.

Swan, T. (1960). Economic control in a dependent economy. *Economic Record*, 36:51–66.

Taylor, J. B. (1999). A historical analysis of monetary policy rules. In Taylor, J. B., editor, *Monetary Policy Rules*, pages 319–341. University of Chicago Press, Chicago.

Tinbergen, J. (1952). *On the Theory of Economic Policy*. North Holland, Amsterdam, 2d edition.

Tobin, J. (1956). The interest elasticity of the transactions demand for cash. *Review of Economics and Statistics*, 38(3):241–247.

Tobin, J. (1958). Liquidity preference as behavior towards risk. *Review of Economic Studies*, 25(2):65–86.

Tobin, J. (1980). *Asset Accumulation and Economic Activity*. Basil Blackwell, Oxford.

Index

About the Author

Thomas R. Michl is Professor of Economics at Colgate University. He received his B.A. from Oberlin College and his M.S. and Ph.D. from the New School for Social Research. He currently is a member of the Economic Advisory Committee of the Fiscal Policy Institute in Albany, New York, and a member of the Editorial Board of the *Review of Radical Political Economics*. His publications include *Growth and Distribution* (1999) with Duncan K. Foley, as well as numerous journal articles.